ST PETERSBURG

K L M Royal Dutch Airlines

To Leonard and Philip

ACKNOWLEDGEMENTS

Phil and Barb Penningroth; Carlichka 'Gospodin' Gottlieb; Dr Brockman, Patrushka Lanza, Eleanor and Gorsky; Lyoni Craven; 'Bashkaus' Bill; Ted Steinberg; Anatoly Valushkin and Svetlana Romashkova; Dr Barbara Stephens; John Porterfield; Richard Neill; St Petersburg Circus—Sonin and Natasha; Vladimir Uspensky; Sasha, Tanya & Andrei—The Frishkadelkamis; Richard Bangs; Larissa Vilenskaya; Bob Liljestrand; Val Ossipov; Robert Trent Jones, II & Gudren; Steve Robertson & Jim McCutcheon; Linda Jassim; Dominique Jando; Gene Sawyer; Sloane, Stephen, Buddy & Mary Beth; William Garson; Richard Burgi & Gus; Lori and Jan; Nikulin & The Moscow Circus; Schneer; The Staub Family; Yuko, Ari & Aidan; Andy and Hank; Margareta, Wouter, Fleur & Peter; Angliisky Misha, Nadiya, E.J. & Anna; Karen, Tom, Connie & Dustin; Peggy Burns; Robert & Alexandra Baker; Tovarishi Magnus Bartlett, Anna Claridge & Sally-Ann Imémé. In special memory of Mek Morsey, Brian Seeholzer, Matt Valensic, Babushki Anna & Evelyn and Dyedushki Mitro & Milford; Anna Akhmatova, sobaka Victoria von Ruppach; koshki Harry & Nicholas I—and a hearty spasibo to all those who helped in THE BIG CABBAGE—BOLSHAYA KAPUSTA!!!

ST PETERSBURG

Masha Nordbye

Photography by Patricia Lanza

British Library Cataloguing-in-Publication Data
A catalogue record for this book is available from the British Library

Distribution in the United Kingdom, Ireland and Europe by Hi Marketing Ltd, 38 Carver Road, London SE24 9LT, UK

Grateful acknowledgement is made to the following authors and publishers for permissions granted:

North Point Press for
The Noise of Time, translated by Clarence Brown, © Princeton University Press, 1965. Published by North Point Press and reprinted by permission

Princeton University Press for
The Road to Bloody Sunday: The role of Father Gapon and the Assembly in the Petersburg Massacre of 1905 by Walter Sablinsky,
© Princeton University Press 1976

Chatto & Windus and A P Watt Ltd for
The Overcoat by Nikolai Gogol, translated by Constance Garnett

Random House Inc. and William Heinemann Ltd for
Among the Russians, © Colin Thubron, 1983

Editor: Stefan Cucos
Illustrations Editor: John Oliver
Maps: Tom Le Bas and Bai Yiliang
Design: Teresa Ho
Cover Concept: Raquel Jaramillo and Aubrey Tse
Excerpts: Andrew Coe
Photography by Patricia Lanza
Additional photography courtesy of: Masha Nordbye; 19, 26, 37, 80, 116, 117, 179, 186, 194, 199, 202, 203; Cox & Kings Travel Ltd: 56, 72

Produced by Twin Age Ltd, Hong Kong
Printed in Hong Kong by Sing Cheong Printing Co Ltd

Gardens of Catherine the Great's Palace, Pushkin

Contents

(Following pages) The Hermitage on the River Neva

Introduction   —Andrew Coe

Between the slate gray skies and leaden waters of the Gulf of Finland (an arm of the Baltic Sea) lie the white columns and baroque decorations of St Petersburg, one of the most beautiful cities in the world. It comes as a shock to see the ornate structures of St Petersburg in these surroundings, only 800 kilometers south of the Arctic Circle. This disorientation is at the heart of St Petersburg's character, because the city has only a loose cultural connection with the flat pine forests—the typical Russian landscape—that spread out to the east. Where St Petersburg really finds its soul is in the Neva River which winds around the 44 islands of the city. In those dark waters, St Petersburg sees its own mirror-image: huge, pale and ornate structures rippling on the waves. St Petersburg is a city passionately absorbed with itself, and this spirit of city-centrism has led to some of the great artistic achievements of Russian culture and also to some of the most violent political upheavals.

The Neva (67 kilometers long) is a broad and muddy river that flows west over a marshy plain from the enormous Lake Ladoga into the Gulf of Finland. Its mouth widens into a delta price made up of 101 islands; today, only 44 islands comprise St Petersburg. The Finnish border is only 175 kilometers away to the northeast, and Moscow is 540 kilometers in the opposite direction. St Petersburg is on the same latitude as Anchorage, Alaska, and during the winter the sun shines blearily on the horizon for a few hours around noon. In June and July the sky is light 24 hours a day, nobody can sleep, and the city celebrates this astronomical bounty with its 'White Nights' cultural festival.

As you walk along the embankments, one of the first things that strikes you is the light that washes over the city. Joseph Brodsky, the Nobel prize-winning poet who was born in St Petersburg, said: 'It's the northern light, pale and diffused, one in which memory and eye operate with unusual sharpness. In this light...a walker's thoughts travel farther than his destination...' The next thing you notice is the unusual unity of the buildings. In the heart of the city, none of the buildings are more than four or five stories and while they may have been built in different styles, they all embody an aspiration for grace and elegance. The spaces between the buildings have been designed in harmony as well: the river is lined with heavy brown granite embankments that provide a solid base for the airy structures that rise above them, and even the bridge railings are small masterpieces of ornate ironwork. The last thing that a pedestrian will remark is the sheer size of St Petersburg's great buildings. The white pilasters of the Hermitage—one of the greatest museums in the world— seem to stretch for kilometers along the south embankment of the Neva. In the outskirts, the imperial retreats at Petrodvorets and Pushkin rival Versailles for grandeur.

These unique characteristics of St Petersburg are the legacy of Peter the Great, who founded the city in 1703. He built the city on the swampy islands at the mouth of the Neva River first as a fortress to repel the Swedish army. When the Swedes were no longer a threat, the city became a window on the West. From this perch on the edge of the imperial domain, Russia could venture into Europe, learn of the great intellectual and technological advances being made, and begin to drag itself out of the Middle Ages. Momentoes to Peter the Great are scattered throughout the city. On the Petrogradskaya Storona sits his cabin, the first house in the city, a simple Dutch-style dwelling. From here he directed the building of Peter and Paul Fortress. The Kunstkammer in the Museum of Anthropology and Ethnography contains Peter the Great's collection of 'monsters', freak animal and human embryos—a tribute to his restless curiosity and to his bloody-mindedness. Next to the Admiralty Building stands the enormous statue of Peter the Great known as the Bronze Horseman, a figure that has brought solace and madness to characters in Russian literature from Pushkin and Gogol to the present day. When it was known as Leningrad, the city's residents would still refer to it as 'Peter' and in doing so reject another leader whose name was also entwined with the city.

In the Russia, the people of St Petersburg have a reputation for aloofness and arrogance and for being less than totally Russian. Ask a Muscovite about St Petersburg, and he will say, 'Forget about it; Moscow is Russia; Moscow is where it's happening.' He is right: Moscow is where you find all the latest cultural and political ideas in the air. St Petersburg residents do not mind, however. Their city is not exactly a backwater: it is a huge and bustling seaport and industrial center of 5,000,000 inhabitants. If St Petersburg is not on the cutting edge, that's all right, because the city has enough cultural patrimony to last centuries. Every time somebody reads Gogol or Dostoevsky or sees a performance of *Boris Godunov*, *The Nutcracker* or *Swan Lake*, St Petersburg's bounty flowers again. And St Petersburgers still have the graceful streets, the buildings scaled to human size and the reflection in the Neva.

History

The delta at the mouth of the Neva River was settled long before the founding of St Petersburg. The Neva was an important trading route between Northern Europe and Asia, and Finns, Swedes and Russians established settlements there at one time or another and frequently fought over the land. In the early 17th century, Russia's 'Time of Troubles', the nation's military power was so debilitated that Mikhail, the first of the Romanov czars, was forced to sign a treaty ceding the land to Sweden in 1617.

After Peter the Great returned from his tour of Holland, England and Germany, one of his first actions was to oust the Swedes from the Neva delta. In the winter of 1702–1703, Russian forces attacked and captured Swedish forts at Nyenshatz, a few miles upstream from the river's mouth, and Noteborg on Lake Ladoga. Peter ordered that the keys to the forts be nailed to their gates, and these two keys, hanging from a sailing ship, became the symbol of the future St Petersburg. On May 16, 1703, seven weeks after ousting the Swedes, Peter the Great lay the foundation stone of the Peter and Paul Fortress on an island near where the Neva divides into its two main branches. The primary role of the new settlement was as a military outpost, but right from the beginning Peter had greater designs.

While the construction of the fortress was underway, Peter lived in a rough log cabin nearby and from it planned his future capital. He decided that the hub of the new city was to be on the opposite bank of the Neva, at the present site of the Admiralty. Here he founded Russia's first great shipyard, where he built his navy. The construction of the city was to begin along the banks of the river and radiate inland along broad avenues from the shipyards. Peter's project was hampered from the start by the occasional flooding of the Neva and by the lack of workers willing to move to the cold and isolated swamp. With typical ruthlessness, he ordered the conscription of 40,000 laborers to lay the foundations and dig the canals. It is estimated that approximately 100,000 people died from disease, exhaustion and floods during the first few years. 'The town is built on human bones', the saying goes.

In 1712, three years after the Swedes were finally and decisively defeated, Peter the Great decreed that St Petersburg was now the capital of the Russian Empire. Unfortunately, the aristocracy and merchants did not share his enthusiasm. Peter did not have the time or patience to persuade them, so he simply commanded the thousand leading families and five hundred of the most prominent merchants to build houses in the new capital. Aside from the Peter and Paul Fortress and Peter's cabin, the notable buildings of this era still standing are the Menshikov and Kikin Palaces, the Alexander Nevsky Monastery and the Monplaisir Palace at Petrodvorets. The construction of St Petersburg was the first time—but certainly not the last—that the hand of the State intervened on a national scale in the lives of the Russian masses.

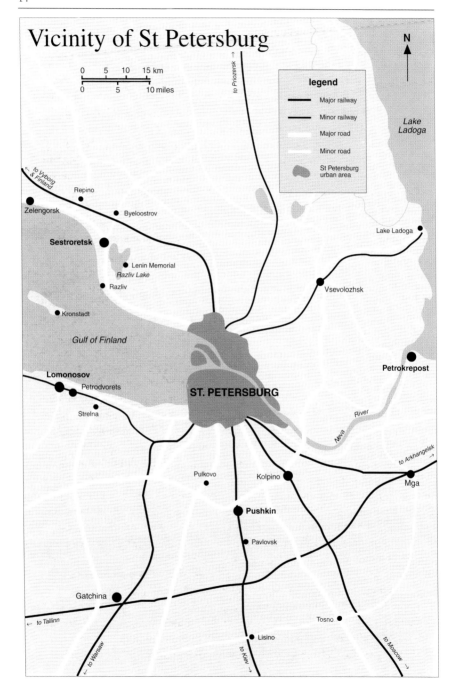

Vicinity of St Petersburg

N

0 5 10 15 km
0   5   10 miles

legend

Major railway
Minor railway
Major road
Minor road
St Petersburg urban area

Lake Ladoga

to Priozersk →

← *to Vyborg & Finland*

Repino
Zelengorsk ●
● Byeloostrov
Sestroretsk ●
● Lenin Memorial
Razliv Lake
● Razliv
● Kronstadt

Gulf of Finland

Lomonosov ●
● Petrodvorets
● Strelna

ST. PETERSBURG

Lake Ladoga ●

● Vsevolozhsk

Petrokrepost ●

Neva River

to Arkhangelsk →

Pulkovo ●
Kolpino ●
Mga ●

● **Pushkin**

● Pavlovsk

Gatchina ●

Tosno ●

← *to Tallinn*

to Warsaw
to Kiev →
● Lisino
to Moscow →

By 1725, the year of Peter's death, St Petersburg had a population of 75,000 unwilling subjects. For the next few years, the future of the new capital was shaky due to the lack of a strong hand like Peter's. The council which ruled Russia under the twelve-year-old Peter II moved the imperial court back to Moscow and thousands of people thankfully left the half-built city. They stayed away until Peter II's early death, after which Empress Anna took the reins and in 1732 decreed that the capital would return to St Petersburg. Under Anna, the second great phase of the construction of St Petersburg began. She hired Bartolomeo Rastrelli, the son of an Italian sculptor hired by Peter the Great, to build her a Winter Palace (no longer standing), the first permanent imperial residence in the city. She also ordered the construction of an 80-foot long and 33-foot high ice palace complete with rooms and ice furniture on the frozen Neva. This was built for a courtier who had been unfaithful to her and was forced to marry an ugly Kalmyk tribeswoman from Central Asia in a mock ceremony. They were stripped naked and had to spend the night in the ice palace with only each other for warmth.

Anna died the same winter, and after the brief rule of another child czar, Ivan VI, the Empress Elizabeth, daughter of Peter the Great, took the throne and built many of the most important buildings in St Petersburg. By this time (1741–61), Rastrelli and other imported European architects had developed a style that later became known as Elizabethan rococo. Like a wedding cake, the basic structures disappeared underneath an ornate icing of pilasters, statuary and reliefs. The other recurrent theme was size. These buildings did not reach for the heavens like the churches of the Moscow Kremlin; they sprawled across acres of flat countryside. Huge architectural clusters like the Winter Palace and the Hermitage and the palaces at Peterhof and Pushkin, all painted an ethereal turquoise, were testament mostly to Elizabeth's power to do as she pleased. By the end of her rule, St Petersburg looked more like a stage set, with broad avenues built for parades and palaces like props for some grandiose drama, than a working city.

After Elizabeth's death, another weak czar, Peter III, took the throne and quickly died after forging an unpopular alliance with Prussia. The sceptre was handed to his wife, Catherine II, an independently-minded German princess who ruled the empire for 24 years. Under Catherine, later dubbed 'the Great', St Petersburg solidified its position as the artisitic and political center of the empire, as intellectuals flocked to the now-thriving academies of Arts and Sciences. The latest political ideas from Western Europe were hotly debated among the aristocracy, and the streets and squares of the city were dotted with sculptures crafted by the finest European artists, including the enormous 'Bronze Horseman' sculptural portrait of Peter the Great cast by the Frenchman, Falconet. At the end of Catherine's reign in 1796, there was a profound sense of achievement in St Petersburg; in less than a century it had become one of the leading cities in the world. But there was also unease: the winds of change were blowing, and no one knew how to reconcile the new political ideas of St Petersburg with the profoundly conservative and deeply religious Russian countryside.

Catherine's son, the mentally unstable Paul I, built a fortress variously known as the Mikhailovsky or Engineer's Palace to protect himself from conspirators against the throne. His paranoia proved justified, because in 1801, just 41 days after he moved in, his own courtiers strangled him to death. His successor was Alexander I, whose liberal reforms during the first half of his reign were wildly popular among the aristocracy and intelligentsia. The latter half of Alexander's rule was less successful, and a number of revolutionary cells were formed within the aristocracy to overthrow the imperial system. When Alexander died in December, 1825, these cells were violently opposed to the accession of his anointed successor, his younger brother Nicholas, who was known to be a conservative and sympathetic to the Prussians. A group of guards officers, later known as 'Decembrists', took over the Senate Square and demanded a constitutional government. Nicholas ordered the army's cannons to fire on them, and the Decembrists fled in confusion. The main plotters were arrested and interned in the Peter and Paul Fortress, where five of them were executed and 115 were sent to Siberia. In 1849, this fortress was also the prison for the writer, Fyodor Dostoevsky, and the rest of the Petrashevsky Circle of socialist revolutionaries. Under Nicholas's orders, they were sentenced to

Portrait of Catherine the Great at the Palace, Pushkin

death, led before a firing squad and then reprieved at the last minute and exiled to Siberia.

The period from Nicholas I through the Russian Revolution in 1917 was an era of more or less constant political repression of the aristocracy and intelligensia. Paradoxically, in St Petersburg it was the time of a great flowering of creativity that has given us some of the masterpieces of world literature, music and ballet, with writers like Pushkin, Gogol and Dostoevsky; the 'Mighty Band' of the composers Rimsky-Korsakov, Mussorgsky and Borodin; and the choreographers of the Mariinsky Ballet, whose dances are still performed today.

Political turmoil proceeded apace with the artistic ferment during the latter half of the 19th century. St Petersburg was the center, of course, and a number of prominent revolutionary theorists, including the anarchist, Mikhail Bakunin, and the writer, Nikolai Chernyshevsky, spent time in the Peter and Paul Fortress. In March of 1881 these activities finally bore fruit when a terrorist cell called the People's Freedom Group succeeded in mortally wounding Czar Alexander II with a bomb on the banks of the Katerininsky Canal. The Church of the Resurrection, inspired by St Basil's in Moscow, was built on that spot by his son Alexander III to commemorate the assassination. This led to more decades of oppression under Alexander III and Nicholas II, which only served to heighten the political unrest. By this time the imperial system was not only unpopular among the St Petersburg elite but throughout Russian society.

Russia got a prelude of its future in 1905, when a series of strikes by soldiers and workers led to a huge demonstration in St Petersburg. A radical priest named Father Gapon led thousands of workers in a march to the Winter Palace to present a petition to Nicholas II. As they entered Palace Square, soldiers opened fire and hundreds of un-armed protestors were killed. 'Bloody Sunday' shocked the nation and galvanized the revolutionary movement. Socialist intellectuals and workers formed mass parties for the first time and demanded a share of the power. Nicholas gave them a weak advisory body named the *Duma*, which was accepted by the moderates but not by the extreme left, and arrested as many revolutionary rabble-rousers as he could. Trotsky went to jail and Lenin escaped to Switzerland.

When Russia went to war against Germany in 1914, St Petersburg's name was changed to Petrograd to avoid the Germanic implications of having a 'burg' at the end of its name. World War I was disastrous for the Russian empire. The long and bloody war in the trenches sapped the economically and politically weak nation. Back in St Petersburg, the czar and the *Duma* fought for power, while the hypnotic priest, Rasputin, played mind games with the czarina and her circle, and the people starved. On March 12, 1917 the people of the capital rioted. They killed policemen, broke open the jail and set the courthouse on fire. The soldiers stationed in the city refused to quell the rioters; instead, they joined them. Two days later the Czar abdicated, and Russia was ruled by the Provisional Government led by the socialist leader, Alexander Kerensky.

In April, 1917 Vladimir Lenin arrived in Petrograd's Finland Station after a decade of exile and plotting and was met by a cheering mass of thousands. From the top of an armored car in front of the station Lenin gave a speech rallying his Bolshevik Party and their allies, the Soviets of Workers and Soldiers, against Kerensky's government. There followed months of agitation and attempted revolution which culminated in the night of November 7, 1917. The battleship, Aurora, under the control of the Bolsheviks, fired one shell at the Winter Palace, giving the signal for the Bolshevik troops to storm the palace and the other principal government buildings. The party of Lenin, Trotsky and Stalin was in command of the Russian Empire. A month later Lenin ordered the formation of the Extraordinary Commission for the Suppression of Counter-revolution, the Cheka—later known as the KGB—and the Soviet state as we know it was born.

That was the easy part; the hard part was consolidating power. For the next three years, civil war raged through the nation. The Soviets were attacked by first the Germans, then the White Russian army and the British Royal Navy. During that time, Petrograd's population dropped from two and a half million to 720,000, due to hardship. In March of 1918, Lenin moved the Soviet government to Moscow, because Petrograd was vulnerable to a German attack - and perhaps also because of his distaste for the artificial imperial city.

On Lenin's death in 1924, Petrograd, which had been given the honorific 'The Cradle of the Revolution', was renamed Leningrad, after a man who publicly despised the city and spent less than a year of his life there. Ominously, that same year there was a great flood in his name-sake city. During the next two decades Moscow became the center of the cultural and political life, while Leningrad became identified as a center of shipbuilding and industry; by 1939 it had more than 3,100,000 inhabitants. Its tradition of political assassination nevertheless continued with the 1934 shooting of Leningrad party leader, Sergei Kirov, at the Smolny Institute. Some say that Stalin was behind the shooting, and he certainly used it as the excuse to start the purges of 1934–36 in which thousands of Communist Party members were killed.

Leningrad received its next great blow during World War II. For 900 days from September, 1941 to January, 1944 the German Army laid siege to the city and hundreds of thousands of inhabitants died, adding more bones to the foundations. (See The Siege of Leningrad, page 94). Stalin instigated another purge in 1948–49, known as 'The Leningrad Affair', in which many of the city's top party members vanished forever or were sent to Siberia. In this purge it was apparent that the Moscow leadership remained suspicious of the Leningrad party hierarchy, because they retained some of the idealism of the original revolutionaries.

The years following the war were devoted to reconstruction of the center and the development of huge satellite suburbs to the south. Luckily, the government banned high-rises in the center of the city sustaining Catherine the Great's edict that no building shall be higher than the Winter Palace. The population now approaches five million, and the city is the second most important industrial centre after Moscow. Culturally, it has not scaled the same heights as it did in the 19th century, but its great ballet tradition at the Kirov (renamed Mariinsky in 1992) and many literary talents keep hopes alive.

Old St Petersburg

It is interesting to speculate on what would have happened to the former Soviet Union if Lenin had kept the capital in Petrograd. It is doubtful that the Soviet Government would have been able to keep as firm a grip on the lives of every inhabitant across the 6,000-mile-wide nation as it did in Moscow. Lenin's whole career was aimed at taking power and holding it, and the goals of Revolutionary Socialism were definitely secondary. If he had stayed on the Baltic—in a city Dostoevsky called 'the most abstract and premeditated city on the whole round world'—it is possible that the northern light and the extravagant, un-Russian architecture would have tempered the cold and brutally realistic tempers of Lenin, Stalin and the other Soviet leaders, and they would have crafted a more fanciful and less totalitarian system.

Perestroika

On March 11, 1985, 54-year-old Mikhail Sergeyevich Gorbachev was elected the new general secretary of the Communist Party. Following in the footsteps of such past rulers as Ivan the Terrible, Peter the Great, Stalin and Brezhnev, Gorbachev inherited a stagnating economy, an entrenched bureaucracy and a population which had lived in fear and mistrust of their previous leaders. As Peter the Great had understood, modernization meant Westernization, and Gorbachev reopened the window on the West.

His first actions were to shut down the production and sale of vodka and ardently pursue Andropov's anti-corruption campaign and, in 1986, he introduced the radical reform policies of *perestroika* (restructuring), *demokratizatsiya* (democratization) and *glasnost* (openness), now household words. Gorbachev emphasized that past reforms had not worked because they did not directly involve Soviet citizens. *Perestroika* introduced the profit motive, quality control, private ownership in agriculture, decentralization and multi-candidate elections. Industry concentrated on measures promoting quality over quantity; private businesses and cooperatives were encouraged; farmers and individuals could lease land and housing from the government and keep the profits from produce grown on private plots; hundreds of ministries and bureaucratic centers were disbanded. A law was passed that allowed individuals to own small businesses and hire workers so long as there was 'no exploitation of man by man.'

With the fostering of private business, about 5 million people were employed by over 150,000 cooperatives. After April 1, 1989 all enterprises were allowed to carry on trade relations with foreign partners, triggering the development of joint ventures. Multi-million-dollar deals were established with Western companies such as Chevron, Pepsi, Eastman-Kodak, McDonalds, Time-Warner and Occidental.

In a powerful symbolic gesture, Andrei Sakharov and other political prisoners were released from internal exile. (After winning the 1975 Nobel Peace Prize, Sakharov, the physicist and human rights activist, was banished for nearly seven years to the city of Gorky. He died in Moscow on December 14, 1989.) One hundred Soviet dissidents from 20 cities were allowed to form the 'Democratic Club,' an open political discussion group. *Glasnost* swept through all facets of Soviet life. For the 40 million Russian Orthodox and people of other religious beliefs, Gorbachev stated that 'believers have the full right to express their convictions with dignity.'

At the 1986 Iceland Summit, Gorbachev proposed to sharply reduce ballistic missiles, and in December, 1987, he signed a treaty with US President Ronald Reagan to eliminate intermediate nuclear missiles. In January, 1988, the Soviet Union announced its withdrawal from Afghanistan. Nine months later Andrei Gromyko retired and

Gorbachev was elected as executive president of the Supreme Soviet, a new post which carried broader constitutional powers and replaced the former honorary chairmanship of the Supreme Soviet; the president now had the right to propose legislation, veto bills passed by Congress, appoint and fire the prime minister and other senior government officials and declare states of emergency (with the approval of the republics).

Gorbachev was faced with a budget deficit of over 100 billion rubles. The severe shortages created a virtual black-market economy, providing goods for up to 85 per cent of the population. On November 1, 1989 the government drastically cut the bank ruble exchange rate by 90 per cent in order to curb black-market exchanges (up to 20 times above the official rate) and to bring the ruble closer to an open exchange on the world market. The prime minister stated that 43 million people (15 per cent of the population) were living below the poverty level. There were also an estimated 23 million people unemployed, the new paradox of this modern Soviet society.

Compounding failing measures and political contradictions, the nation was also rocked by a series of disasters: Chernobyl, the earthquake in Armenia, ethnic unrest, and extensive strikes in mines and factories across the country (a 1989 law legalized strikes). But Gorbachev remained confident and pressed on with *perestroika*. 'This is a turbulent time, a turbulent sea in which it's not easy to sail the ship. But we have a compass and we have a crew to guide that ship, and the ship itself is strong.'

The Communist Party

The Bolshevik Party, formed by Lenin, began as a unified band of revolutionaries whose 8,000 members organized the mass strike of the 1905 St Petersburg revolt. By October 1917, the Bolshevik Party (soon renamed the Communist Party) had over 300,000 members, many of whom became the leaders and planners for the newly formed Soviet State.

Before the fall of Communism, there were over 20 million Party members, a third of them women. Membership was opened to any citizen who 'did not exploit the labor of others,' abided by the Party's philosophy, and gave three per cent of their monthly pay as dues to the Party. Members were also required to attend several meetings and lectures each month, provide volunteer work a few times a year and help with election campaigns. Approximately 200,000 of these members were full-time officials, apparatchiks, paid by the Party. The Komsomol, or Communist Youth Organization, had 40 million additional members, while 25 million school children belonged to the Young Pioneers. Eligibility for party membership began at the age of 18.

Elections and Economy

On March 26, 1989 there was a general election for the new Congress of People's Deputies—the first time since 1917 that Soviet citizens actually had a chance to vote in a national election. One thousand five hundred delegates were elected together with an additional 750, who were voted in by other public organizations. The 2,250-delegate body then elected 542 members to form a new Supreme Soviet.

Ousted a year earlier from his Politburo post for criticizing the reforms, the Congress candidate Boris Yeltsin won 89 per cent of the Moscow district vote. As Moscow crowds chanted, 'Yeltsin is a Man of the People' and 'Down with Bureaucrats,' a surprising number of bureaucrats had, in fact, lost to people like the Church Metropolitan of Leningrad. Andrei Sakharov was also elected. One interesting aspect of the election rules was that even candidates who ran unopposed could lose, if over half the votes pulled a lever of 'no confidence,' a privilege not enjoyed by voters in most Western countries.

At the beginning of 1990, Soviet citizens once again headed for the polls to elect their own regional and district officials, this time with the additional opportunity to choose candidates from other independent and pro-democracy movements. Scores of Communist Party candidates suffered defeat at the hands of former political prisoners, adamant reformers, environmentalists and strike leaders. Yeltsin was voted in as President of the Russian Federation, the Soviet Union's largest republic, which has more than half the country's population and Moscow as its capital. On February 7, 1990, after 72 years of Communist rule, the Soviet Communist Party's Central Committee voted overwhelmingly to surrender its monopoly on power.

Yeltsin's ascent underscored the fact that, for all Gorbachev's unprecedented reforms and innovative policies, he had not been able to bring the country's economy out of stagnation. Food and fuel were in critically low supply; ration coupons were being issued for meat, sugar, tea and soap. Modernization still did not approach Western standards, there were few computers, and most areas still used the abacus. It was estimated that 40 per cent of the crops had been wasted because of poor storage, packing and distribution methods. Many Soviets felt that their living conditions worsened: 'We live like dogs. The leash has become longer but the meat is a bit smaller, and the plate is two meters further away. But at least we can now bark as much as we want.' In June 1990, Yeltsin resigned from the Communist Party, declaring that 'in view of my...great responsibility toward the people of Russia and in connection with moves toward a multi-party state, I cannot fulfill only the instructions of the Party.'

Attempted Coup of August 1991

Gorbachev banned Yeltsin's rally of support in March, 1991, and renewed censorship of the print and television media. The people in Moscow demonstrated anyway and troops were sent in. One of Gorbachev's aides said, 'March 28 was the turning point for Mikhail Sergeyevich. He went to the abyss, looked over the edge, was horrified at what he saw and backed away.' Gorbachev had to move closer to an alliance with Yeltsin to survive.

Those in the government became uneasy with the upcoming republics treaty. Much of Moscow's power would be usurped if it was signed. The bureaucratic leaders realized they could lose their jobs and began planning ways to undermine Gorbachev's power. Even though he had created an unprecedented wave of changes, Gorbachev's popularity at home had now fallen to practically zero. After five years of promises, reforms had only made the living standard of average citizens worse.

On Sunday afternoon of August 18, 1991 Gorbachev, who had left for a vacation in the Crimea to work on the Union treaty, was told that Yuri Plekhanov, a top KGB official, had arrived to see him. Gorbachev, sensing something amiss, tried to use the phones, but all five lines were dead. Then Valery Boldin, Chief of Staff, entered the room, saying that Gorbachev had to sign a referendum declaring a state of emergency within the country. If he did not sign, the Vice President would take over leadership duties. Since Gorbachev refused to go along with the conspiracy, thousands of troops were sent into Moscow. Ironically, after all the planning, the coup members failed to arrest Boris Yeltsin who, that morning, had rushed off to his office in the Parliament building 45 minutes earlier than usual.

The next morning, the coup leaders went public and announced that Gorbachev, 'with serious health problems,' could no longer govern. But it became obvious from the onset that the coup was ill-planned. None of the opposition leaders were ever arrested. Yeltsin, holed up in the White House, was receiving calls from around the world. At one point, Yeltsin went outside and climbed on top of a tank in front of 20,000 protesters appealing for mass resistance; he named himself the 'Guardian of Democracy.' The crowd swelled to well over 100,000. By the end of the day, troops were switching over to Yeltsin's side, and many of the élite commando divisions were now protecting the White House.

By August 20, the coup attempt was weakening as many of the planners had come down with 'coup flu' and stayed home. Crowds of people raised the old Russian flag with its white, blue and red colors. Tank divisions descended upon the White House later in the day. Swarms of people blocked their way; after three were killed, the tanks finally retreated, refusing to fire on their own people.

Three days after the attempted coup, Yeltsin announced that the coup had failed. He sent officials to the Crimea to return Gorbachev safely to Moscow. By the end of August, 1991, Boris Yeltsin stood in the White House and declared, 'I am now signing a decree suspending the activities of the Russian Communist Party!' All Communist newspapers such as *Pravda* were temporarily shut down. Gorbachev followed by issuing decrees to end Soviet Communist rule. These decrees dissolved the Party's structure of committees and policy-making, which included the Central Committee. Archives of the Party and the KGB were seized. In addition, the government confiscated all the Party's assets and property throughout the country. It would take two years before the Communist Party could regain any of its powers.

The End of the Soviet Union

The Soviet Union ceased to exist on December 21, 1991. The great ideological experiment begun by Lenin's Bolshevik Revolution, constituted on December 30, 1922, ended nine days short of its 70th year. 'One state has died,' said Russian television, 'but in its place a great dream is being born.' The birth was the Commonwealth of Independent States. Four days later, symbolically on December 25, 1991, Gorbachev, the eighth and final leader of the Soviet Union, submitted his resignation. He no longer had a Soviet Union to govern. Boris Yeltsin claimed his office in the Kremlin.

In his largest crisis since the attempted 1991 coup, Yeltsin dissolved the obstructionist Russian legislature at the end of September, 1993, and moved to replace it with a new elective body, the Federal Assembly. Leaders of the Supreme Soviet, an organ left over from the socialist era, instantly declared Yeltsin's order unconstitutional and voted to impeach him; Vice President Alexander Rutskoi, was elected acting president.

When Yeltsin's opposition barricaded themselves in the White House, the patriarch of the Russian Orthodox Church, Alexi II, was called in to mediate between the two factions. After nearly two weeks of unsuccessful negotiations and mounting violence that culminated in the bloody raid of the central television station, Yeltsin ordered commandos, backed by tanks, to attack the White House. A few days later, the leaders of the White House coup against Yeltsin surrendered. Half a year later, the White House hard-liners arrested for attempts to topple the government in 1991 and 1993 would be pardoned by the new parliamentary house, the *Duma*.

Russia Today

On December, 12, 1993, the country's lawmakers were elected in the first true multi-party balloting. A new Russian constitution was also voted in which gave the president more power and Parliament less. The new constitution also granted Russia's 149 million citizens many economic freedoms and civil liberties long stifled since the Bolshevik take-

over; some of these included the right to own land, the right not to be wiretapped, and the freedom to travel freely at home and abroad. The Federal Assembly, with the Federation Council as its upper chamber and the *Duma* its lower, came into being. The country would no longer be ruled by the Soviets or councils, a bureaucratic legacy of the Bolsheviks. Despite the collapse of the Soviet Union two years earlier, the Soviet system had still been operating. A month later, those elected, from Communist to Women's parties, assembled in Moscow to launch the new parliamentary democracy. Yeltsin stated: 'We must preserve this for the sake of national peace and to make sure dictatorship never returns to Russia.'

Even though in the *Duma* ,Yeltsin's opponents appeared to hold the majority, they were forced to compromise with Yeltsin backers. One of the *Duma* members, and Yeltsin's strongest opponent, Vladimir Zhirinovsky, leader of the ultra nationalist and (misleadingly named) Liberal Democratic Party, was described as a neo-Facist who advocated party dictatorship, Russian military expansion to create another Russian empire, the expelling of millions of non-Russians and ending payments on foreign debt. He also wanted only blonde native Russian-speaking newscasters and promised cheap vodka for all. As one would imagine, this man shocked the world by winning nearly a quarter of the Russian vote among party lists in the elections (many say as a protest vote by a population feeling the pain of reform); he also planned to run in the 1996 presidential elections. Other men elected were reactionary journalist Alexander Nevzorov, weightlifting champion Yuri Vlasov, and psychic healer Anatoly Kashpirovsky.

The upper chamber, the 178-seat Federation Council, roughly equivalent to the US Senate, met under the new state symbol, the two-headed eagle. First Deputy Prime Minister Vladimir Shumeiko, a close ally of Yeltsin, was elected to the first Speaker's post. In addition to the sweeping changes, criminals were now allowed to choose a trial by jury, and those juries could also challenge the power of the State.

In Russia today, since the days of Gorbachev's *perestroika*, too many new processes have been started, too many private industries have broken out of old-style government central control, and, for the first time since Communist rule, the people themselves are able to freely activate their own potentials and voice their concerns. The cradle to Russian revolutions, St Petersburg once again finds itdelf the defender of determination and freedom. As Anna Akhmatova, the renowned poet, wrote of the city she so dearly loved, inspired by the statue of Peter the Great:

> You are free, I am free
> Tomorrow is better than yesterday
> Under the cold smile
> of Emperor Peter.

The Virgin of Vladimir *by Rublev*

Culture

A political and social history tells only half the story of St Petersburg. Of equal consequence are the literary and artistic creations set in St Petersburg, because in them writers and artists have created a parallel city that lives just as much in the minds of the inhabitants as today's crowded, slightly shabby metropolis. Since the reign of Elizabeth, the realms of fiction, poetry, symphony, opera and ballet have all collaborated to produce a St Petersburg of the mind that is one of the great artisitic creations of humankind.

Literature

In the earliest years of St Petersburg, the fate of the city was too doubtful to allow the production of great works of art. Peter the Great emphasized the practical sciences, particularly engineering, and his image of the city as a glorified barracks left little room for the arts. St Petersburg's first great fight to Russian culture, Mikhail Lomonosov, arrived in the city in 1736 and went on to become the director of the Academy of Sciences.

Lomonosov was a kind of Russian Benjamin Franklin—a chemist, physicist, geologist, educator, historian and poet. He also had studied in the West and was a friend of the French philosopher, Voltaire. Lomonosov devoted his life to bringing the ideas of the European Enlightenment to Russia and at the same time tried to advance Russia's cultural thought in distinctly Russian ways. Of all Lomonosov's achievements, his greatest in the cultural sphere was his Russian grammar, which codified and encouraged the use of the language of the common people in Russian literature.

If Lomonosov was the genius of the 18th century, then Alexander Pushkin was the soul of the 19th century. Pushkin was born into an aristocratic family descended on one side from a Negro slave who was a favorite in the court of Peter the Great. In his 20s he led a life of aristocratic dissoluteness in salons and bordellos of the imperial capital and began to write light romantic poetry. Many of his friends were politically active young officers associated with the Decembrist group, which Pushkin was never asked to join because they considered him too frivolous for their revolutionary mission. Nevertheless, he wrote some mildly seditious poems and was exiled to the Caucuses in 1820. During his exile from St Petersburg he wrote some of his most famous works, including his epic *Boris Godunov*, the story of the pretender to the Russian throne at the start of the 'Time of Troubles' in the early 17th century. At the end of his exile he began his masterpiece *Eugene Onegin,* a novel in verse about two star-crossed lovers, Onegin and Tatyana. Pushkin's last completed work was the apocalyptic poem *The Bronze Horseman* (see page 178), which is revered as the great work about St Petersburg. In it a young govenment clerk watches a huge storm cause a flood in St Petersburg which destroys most of the city and kills thousands, including his fiancée. Driven mad by grief, he comes upon Falconet's statue of Peter the Great, The Bronze Horseman, and he associates Peter's terrible imperial power with the destructive force of the flood. The mad clerk shakes his fist at the statue, and the horseman comes to life in a rage and chases him out of the square with a great clattering of bronze hoofs. In 1836 Pushkin was mortally wounded in a pistol duel over his wife's honor and died in January, 1837 at the age of 36. Immediately upon his death he was lionized as the greatest Russian writer, and that acclaim continues to this day.

Pushkin's mantle was inherited by Nikolai Gogol, a Ukranian-born writer, whose work is difficult to classify. At times, as in his play *The Inspector General,* he satirized the vast bureaucratic state that had taken over the Russian Empire. His famous short story *The Overcoat* is more enigmatic. A petty government clerk in St Petersburg invests all his savings in a new overcoat, but as he is returning home late at night he loses it to a band of robbers. After he discovers that none of his superiors will help him find his coat he dies of grief, only to reappear on the streets of St Petersburg as an avenging ghost. Gogol followed *The Overcoat* with *Dead Souls,* which was to be the first volume of a projected trilogy envisioned as a sort of Russian 'Divine Comedy' about sin, atonement and salvation. As he wrote the second volume, he began to go mad, thinking that the flames of hell were licking at his heels, and eventually threw the pages into the fire. He died in 1852 after doctors applied leeches and bled him to death.

The next great St Petersburg writer was Fyodor Dostoevsky, who, although anguished and epileptic, managed to live to a full lifespan. Dostoevsky studied to be a military engineer and fell in with the Petrashevsky Circle of socialist revolutionaries in St Petersburg. After being condemned to death and reprieved at the last minute, Dostoevksy was exiled to Omsk, Siberia, for four years. When he returned, he wrote *Memories from the House of the Dead* about his Siberian experiences and the acclaim at its publication in 1860 launched his career as a writer. Most of Dostoevsky's novels were written in serial form for magazines, so he could stay one step ahead of his many creditors. He took his subject matter from popular melodramas and sensational newspaper stories and wrote about them with the methods of psychological realism, a form that he pioneered. His greatest novel, *Crime and Punishment* tells the story of Raskolnikov, an impoverished former student, who murders an old woman—a pawn broker, and feels such guilt that by the time he is finally brought to justice he welcomes it.

CATHERINE THE GREAT

Peter the Great propelled Russia into the beginning of the 18th century. Catherine II completed it by decorating his creation in European pomp and principle. Catherine was a German princess who was given in marriage to Peter III, the homely grandson of Peter the Great. When her husband died of mysterious circumstances in 1762, Catherine became the first foreigner ever to sit upon the Russian throne. Catherine was clever and adventurous and had fallen (instead of with her husband) deeply in love with her new homeland. She immersed herself in the problems of politics and agriculture and worked toward basing the government on philosophic principles rather than on religious doctrines or hereditary rights. Because of her European roots, Catherine held a fascination for France and avidly worked to link French culture with that of her adopted nation. She read Voltaire, Montesquieu and Rousseau and sent emissaries to study in foreign lands; she also began the education of noblewomen. The Russian aristocracy soon incorporated French culture into their daily lives, giving the noblemen a common identity. The French language also set them apart from the Russian peasantry.

Catherine described her reign as the 'thornless rose that never stings'. Along with autocratic power, she ruled with virtue, justice and reason. By the publication of books and newspapers, and instruction by Western-trained tutors, education spread throughout the provinces, where before much of the learning originated from the Church. This allowed Russian culture to cut loose from its religious roots. Paper money was introduced, along with vaccinations; the day of Catherine's smallpox vaccination became a national feast day.

Scientific expeditions were sent to far eastern lands and hundreds of new cities were built in Russia's newly conquered territories. Along the coast of the Black Sea, the cities of Odessa, Azov and Sevastopol were constructed on the sites of old Greek settlements. With the formation of the Academy of Sciences, Russia now contributed to the Renaissance Age and would never again stand in the shadows. One of the most important figures of the time, Mikhail Lomonosov, scientist, poet and historian, later helped to establish Moscow University.

Catherine spared no expense to redecorate St Petersburg in the classical designs of the time. Wanting a home for the art that she began collecting from abroad, Catherine built the Hermitage. It was connected to her private apartments and also served as a conference chamber and theater. Besides the exquisite treasures kept within, the Hermitage itself was constructed of jasper, malachite, marble and gold. The Empress also had an extravagant reputation which filtered into her love life as well; she had 21 known lovers.

Unfortunately it became increasingly difficult for Catherine to maintain her autocratic rule while at the same time implement large-scale reform. Her sweeping plans for change planted the seeds for much more of a blossoming than she bargained for. The education of the aristocracy created a greater schism between them and the working class and her reforms further worsened the conditions of the peasantry. As the city took the center of culture away from the Church, more and more Old Believers were left disillusioned with her rule. Catherine tore down monasteries and torched the old symbols of Moscovy. In an Age of Reason, she had a deep suspicion of anything mystical.

Huge sums of money were also spent on constructing elaborate palaces for her favorite relations and advisors. One of these was Prince Grigory Potemkin, her foreign minister, commander-in-chief and greatest love for almost two decades. It was he who organized a trip for Catherine down the Dnieper River to view the newly accessed Crimean territories. The prince had painted façades constructed along the route to camouflage the degree of poverty of the peasants. These "Potemkin Villages" were also to give the appearance of real towns in the otherwise uninhabited areas. Finally in 1773, Pugachev, a Don Cossack, led a rebellion of impoverished Cossacks, peasants and Old Believers against the throne and serfdom. Pugachev was captured and sentenced to decapitation, but ended up exiled in Siberia.

It was not only the peasantry and the Church that felt alientated. The aristocracy too grew dissatisfied with the new European truths and philosophies. Those who yearned for more considered themselves a new class, the intelligentsia. Searching for their own identity amidst a surge of French principles, the intelligentsia proceeded not only to understand Voltaire's logic but to incorporate the heart and the spirit as well.

By grasping the ideals of a foreign Enlightenment, Catherine II unknowingly gave birth to Russia's own. The catalyst of change, along with teaching people to think for themselves, brought despotism into deeper disfavor and paved the road to revolution. After the fall of the Bastille, Catherine turned her back on France. In a panic, she tried to dispose of all that she had helped create. Censorship was imposed throughout Russia, and Catherine attempted to slam shut the window to the West less than a century after Peter had opened it. But from this period of discontent and new search for meaning, Russia would give birth to some of the greatest writers and thinkers of all time. The West would be captivated by the works of Pushkin, Dostoevsky and Tolstoy, and Lenin would later lead Russia out of five centuries of autocratic rule. Peter the Great had built the wheels and Catherine set them in motion; there was to be no turning back.

Late in life Dostoevsky became a devout believer in Orthodox Christianity. Luckily for world literature, he never lost his commitment to artistic realism, so his novels show the passionate struggle of trying to reach an ideal goal but never attaining it. When Dostoevsky died in 1881, thousands of Russians, ordinary citizens and fellow writers alike, accompanied his coffin to the Alexander Nevsky Monastery for a hero's burial.

After the Revolution, the center of literary activity moved to Moscow, although Leningrad continued to produce great writers. In partial reaction to the Soviet State, many of these, like the poet Anna Akhmatova, produced intensely personal visions rather than huge, all-encompassing epics.

Ballet

Russia made ballet a great art. Before the 19th century, ballet was little more than a music-hall phenomenon and distinctly inferior to opera. Russia's ballet tradition started in 1738 when the Empress Anna granted Jean-Baptist Landé, a French dance instructor, permission to open a dance school for children of the aristocracy. The Imperial Ballet School grew in importance but did not produce any significant innovations until Charles Didelot took over in 1801. Didelot was another French émigré, and he reorganized the school following the French classical model. The Imperial Ballet had the advantage of royal patronage and this prestige gave Didelot the impetus to raise the form to a higher level. He introduced elaborate narrative ballets with complicated sets that turned the performances into great theatrical experiences. The new Russian ballets, and the ballerinas, provided inspiration for a whole generation of writers, particularly Pushkin.

The next great era of Russian ballet began in 1847 when Marius Petipa joined the Imperial Ballet. In 1869 he became ballet master and choreographer and for the next 34 years he was the guiding light of Russian ballet. He choreographed over 60 ballets, many of them with Russian themes, and worked with many Russian composers in producing distinctly Russian works of art. His most popular creations include *The Sleeping Beauty*, *The Nutcracker* and *Swan Lake*, all with music by Tchaikovsky. As news of his work spread throughout the dance world, Russian ballet became known for these exciting, large scale spectacles. His dancers also became world-famous and the standard for excellence: Anna Pavlova, Mikhail Fokine (who went on to become a choreographer) and Vaslav Nijinsky.

Vaganova Ballet School Museum

The Imperial Ballet lost some of its brightest stars when many dancers emigrated with Serge Diaghilev and his Ballets Russes company. Since the 1918 Revolution, the Moscow Bolshoi Ballet, with its flamboyant and emotional productions, has been considered the top Russian company. However, the Mariinsky (Kirov) in St Petersburg continues to follow a more elegant and classical tradition and produce stars, and emigrés, like Rudolph Nureyev, Natalia Makarova and Mikhail Baryshnikov.

Music

The development of Russian music in St Petersburg followed the same patterns as literature, only later. In the 1830s and 40s, Mikhail Glinka, a close friend of Pushkin, composed many symphonies and two operas based on Russian folk songs from his childhood. Glinka put these folk themes together with many of Pushkin's poems and produced some of the first distinctly Russian musical works. One of his most famous pieces is *Ruslan and Ludmilla*, an opera based on Pushkin's mock-romantic epic about the court of Kievan Russia.

By the mid-19th century, St Petersburg had become a major musical center and Berlioz, Verdi, Strauss and Wagner conducted their work there. In response to this invasion of Western talent, particularly Wagner, whom they believed had imperial aspirations, a group of Russian composers banded together to promote their own 'Russian' music. Known as the 'Mighty Band', they included Nikolai Rimsky-Korsakov, Alexander Borodin and Modest Mussorgsky. The 'Band' followed Glinka's example and composed music based on folk songs and themes from Russian literature. Borodin's most famous work was the opera *Prince Igor*, which was based on old Russian heroic song and included the famous Eastern dance number, the Polovetsian Dances. Rimsky-Korsakov also wrote a number of operas based on mythic-historical themes from early Russian history and folklore. Mussorgsky, an epileptic like Dostoevsky, was the most artistically ambitious of the 'Band'. He began by writing works based on Gogol's stories, which he considered were the closest to the Russian soul. Another piece tried to reproduce musically the babble in the marketplace at Nizhny Novgorod. Mussorgsky's two greatest works are the operas *Boris Godunov*, based on Pushkin's poem, and *Khovanshchina*, the first part of yet another unfinished trilogy. *Khovanshchina* is a kind of tone poem rendition of Russian-style chaos and social anarchy set at the end of the Time of Troubles just before Peter took the throne. While Mussorgsky was finishing this piece, he went mad and died a few weeks after Dostoevsky in

1881. He was buried near the writer in the Alexander Nevsky Monastery.

As in the other arts, music during the post-Revolution period, particularly after 1928, was marked by a decline in quality, not just in Leningrad but in all of the Soviet Union. Leningrad's greatest musical genius of the 20th century was Shostakovich, who produced works like *The Symphony of Socialism* described here:

It begins with the Largo of the masses working underground, an accelerando corresponding to the subway system; the Allegro, in its turn, symbolizes the gigantic factory machinery and its victory over nature. The Adagio represents the synthesis of Soviet culture, science and art. The Scherzo reflects the athletic life of the happy inhabitants of the Union. As for the Finale, it is the image of the gratitude and enthusiasm of the masses. The abstraction has finally swallowed the people whole, and not a trace of humanity remains.

It is too early to tell if the current perestroika will lead to a new flowering of culture in St Petersburg and, if it does, what arts will flourish. Times are so hard economically that people may not have time to step back and look at themselves. However, at least they have the room to create.

PETER THE GREAT

Peter the Great, one of Russia's most enlightened and driven rulers, pulled his country out of her dark feudal past into a status equal with her European neighbors. Possessing an intense curiosity toward foreign lands, he opened Russia's window to the West and became the first ruler to journey extensively outside Russia. Standing at six feet seven inches, with a passionate will and temper to match his great size, Peter I, against all odds, also built a city that became one of the most magnificent capitals in all of Europe.

Peter's father, Czar Alexei, ruled the Empire from 1645 to 1676. Alexei's first wife had 13 children; but only two, Fyodor and Ivan, were destined to inherit the throne. Natalya Naryshkin became Alexei's second wife and gave birth to a son named Peter in 1672.

When Alexei died, his son, Fyodor III, succeeded to the throne and reigned from 1676 to 1682. During this time, his half-brother, Peter, along with ill-favored Natalya, were sent away from Moscow to live in the country. Instead of the usual staunch upbringing within the Kremlin walls, Peter had the freedom to roam the countryside and make friends with peasant children. When Fyodor died, a rivalry broke out between the two families as to which son would gain the throne. Peter won the first battle and was proclaimed czar at the age of ten. But soon Ivan's side of the family spread rumors to the Streltsy, or Musketeers (the military protectors of Moscow), that the Naryshkins were plotting to kill Ivan. The Streltsy demanded that Peter's half-brother be crowned, too. So, for a time, the throne of Moscovy was shared by the two boys, the feeble-minded Ivan V and the robust Peter I. In actuality, however, it was Sophia, Peter's older half-sister, who ruled as Regent for seven years with the help of her lover, Prince Golitzin.

Peter spent most of this time back in the country, mainly engaged in studies that had a practical use. One fateful day, the young boy discovered a wrecked English boat that could sail against the wind. He had the boat repaired and learned how to maneuver it. Infatuated now with sailing, he also immersed himself in the study of mathematics and navigation. In addition, the young czar worked well with his hands and became an accomplished carpenter, blacksmith and printer; he even mended his own clothes. As a child, he loved to play soldiers, and drilled his companions in military maneuvers, eventually staging mock battles with weapons and in uniforms supplied by the royal arsenal. Peter was also fascinated with the techniques of torture. Later in his reign, fearing an assassination attempt, he would torture his first son, Alexei, to death.

Peter the Great in England *by Sir Godfrey Kneller, 1698*

Sophia was eventually removed from court affairs and sent off to live in Novodevichy Convent outside Moscow. When Ivan died, Peter I, at the age of 22, assumed the throne as the sole czar and took up his imperial duties with earnest. On the throne, his first real battle was against the Turks. His plan was to take the Sea of Azov at the mouth of the Don in order to gain access to the Black Sea. Peter built a fleet of ships, and for the first time in her history, Russia led a surprise attack from the water. The Turks were defeated and Russia had her first southern outlet to the sea.

After this successful campaign, Peter set off on a long journey to the West. He traveled to England, France, and Germany, and worked as a shipbuilder in Holland. Back home, the Streltsy, with the help of Sophia, began to organize a secret revolt to overthrow the Czar. Peter caught wind of their plans; upon his return, he captured and tortured almost 2,000 men and dissolved the corps. By this time, the now cultured ruler had lost interest in his first wife and sent her off to a convent in Zagorsk, the equivalent of divorce.

Peter was greatly impressed by Western ways and, to him, change symbolized Russia's path to modernizaton. Knee-length coats became the new fashion. One of the new state laws prohibited the growing of beards. Since the church taught that man was created in God's image (ie with a beard), many believed Peter I to be the Antichrist.

But Peter was as determined as ever to pull Russia out of her isolation. He tolerated new religions, allowing the practices of Catholics, Lutherans and Protestants, and even approving of the sacreligious scientific stance taken by Galileo. He exercised state control over the Russian Orthodox Church by establishing the Holy Synod. This supremacy of the Czar over the Russian Church lasted from 1721 until 1917. In 1721, Peter also declared himself Emperor of All Russia.

During the Great Northern Wars, while chasing the Swedes out of the Baltic area, Peter the Great began building the first Russian Navy on the Gulf of Finland. It was during this time that he met and fell in love with a good-natured peasant girl named Catherine, whom he later married; Empress Catherine ruled for two years after his death.

In 1703, Peter began the fanatic building of a new city in the north at a point where the Neva River drained into Lake Ladoga. The city was constructed on a myriad of islands, canals and swamps. The conditions were brutal and nearly 100,000 perished the first year alone. But within a decade, St Petersburg was a city of 35,000 stone buildings and the capital of the Russian Empire. Peter commissioned many well-known foreign architects: the Italian Rastrelli, the German Schlüter, the Swiss Trezzini and the Frenchman Leblond, who created Peter's Summer Palace of Petrodvorets. Montferrand later designed St Isaac's Cathedral, which took over 100 kilos of gold and 40 years to build. Peter brought the majesty of the West to his own doorstep. It was no small wonder that St Petersburg was nicknamed the Venice of the North.

Peter died looking out from his 'window to the West'. Today in St Petersburg stands a monument to the city's founder, a statue of Peter the Great as the Bronze Horseman. The statue, made by the French sculptor, Falconet, shows Peter rearing up on a horse that symbolizes Russia, while trampling a serpent that opposes his reforms. Pushkin wrote that Peter 'With iron bridle reared up Russia to her fate'. By a great and forceful will, Peter the Great had successfully led Russia out of her darkness into the light of a Golden Age.

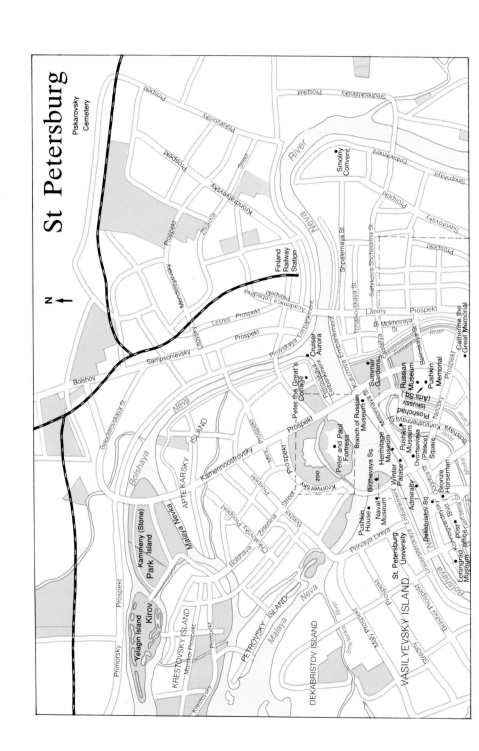

St Petersburg

N

Piskarovsky
Cemetery

Piskarovsky   Prospekt

Prospekt

Prospekt

Sredneokhtinsky   Prospekt

Prospekt

Sinopskaya

Krondtalyevsky

Street

Zhukova

Smolny
Convent

Embankment

Neva   River

Prospekt

Suvorovsky

Mendeleyevskaya

Akademica Lebedeva

Finland
Railway
Station

Shpalernaya St.

Liteiny   Prospekt

Tchaikovskaya St.

Prospekt

Catherine the
Great Memorial

Lesnoi   Prospekt

Saltykova-Shchedrina St.

Mokhovaya
St.

Prospekt

Sampsonievsky   Prospekt

TROYSKY

Belostrovskaya St.

Bolshoy

Pirovskaya Embankment

Cruiser
Aurora

Petrovskaya
Embankment

Kutuzova Embankment

Summer
Gardens

Fontanka   River

Belinskaya

Pestelya

Russian
Museum

Pushkin
Memorial

Peter the Great's
Cottage

Ploschad
Iskusstv
(Arts Sq.)

Nevsky   Prospekt

Bolshaya   Neva

ISLAND

Prospekt

Branch of Russian
Museum

Naberezhnaya St.

River   Konyushennaya St.

Bolshaya   Konyushennaya St.

River   Moika

KAMENNY

Kamennoostrovsky   Prospekt

Kronversky   Prospekt

Peter and Paul
Fortress

Birzhevaya Sq.

Hermitage
Museum

Pushkin
Museum

Dvortsovaya

Winter
Palace

Gogolya St.

(Palace)
Square

APTEKARSKY

zoo

Malaya Nevka

Naval
Museum

Admiralty

Bronze
Horseman

Kamenny (Stone)
Park / Island

Zelenina

Bolshoy

Pushkin
House

Pervaya Liniya

St. Petersburg
University

Embankment

Dekabristov Sq.

Leningrad
post
office

Komsomolov   Blvd.

Ulitsa Gertsena

Yelagin Island

Kirov

Prospekt

Bolshaya

Otkalovsky Prospekt

Bolshaya

Neva

Universitetskaya

Bolshaya

Bolshoi Prospekt

KRESTOVSKY ISLAND

Morskoi Prospekt

Prospekt

PETROVSKY ISLAND

Malaya   Neva

River

VASILYEVSKY ISLAND

Sredny

Krestovsky

Smolenka

Maly Prospekt

Primorsky   Prospekt

DEKABRISTOV ISLAND

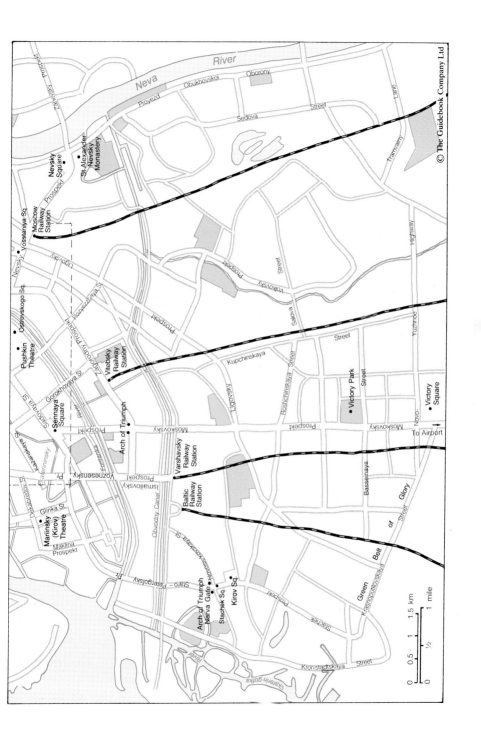

Facts for the Traveler

Planning Your Trip

INTOURIST

Many travelers organise their stay through Intourist, one of the largest Russian travel agencies for foreigners. An Intourst branch is located in most cities that are officially open to tourists. When visitors stay in Russian Intourist hotels, which have an Intourist service desk, hotel reservations must usually be prepaid before entering the country. Tourist visas are not generally issued by a Russian embassy or consulate without a confirmed hotel reservation or proof of Russian sponsorship. It often takes up to one month for reservations and itineraries to be confirmed. Once you have confirmed and paid for your Intourist itineraries, the travel agency will issue Intourist vouchers—booklets containing coupons for hotels, transfers and tours.

GROUP TOURS

There are a multitude of package and special interest tours from which to choose. The advantage of a group tour, especially if it is your first trip and you do not speak the language, is that everything is set up for you. Travel agencies handling Russian excursions have a list of available package tours. Most group tours have preset departures and a fixed length of stay, and usually visit St Petersburg and Moscow. The group rate includes round trip airfare, visa processing fees, first-class accommodation, up to three meals a day, transportation within Russia, sightseeing excursions and a bilingual guide. (Any last minute changes in your itinerary can delay the process for weeks.)

Adventure tourism has also opened up a whole array of other opportunities. Trips include rafting, hiking, climbing, biking, kayaking, horse riding and even arctic expeditions The following US adventure travel companies organise trips to Russia:

> **Boojum Expeditions** (Horse) Tel./fax (406) 587–0125.
> **Direct Action/Wild World** Tel. (201) 796–6861.
> **Mountain Travel/Sobek the Adventure Co** 6420 Fairmount Avenue, El Cerrito, CA 94530 Tel. (800) 227–2236.
> **REI Adventures** Tel. (800) 622–2236.
> **Zegrahm Expeditions** (Arctic) Tel. (800) 628–8747 or (206) 285–4000.

INDEPENDENT TRAVEL

Compared to many countries, independent travel in Russia is not easy. A person cannot just go to the Russian embassy or consulate, pay a processing fee and be on their way. In order to issue a visa, the embassy will first check your proof of reserved hotel accommodation or official sponsorship. The visa will be for the same dates as your hotel reservations although it can be extended while in the country. The reason given for this is because hotel space in the country is limited, many are prebooked far in advance, and the government does not want visitors with no place to stay. Recently motels, hostels, bed and breakfasts and even camp sites have sprung up, but these also should be booked in advance—cheaper places are in big demand! The easiest way is to book a place to stay through a travel agency, which can also arrange visas and internal travel. The independent traveler can also arrange home-stays or hostel accommodation; the only drawbacks are that the places may not be centrally located, or the hosts may not speak much English (see the Practical Information hotel section for these listings, page 157).

When to Go

Hotel prices and itineraries of many of the tour programs change depending on the season. Peak season is from May to September. Alternatives are to go in the spring (1 April-15 May) or fall (1 September-31 October) when prices are lower and the cities less crowded. The summer White Nights in St Petersburg are spectacular but, at the same time, the summer in Moscow can be humid and dusty. An Indian summer in the fall can be lovely. If you do not mind the cold and snow, the winter season is cheapest and accommodation most readily available. The rainiest months for both cities are July and August.

Getting There

By Air

There are two major airports in St Petersburg: Pulkovo I is for domestic flights and Pulkovo II for international. They are about five kilometers apart. Another smaller airport, Rzhevka, provides flights for northwest Russia.

■ INTERNATIONAL FLIGHTS
Most major airlines fly to St Petersburg (Pulkovo II) and Moscow (Airport Sheremetyevo II). Moscow is connected with over 120 cities in Europe and 70 countries around the world. Inquire at travel agencies and call around the different airlines to find the best rates. The advance-purchase (14- to 21-day APEX) fares usually give the best rate. **Delta's** flight to St Petersburg or Moscow from New York (either non-stop or with a stop

in Frankfurt) costs approximately $800 return; Los Angeles to Moscow is about $1000 return. **British Airways** offers flights to St Petersburg and Moscow from London for about $600 (£400) return. British Airways also offers daily fights between New York and Moscow ($800 return) and Los Angeles and Moscow (about $1000 return). **KLM** flies through Amsterdam to Moscow, **Lufthansa** through Frankfurt, and **SAS** through Stockholm or Copenhagen. **Aeroflot** also flies from most major cities to St Petersburg and Moscow; San Francisco to Moscow tickets are about $1000 return. Flights to Khabarovsk in eastern Siberia (where, in Vladivostok, you can pick up the Trans-Siberian railway) are also available from San Francisco. From the east coast of the United States, flights to Moscow start at about $800 return. The above fares are quoted for low season APEX with restrictions. Rates are higher in peak season.

Aeroflot is the largest airline in the world, carrying 100 million passengers each year. You can fly from and to destinations in Asia and Europe on Aeroflot with stopovers in Moscow (a transit visa and hotel confirmation are required). Even though Aeroflot has the reputation of being the airline of the people, and not of luxury, in-flight conditions have improved, but may not equal the standards of other overseas carriers. Since flying, especially from points outside Europe, involves large time differences, consider a stay in a European city for a day or two to recover from jet lag. Stopovers are sometimes included or provided for a minimal extra charge. (See Practical Information section for airline locations and phone numbers, page 155.)

■ DOMESTIC FLIGHTS

The airports used for internal flights are much more crowded and chaotic than the international airports. Special preference is usually given to foreign groups at the check-in, and Intourist waiting areas are provided. Passports and visas are required at the check-in. Boarding passes are issued, either with open seating or with seat numbers and rows written in Cyrillic. Groups are usually seated first on the plane. Remember that the locals are quite assertive and will push vigorously to board the plane, especially with open seating. On internal flights, there is one class and no non-smoking sections. Sometimes the only meal consists of seltzer water, bread and cucumbers! Bring along some snacks. There is no airport departure tax.

By Train from Helsinki

Another pleasant way to travel is to take a train from a European city to St Petersburg or Moscow. **Finnair** flies daily from New York to Helsinki from about $700 return. After a few relaxing days in Helsinki, take the train to St Petersburg or Moscow. (Finnair also flies daily from Helsinki to St Petersburg or Moscow.) Two trains leave daily for St Petersburg, one Russian and one Finnish. The Russian one leaves at 15.06 and arrives at 23.15. The Finnish train departs at 06.25 and arrives at 13.45; both arrive the same day as departure, with a one-hour advance time change. For soft berth, one way is approximately $130/265FM (first class $245/491FM). The Moscow train leaves each day at 17.08, arrives the next morning at 09.10 and costs about $250/506FM ($375/760FM first class) each way. If the train has hard berths, these are usually cheaper. Instead of dealing with reservations at the last minute in Helsinki, you can book and pay for the train through your travel agency (strongly recommended as the trains fill up in advance). You can also book space directly. The address is Finnish State Railways, Ticket Office, Railway Station, SF-00100 Helsinki, Finland, fax (358-0) 707-4240; telex 12-301124. A handling fee is charged. Return trains leave Moscow at 18.17 and arrive in Helsinki at 09.02 the next day. Russian trains from St Petersburg depart at 06.25 and arrive in Helsinki at 12.07 the same day. The Finnish train leaves at 15.55 and arriving Helsinki 21.26.

By Train from Moscow

The Red Arrow trains between St Petersburg and Moscow are a wonderful way to travel. Board the sleeper at night and arrive the next morning for a full day of sightseeing. Since there are several train stations in each city, make sure you know which one you are departing from. (See page 155 for a complete list of St Petersburg train stations.) In St Petersburg, trains for Moscow leave from the *Moskovski Vokzal*, the Moscow station. (*Vokzal* stems from the London station, Vauxhall.) In Moscow, trains for St Petersburg leave from the *Leningradski Vokzal*, the Leningrad station.

The trains always leave on time with a broadcasted warning five minutes before departure—and that is all! So do not miss the train! First class has two berths to a compartment and second class has four. This is an excellent way to meet Russians. A personal car attendant will bring tea (brewed in the car's samovar) and biscuits, and wake you up in the morning. Remember to turn off the radio at night or the National Anthem will blast you awake at 6 am. The compartments are not segregated. If there is a problem, the attendant can usually arrange a swap. It is difficult for foreigners to buy train or plane tickets direct from local stations or ticket counters. Tickets are usually bought through Intourist or a hotel service desk. Each city visited must be listed on your visa. If you have some Russian friends, they can purchase a ticket in rubles at local ticket offices. If you have a ticket for rubles, the train attendant will also charge a minor fee for sheets and towels once you have settled in the compartment.

By Ferry and Bus

Numerous ferries leave for Sweden once a week on Monday, for Germany once a week on Wednesday, and for Finland three times a week on Tuesday, Thursday and Sunday. There is also a ferry to Tallin, Estonia. The journeys take about 14 hours; overnight cabins are available. Ferries leave from the Sea Passenger Ship Terminal on Vasilyevsky Island. For schedules, call the Baltic Shipping Company at 1 Morskoy Slavy Prospekt, tel. 355-1310/1616, tickets 355-1312.

Another option is an express bus to Finland. Finnord, at 37 Italyanskaya Street, tel. 314-8951, is open 9 am-6 pm. Sovavto Express Bus is at tel. 298-1352 and at Hotels Grand Europe, Astoria, Pulkovskaya and Helen with daily departures to and from Helsinki.

Visas

All travelers to Russia must have a visa. There are three types of visas: tourist, business and visitor. A tourist visa application can be collected from a travel agent or at a Russian embassy or consulate. Three passport size photos and a photocopy of the information page of your passport are also required. Once confirmation of your hotel or sponsored stay is received, the visa is issued. Depending on how quickly you need the visa returned to you (from two hours to two weeks or more), a corresponding processing fee is charged that you must send in with the application. Call your local Russian embassy or consulate; information for visas is usually given on a recorded message. Independent travelers are advised to book at least six to eight weeks in advance to guarantee space and the best rates in hotels. Each city you plan to visit must be written on the visa. Once in Russia, you can lengthen your stay or visit additional cities by making arrangements with the service desk at your hotel.

If you are sponsored by a Russian organization, you are entitled to a business visa. Ask the organization to fax you with an invitation and dates of stay. Give this to the Russian embassy or consulate; they will usually issue a business visa without proof of hotel stay. Multi-entry visas are also issued with the proper papers. If hosted by a relative or friend, you can enter on a visitor's visa. You must send your host a visa application filled out in duplicate (not a photocopy). The host must then take it to his own travelers' organization, OVIR, which will issue a visitor's invitation for you after several months. The traveler is only allowed to travel to the cities and stay with the persons designated on the visa. You must make these arrangements far in advance.

On arrival, all visitors to Russia must register their visa and passport with OVIR. If you are staying in a hotel, the registration desk will do this for you upon checking in. (Your passport and visa may be held for a few hours or days at the hotel registration desk.) If staying elsewhere, you should go directly to OVIR: Visa Registration Department 4 Saltykova-Schedrina Street, tel. 278-2481. (Open 10 am-6 pm; closed Saturday and Sunday.)

Russian embassies and consulates are known for issuing visas at the last minute—do not panic, this is quite common. Try to apply as far in advance as possible. You may need visas to go to other Commonwealth states outside of Russia and to the three Baltic countries, before you enter their borders. Check first before you try to go.

See Practical Information section for addresses and phone numbers of Russian Embassies and Consulates, page 153.

Customs

Visitors arriving by air pass through a passport checkpoint in the airport terminal. Those arriving by train do this at the border. Uniformed border guards check passports and stamp visas. (A passport is never stamped. One page of the visa is removed upon arrival. The rest of it is turned in upon leaving the country.) Russian custom declarations are issued during your flight or train ride, or one can be picked up from stands located near the baggage claim area in the airport. Fill in exactly how much foreign currency you are bringing into the country (there is no limit unless it is ridiculously high). Declare your valuables (gold, silver, jewelry), otherwise they could be confiscated on departure if there is no proof you brought them into the country. An inspector will look through your luggage in varying degrees and stamp your declaration. Do not misplace it! You need it to exchange money and leave the country. On departing, another declaration (same format) must be filled out, which is compared to your original. Make sure you are not leaving the country with more foreign currency than you declared upon arrival. Even though Russian customs has become considerably easier and faster than in past years, your bags may be thoroughly searched when you leave. Do not overwrap items as they may be picked for inspection.

It is forbidden to bring in what is considered anti-Russian material and pornography. You may be asked to show all your printed matter. Drugs, other than medicinal, are highly illegal. Any video or small-film camera, VCR, personal computer or typewriter should also be noted on the customs form. You must exit with these items (unless you have official permission to leave them) or else be subject to a huge duty up to the full value of the items in question. You cannot leave with antiques, icons or expensive works of art unless you have permission from the Ministry of Culture.

Time Zones

Russia has 11 time zones. St Petersburg and Moscow are in the same time zone. Many train and plane schedules are listed throughout the country as Moscow time. Always check to see what time is actually meant by the listing. There is an 11-hour time difference from the west coast of the US, eight hours from the US east coast, three hours from London, and Helsinki is one hour behind.

Money

CURRENCY

The Russian currency is the *ruble*. It comes in note denominations of 100, 200, 500, 5,000, 10,000, 20,000, 50,000 and 100,000 (as inflation progresses, higher notes appear). 1, 5, 10, 20, 50 and 100 rouble coins also exist. (Due to high inflation, some establishments have begun weighing the bricks of money, instead of counting the bills.)

CURRENCY EXCHANGE

It is illegal to enter or exit the country with Russian currency. (Small amounts of bills and change are excepted as souvenirs.) Officially, foreign currency can only be converted into rubles at exchange offices in the country at fixed rates. You can convert hard currency to rubles at the airport or, more easily, in your hotel (bring some cash with you; often traveler's checks and credit cards are not accepted). Some banks and street kiosks also exchange foreign currency. These kiosks, or 'private exchange markets', are now popping up around the city, and many of them advertise 'We buy Dollars, Finn and Deutschmarks'. Rates vary from place to place; when the banks are closed at night and on holidays, the rates naturally go up. Be aware that some kiosks do not have a license, so they will not stamp your declaration form. The customs declaration form should be presented when money is legally exchanged. The date and amount converted is noted on the form. You can re-exchange your unused rubles at the end of your stay (not before) at the airport or border. Remember when exiting that you cannot convert more rubles than you officially exchanged. As it is considered illegal to change foreign currency on the black market, should the opportunity present itself, be discreet (see the Hazards section, page 63). Since the ruble is worth less and less, many places prefer direct payment in foreign currency.

In addition to exchange offices in your hotel, the **Credobank**, at 26 Mokhovavya Street (tel. 275-0606), Astoria Hotel and Finland Railway Station, buys and sells currencies. It is open from 9.30 am-1 pm and from 2-6 pm. You can also exchange currency (into rubles) at: **Lada Bank**, 6 Zanevsky Prospekt (9.30 am-12.30 pm); **Russian Bank** at 15 Bolshaya Morskaya Street (9 am-3 pm; closed 12.30-1.30); and a bank at 10 Millionnaya Street (near Hermitage), open 10 am-1 pm, 2-5 pm.

TRAVELER'S CHECKS AND CREDIT CARDS

Traveler's checks and credit cards are now accepted at some banks, restaurants and shops. It is advisable to bring cash, especially small notes and change. At times, it can be difficult to change traveler's checks into foreign cash. You should have rubles for regular stores and local transportation.

(Preceding pages) St Petersburg's Neva river

American Express is located in the Grand Hotel Europe (tel. 119-6009). Here you can cash traveler's checks or get money with your AMEX card. You also need a personal check to get money with the credit card—the money comes out of your checking account. Bear in mind that a five per cent commission is charged on all exchanges. Get to the office early, as they may run out of foreign currency—and be warned that often one can exchange for rubles only! It is strongly advised to bring more cash than traveler's checks. If no one has dollars, try the **Vnesheconombank** at 29 Bolshaya Morskaya Street. Small amounts (under $100) can usually be cashed at some stores with a purchase.

Credit cards are increasingly being accepted by many businesses (but not traveler's checks; foreign cash is wanted). There is a Visa cash machine at the **St Petersburg Savings Bank** at 70 Fontanka Embankment. The Bureau de Change is in room 73 and is open 9.30 am-noon. You can also get a cash advance from Visa card (you may need a personal check) The commission is five per cent. Other offices can be found in **Hotel Pulkovskaya** (9 am-9 pm) and at 38 Nevsky Prospekt; open 10 am-6 pm, closed Sunday.

What to Pack

LUGGAGE ALLOWANCE

For your own convenience, travel as lightly as possible. Most airlines departing the US allow up to two pieces of luggage and one carry-on bag. Other airlines allow 20 kilos check-in luggage and one carry-on bag. Baggage allowance is very strictly controlled on exiting Russia. Often, all bags are weighed, including your carry-on. Anything over 20 kilos (coach class) and 30 kilos (first and business class) may get charged per additional kilo. This is usually the procedure for internal flights as well.

CLOTHES

The season of the year is a major factor in deciding what to bring. Summers are warm, humid and dusty, with frequent thunderstorms, especially in Moscow. Bring a raincoat or an umbrella. Summer evenings with the White Nights are delightful in St Petersburg, but you will occasionally need a sweater or light jacket. Wearing shorts or sleeveless shirts may prevent you from entering a church during services. Winters are cold and damp, with temperatures well below freezing. It can snow from November until April, when the cold arctic winds sharpen the chill. Be prepared with your warmest clothes—waterproof boots, gloves and thermal underwear. Interiors are usually well heated, so dress in layers.

MEDICINE

Take a good supply of medicine, prescription drugs, and remedies for flu and minor illnesses. Recommended items include aspirin or Tylenol, throat lozenges, cold formulas, a course of antibiotics to treat a very bad cold or infection, vitamins (especially C), laxatives, lip salve, travel sickness pills, water-purifying tablets, contact lens cleaners. For an upset stomach take indigestion tablets, Alka-Selzer or Pepto Bismal.Each hotel has a resident nurse or doctor and a small apothecary stand with a few medications for sale.

PERSONAL ARTICLES

Consider taking with you cosmetics, lotions, shampoo, conditioner, razors, shaving cream, toothpaste, lavatory paper, Kleenex, feminine products, water bottle for long trips, soap, washing powder, flat bathtub plug, nylons, sewing kit, scotch tape and strong wrapping tape, pens and an extra pair of glasses or contact lenses.

FILM

Film is expensive and the stock is of a limited range. Bring whatever you plan to use. Since using a flash is prohibited in many museums and churches, have some high-speed film on hand. If you find yourself short of film try some of the major department stores and international shops in this list:

Best, 15 Kupchinskaya Street; **Dom Peterburg Torgovli** ('Trade House'), 21–23 Bolshaya Konyushennaya Street; **Fruzensky Univermag**, 60 Moskovsky Prospekt; **Gostiny Dvor**, 35 Nevsky Prospekt; **Kirovsky Univermag**, 9 Narvskaya Square; **Moskovsky Univermag**, 205–220 Moskovsky Prospekt; **Narvsky Univermag**, 120–138 Leninsky Prospekt; **Passazh**, 48 Nevsky Prospekt; **Shopping Center**, 1 Novosmolenskaya, Embankment.

GADGETS

Voltage varies from 220V to 127V. Sometimes hotels have plugs for 220/110V. Pack a transformer and an adaptor. New hair dryers, travel irons and electric shavers are now made with safety ends that do not fit into many adaptors—check before you go. A duel voltage coil is useful for boiling water and brewing tea and coffee in hotel rooms. Use with *extreme caution*. A personal stereo may be welcome.

DOCUMENTS

Keep your passport, visa, important papers, tickets, vouchers and money in your hand luggage at all times. Also, carry a photocopy of your passport and visa. Bear in mind that you will need to show some identification to get into certain places. Serious photographers with a lot of film should have it inspected separately—Russian X-rays are not always guaranteed film-safe.

Health

Immunizations are not required, unless you are coming from an infected area. Other than the cold, food and pollution, Russia does not have many health risks. Some people may have trouble adjusting to Russian cuisine, which includes heavy breads, thick greasy soups, smoked fish and sour cream. Vegetables and fruit are often in low supply. Bring indigestion or stomach disorder remedies. If you are a vegetarian or require a special diet, bring along what you need, even if it is instant, freeze-dried mixes or nutritional supplements. Do not drink the water, especially in St Petersburg where it is highly polluted. The parasite *giardia lamblia* can cause severe illness. Drink bottled or boiled water. Each hotel usually has its own resident physician. For a serious illness, contact your embassy or consulate. Consider purchasing some type of travel medical insurance before the trip. For medical listings in the Practical Information Section, see page 152.

Safety

Even though some areas of Russia are experiencing unrest, it is considered safe to walk around St Petersburg and Moscow any time during the day or evening, though, as in any big city, you should use common sense and take care of your possessions. Hotels usually have safety deposit boxes by the front desk. It is advisable to lock up your valuables, money, passport and airline tickets even if there is a lock on your suitcase—there are thefts from hotel rooms. In case of loss or theft, notify the service bureau at your hotel. See the Hazards section, page 62

Accommodation

Most group tours are provided with first-class hotel accommodation. Russian hotels usually offer deluxe, first-class or tourist accommodation. For individual travelers, hotels are often the most expensive part of the stay. To visit Russia, you must pay the fixed rate for Russian or Western-style hotels, which can be expensive, costing from $75 to $200 per person per night. (Note that in many instances it costs only a little extra for a double room.) Recently a wider selection of cheaper hotels, hostels and bed and breakfasts has become available (see the Practical Information hotel listings, starting on page 156). One can camp at designated camp grounds, but this must be set up before entering the country and arranged in advance.

Upon arrival, hand in your passport and visa. The hotel registers you in the country and returns everything within a few days. (Notice that the hotel dates of your stay are stamped on the back of your visa. If you exit the country and these have not been stamped, you may be pulled aside for questioning. Make sure a hotel stamp appears on the back of your visa.) The name of the hotel is written in Russian on your hotel card, which can be shown to taxis, for example.

Many of the Russian hotels still have a *dezhurnaya* (hall attendant) on each floor. When you show her your hotel card, she will give you the key. (The 'Westernized' hotels just issue the key at the front desk.) Most rooms are quite adequate, but they sometimes do not match your conception of a first-class hotel, particularly those outside St Petersburg and Moscow. They have a bathroom, TV and phone, but many lack room service. A laundry bag is provided in each room; dry-cleaning services are often not available. There is usually a same-day or two-day service. Western-style hotels usually provide better services. A word of warning: Housekeepers in some of the Russian hotels often lack respect for privacy, and enter the room without knocking, or bring back your laundry at midnight. Use the chain lock!

Most Intourist hotels are accustomed to catering to groups. Many hotels now offer the 'Swedish table', a cafeteria-style restaurant. Check to see if your hotel has one. Here, you can enjoy a quick and inexpensive smorgasbord-type breakfast, lunch or dinner. Western-style hotels have restaurants and cafés, which are easier to get into, but these usually charge much more.

Communications

At the service bureau in your hotel, you can book a call abroad that rings through to your room at a specific time. Be forewarned that these often do not come in exactly at your booking time. Try to reserve a call for the evening; this way, if the call is late, you will be in your room and will not have to miss a tour. There is also a central number in each city that you can dial directly to place a phone order yourself. This may take up to two days. In St Petersburg, dial 314-4747 or 315-0012 and ask for an English-speaking operator. Tell the operator where you are calling. They will tell you when they can place the call. Specify where you can be reached and the operator will call back when the call goes through. Most Western hotels now have satellite dishes hooked up to phone lines in their business centers, or hard-currency international phone booths, which usually require either a credit or prepaid card. In this way, a call can go out immediately—but not cheaply. Always check the fee as some hotels charge for a three-minute minimum. Most hotels are also equipped with fax and telex.

Direct long-distance dialing in St Petersburg is also possible. First dial 8 and wait for the tone. Dial 10 (international), then the country code, area code and telephone number. During peak hours it can be difficult to get through, so be persistent. Also, many hotels do not have direct dialing capabilities. If not, try calling from a friend's home for rubles; this makes it much cheaper.

If you have an AT&T calling card and wish to call the United States, you can try calling a USA Direct number. If this does not connect, try calling Helsinki USA direct— (10-358)-9800-100-10. The AT&T access number out of Russia is 155–5042. This currently works out of Moscow only, but St Petersburg should follow soon. Baltic Communications Limited (BCL) has recently introduced the first international credit card payphones in St Petersburg. The phones are located in key business areas and hotels throughout the city. Customers can pay for calls with major credit cards. Dial 311-8800 or 315-0073 for details. The country code for Russia is 7, St Petersburg 812 + phone number. Many Russian hotels do not have switchboards. Give the person wishing to call you the seven-digit number for the phone in your room.

Local calls can be made from your hotel room, in many establishments, free of charge. Long-distance calls within the CIS can be made (also from your room) once you know the area code. For example, St Petersburg is 812 and Moscow 095. For other city area codes, dial 07. To call St Petersburg from Moscow, dial 8 to get a long-distance tone, then 812 and the seven-digit number. An information operator will sometimes need to know the name (and patronymic), address and date of birth to attempt to track down a personal number!

Special 'long-distance' phones can also be used for calling other cities within the CIS. *Mezhdugorodny*, or intercity phone booths, line the streets. You can also go to the *peregovorny punkt*, the city's long-distance telephone centers, one of which is at 3/5 Bolshaya Morskaya Street. International calls can be ordered too, but this could take some time. Local calls from a pay phone cost, at the time of the writing, 150 rubles for three minutes. One must buy special tokens, sold in kiosks, metro stations and stores throughout the city, for 150 rubles each—in most local phone booths only tokens can now be used. A one-ruble coin can also be used, but are hard to find. Do not lose your residential phone numbers as Russia has never known a phone book. There is, however, *The Traveler's Yellow Pages for St Petersburg*, the first business phone book for the city (and for Moscow). It is sold in many stores and tourist hotels in St Petersburg, as well as InfoServices International, 64 Troika Embankment, St Petersburg 190000 tel: (812) 315-6412 fax (812) 312-2032. It can also be obtained in the US from Michael Dolan at InfoServices International Inc, 1 St Mark's Place, Cold Spring Harbor, New York, NY 11724 USA tel: (516) 549-0064, fax (516) 549-2032. If you do not know where you will be staying and are staying for a length of time, mail to each city can be addressed to either Post Restante or c/o Intourist. The Poste Restante address is : 19044, St Petersburg, 6 Nevsky Prospekt, Your Name, Poste Restante (in Russian: *Pochta Do Vostrebovaniya*).

ALL ABOARD THE BOLSHOI EXPRESS   by Amanda Reynolds Leung

Although today the Commonwealth of Independent States has one of the world's largest rail networks and arguably the most famous of train journeys—the Trans-Siberian—for years it actually lagged behind the railway systems of other European powers. Fourteen years after George Stephenson began building his proto-railway from Stockton to Darlington, and eight years after the engineer's locomotive, *Rocket*, was built, Tsar Nicholas I reluctantly opened Russia's first railroad. The Pushkin to St Petersburg line, inaugurated in 1837, was succeeded by additional tracks including a St Petersburg to Moscow service in 1851. Yet by this date the country could still only boast some 770 miles (1,240 kilometers) of tracks.

Russia's transport and military supply service was shown to be woefully inadequate in 1854 when British, French and Turkish armies inflicted a humiliating defeat on the country in the Crimean War. Historians have noted that more Russian troops died on the freezing foot march to the Crimea, and from disease, than perished in battle.

The reforming Tsar Alexander II instituted a programme of modernisation which included railway building, often inspired by military campaigns. The St Petersburg to Warsaw line was initiated in 1861; a decade later iron sleepers reached the Volga. At the time of his death in 1881, Russia had 14,000 miles (22,530 kilometers) of track. In 1892 the Trans-Siberian route started from Chelyabinsk, it reached Irkutsk in 1898 and the last leg to the port city of Vladivostock was broached in 1916. Until this point, passengers traveled by boat in summer (and sleigh in winter) across Lake Baikal.

The railroads had an enormous economic and strategic importance for the country. The Trans-Caspian line to Central Asia was part of a military campaign to conquer the territory. As the sleepers snaked their way from the Baltic sea through the rolling heartland of Russia and on across the Siberian wilderness ploughing the deserts of Uzbekistan and Kazakstan, markets and trade opened up almost overnight. The railways were responsible for Russia's first speculative boom.

Today, the CIS's network carries some 11 million travelers every day on some 145,000 miles (233,355 kilometers) of rails. Thanks to Lenin's prognosis that Communism was Soviet power plus the electrification of the whole country, a third of the network is now electrified. The most heavily used route is between St Petersburg and Moscow where express trains run the distance in about four hours. The most interesting way is to take the overnight Red Arrow service which departs at midnight and arrives in time for breakfast next morning.

And those travelers who long to recapture the golden era of railway travel and enjoy the sights and history of the CIS can now do so with Cox and Kings' specialized tours. Aiming to revive the stately pace of travel of the Tsars and Grand Dukes who traveled annually left St Petersburg for the South of France, Cox and Kings Travel Ltd bought up a series of carriages built in the 1950s.

Named the Bolshoi Express, this special train, which began serving tourists in 1993, comprises 16 maroon carriages. In addition to six sleeping carriages, travelers can relax in three dining cars decorated in Baltic, Ukrainian and Georgian styles and a 1920's style saloon car with wooden parquet floor. The sleeping cars feature double-berth compartments with brass, oak and mahogany fittings. Thanks to the additional space available on the Russian broad (1.524 metres) gauge track, each room has an armchair, writing table and sofa, with an adjoining small bathroom containing shower and washbasin. For the ultimate in luxury, each carriage has a centrally located suite of two rooms plus bathroom.

Measuring 800 metres in length, the imposing Bolshoi Express makes a lasting impression as it sweeps out of the station to the strains of a jazz band on the platform and passengers tinkling champagne glasses—part of the celebration which accompanies every gracious departure. One of the tour's original features is the use of steam engines for part of each journey transporting travelers back to the golden era of rail travel. En route, travelers are entertained nightly by the train's musicians who play classical and folk music during and after dinner in the saloon and restaurant cars.

Passengers can select between four-day sight-seeing weekends in St Petersburg and Moscow with two nights aboard the locomotive and an optional detour to take in the twelfth-century city of Novgorod or an eight-day tour of the duchies and principalities of ancient Muscovy and medieval Russia—the famed Golden Ring—which takes in Suzdal, Rostov and Yaroslavl as well as the premier cities.

Those with more time on their hands can take the 14-day, 5,000-kilometer ride from St Petersburg through Central Asia to Tashkent. This fascinating journey on the Bolshoi Express was filmed by the BBC as part of its *Great Railway Journeys of the World* series aired in early 1994. The train carried prima ballerina Natalia Makarova on a nostalgic visit through her homeland. The tour takes in the city of Volgograd (formerly Stalingrad) before coasting the Volga delta, settled by the Mongol-Turkic Khazar tribes, to the Caspian Sea for a visit to the Tartar capital, Astrakhan, and on to the deserts of Central Asia. The trip takes in the ancient Silk Road cities of Khiva, legendary Tamerlaine's Samarkand and Bukhara.

Options include a ten-day circular tour starting from St Petersburg and taking in the Baltic states of Estonia, Latvia and Lithuania before reaching Moscow, or an in-depth ride from Moscow to the well- and lesser-known Golden Ring historical and religious centres of imperial Russia—Rostov the Great, Yaroslavl on the Volga, Kostroma, Ivanovo and Suzdal.

The famous Trans-Siberian route which stretches 5,787 miles (9,313 kilometers) from European Russia to the Sea of Japan is often no more than a dream for all but hardy travelers who take the state trains. However, the Bolshoi Express made its inaugural trip from Vladivostock in August 1994.

Cox & Kings Travel Ltd, St James Court, 45 Buckingham Gate, London SW1E 6AF. Tel: 071 873 5003, fax 071 630 6038, telex 23378 COXKIN G.

Mail is usually held for up to two months. Notice that addresses are written *backwards* in Russia. Any mail sent to Russia takes weeks or even more than a month. The city's central post office is at 9 Pochtamtskaya Street. Post offices send telegrams and packages but, if you send packages, do not wrap them fully; the contents are usually inspected before shipping. Mail is slow and erratic, and many travelers arrive home before their postcards! To get mail out quickly, try Federal Express or DHL; see Practical Information for locations, page 152.

Getting Around

ORIENTATION

St Petersburg is 400 miles (640 km) north of Moscow on the same longitude as Helsinki and Anchorage. The city is separated by the **Neva River**, which begins at Lake Ladoga and empties 46 miles (74 kilometres) later into the Gulf of Finland. At the tip of Vasilyevsky Island, it splits into the Bolshaya (Big) and the Malaya (Little) Neva. The right bank of the Neva is known as the Petrogradskaya side (originally known as Birch Island), which includes the Zayachy, Petrogradsky, Aptekarsky and Petrovsky islands. The Kirovsky Islands lie farther to the north. Many of the main points of interest are found on the left bank of the Neva.

St Petersburg was originally spread out over 101 islands; today, because of redevelopment, there are 44 islands, connected by 620 bridges linking over 100 waterways and canals that make up one-sixth of the area of the city. St Petersburg is a treasure house of activity with over 50 museums, 40 theaters and concert halls, 60 stadiums and 2,500 libraries.

ARRIVAL

When arriving in St Petersburg, group travelers are automatically taken by bus to their hotel. Individual travelers staying in Russian Intourist hotels should hold a transportation voucher issued at home before departure. Report to the Intourist desk at the train station or air terminal upon arrival. Whilst the airport is about 45 minutes from the city center, the train station is much more centrally located. For those without transportation, inquire at the Intourist desk or bargain with drivers of taxis or individual cars for a ride into town. If you arrive at a train station and you do not have too much luggage, try riding the Metro to your destination. Reconfirming your departure flight can be done through the service desk at your hotel or by phoning the airlines directly. Reconfirm internal flights as well as they tend to be overbooked. One cannot officially venture more than 35 kilometers outside the city's parameters. Only the cities specified on the visa can be visited. Unless the visa is extended, one must exit the country on the date shown on the visa.

COACH TOURS

Group tourists are shown around St Petersburg by coach. Often the buses are not air conditioned, but all are heated in winter. Individual travelers can sign up through Intourist or their hotel's service desk for city sightseeing excursions; check at these locations for tour listings. Comfortable coach excursions are also offered to areas in the Golden Ring. Always remember the number of your bus; parking lots tend to fill up quickly.

LOCAL BUSES, TRAMS AND TROLLEYS

Local transportation operates from 6 am to 1 am and is charged by distance. Rides are often run on the honor system. You must prepurchase tickets at a special kiosk or from the driver and punch them at a special device on the bus or tram. These get stamped by a device on the wall. Sometimes there are control checks; the fine is minimal. Even if you do not speak Russian, people will help to direct you to the proper bus or stop. Never be afraid to ask, even if in sign language!

METRO

The Metro is the quickest and least expensive way to get around St Petersburg. Trains run every 90 seconds during rush hour. Central stations are beautifully decorated with chandeliers and mosaics. Metro stations are easy to spot; entrances on the street are marked with a large 'M'. Even the long escalator rides are great entertainment. Metro maps can be purchased in the hotels and are posted inside each station (or use the one in this book). To ride the Metro, purchase a token at the ticket counter or through the machines. Other automatic machines give change.If you cannot read Cyrillic, ask someone to write down the name of your destination in Russian. People are always most helpful and will point you in the proper direction. It is time to be adventurous!

TAXI

Unlike many other countries, a taxi ride is not as simple as it seems. Firstly, Russian taxi drivers usually stop and ask you where you want to go. Then the driver decides if he wants to take you! If he does, then the negotiating begins. If you look foreign, he will start out high and in foreign currency, even though payment legally should be made in rubles and each taxi should have a meter. (Note that inflation is increasing faster than meters can be changed or reprogrammed; your ruble fee may be calculated as a few times more than the actual amount on the meter.) Also, taxi fees are higher in the evening. Learn numbers in Russian to negotiate successfully. It is always wise to know the average cost of your journey before you bargain.

Hitching is quite common since taxis are not always available, and local people in private cars are eager to earn some extra cash by picking up paying passengers on their way to work or home. A reasonable ruble contribution for gas is expected. Always use common sense when accepting rides from private cars. To order an official taxi (for rubles), call 312-0022 (inquiries 315-1117). They must have two-hour advance notice but often arrive more quickly. Unfortunately, in more recent times, customers have been robbed by their car or taxi drivers.

CAR HIRE

Many hotels offer car service with a driver. A guide can also be hired for the day. This must be paid in foreign currency. Outside the hotel, you will usually find many cars and off-duty taxi drivers who will be open to a suggestion. Some can be hired for the day to take you around town. Make your payment agreement beforehand. St Petersburg has a few rent-a-car companies (see page 184). It is best to hire a car with driver or use public transportation. You can drive your own car in from Europe. This requires advance planning and permits, since a few borders are crossed and special insurance is necessary.

Hydrofoil on the River Neva

BOAT TOURS

A number of boat tours run through St Petersburg. If your tour does not include any, you can easily go on your own. Opposite the Hermitage Museum are two docks on the Neva. The first is for a boat ride along the Neva (another dock for a cruise on the Neva is opposite the statue of Peter the Great). Here you can buy tickets—the times are posted on the kiosk. It is a lovely cruise from the Hermitage to the Smolny Convent on a double-decker boat that lasts about an hour. The second dock is for hydrofoils, the *Rockets*, to Peter's Summer Palace, Petrodvorets. The ride lasts about 30 minutes and takes you past the city out into the Gulf of Finland. (See also Petrodvorets in Vicinity of St Petersburg section.) A third boat trip takes you on a tour of the St Petersburg canals. This leaves from the Anichkov Bridge off Nevsky Prospekt and cruises along the Fontanka and Moika rivers and Kryukov Canal, and lasts about 75 minutes. Boats depart daily about every 15-30 minutes from May to September. Commentaries are usually in Russian only. Tickets (in rubles) are inexpensive; but often, during nice weather, they sell out quickly. It is advised to buy tickets ahead of the time you wish to leave. Refreshments are sold onboard each cruise for rubles. Special 'White Night' cruises are offered in the summer.

Photography

Under the former Soviet Union, you could photograph anything you wished except for the following: military installations, border areas, airports, railway stations, bridges, tunnels, power and radar stations, telephone and telegraph centers, industrial enterprises and from airplanes while flying over the country. The new government is less strict, but laws and attitudes are still in a state of flux—and old habits die hard. If you are not sure, inquire before you shoot. Ask permission at factories, state institutions and farms—and of individuals, who may not want their picture taken. Bear in mind that local people are sometimes sensitive about foreigners photographing what they perceive as being backward or poor conditions. Always remain courteous.

Hazards

In the big cities you will most likely be approached by people asking 'Do you speak English?' and trying to sell everything from lacquer boxes and caviar to army watches. Some may even want to buy your clothes. The government is trying to discourage speculation, since most want to sell their wares for foreign currency and dealing directly in hard currency is totally illegal. Work out your own bargain, but be discreet. Many will ask to change money; it is best to stay away—or beware and pay attention for sometimes the exchanger will present false or out-of-circulation bills (in 1991, 50- and 100-rouble notes were removed from circulation, and new ones introduced—make sure you receive the legal ones), or will roll lower notes inside higher notes; robberies are on the increase. Some of the most notorious places to get duped are around Gostiny Dvor, Sadko and Sennaya Square. In marketplaces, such as the Klenovaya Flea Market, it has been known for a small group to surround a person and, while pretending to sell souvenirs, others are going through the tourist's shoulderbag. Also, do not carry money in pockets or inside jackets; wear a moneybelt. (Often the bank, hotel or kiosk exchanges are about the same as those on the black market so it does not merit the energy searching for back-alley exchanges. The black market rate is published in the *Commersant* newspaper; it is sold at newsstands in English.) As in any big city, always be on guard. Nowadays in Russia, mafia activities are on the rise, and unfortunately so are crimes against tourists.

Etiquette

Russians appear on the surface to be very restrained, formal, even somewhat glum. But there is a dichotomy between public (where for so many generations you dared not show your true feelings) and private appearance. In private and informal situations or after friendship is established, their character is suddenly charged with emotional warmth, care and humor. They are intensely loyal and willing to help. Arriving in or leaving the country will merit great displays of affection, usually with flowers, bear hugs, kisses and tears. If invited to someone's home for dinner, expect large preparations. The Russians are some of the most hospitable people in the world.

The formal use of the patronymic (where the father's first name becomes the children's middle name) has been used for centuries. For example, if Ivan names his son Alexander, Alexander's patronymic is Ivanovich. Especially in formal or business dealings, try to remember the person's patronymic: Alexander Ivanovich, or Mariya Pavlova (her father's name is Pavel or Paul). As with Western names, where Robert is shortened to Bob, the same is done with Russian first names, once you have established a friendship. Call your friend Alexander 'Sasha', Mikhail 'Misha', and Mariya 'Masha', or use the diminutive form 'Mashenka'.

Complaints

Many restaurants and cafés have a service book (*kniga zhalov*), where you can register complaints. Hotel complaints can be reported to the service desk. Remember that rules, regulations and bureaucracy still play a large role in Russian life—with many uniformed people enforcing them. People here are not always presumed innocent until proven guilty. When dealing with police or other officials, it is best to be courteous while explaining a situation. For example, police in the streets will randomly pull over vehicles to spot check the car and registration. If you are pulled over, it does not mean you did something wrong. If you are kept waiting long, as in restaurants for service, remember that everyone else is waiting too.

Shopping

Please note: Since January 1, 1994 all cash payments in hard currency in Russian stores were banned. Officially payment for all goods must be made in rubles only. However, many establishments accept and prefer payment in hard currency. The official decree doesn't seem to be enforced; and many people, even Russians, pay with hard cash. If you need more rubles they can be purchased in numerous Currency Exchange Offices at the current bank exchange rate. Most local stores open between 8 and 10 am and close between 5 and 8 pm. They close for an hour's lunch sometime between 12 and 3 pm. Restaurants and cafés also close for a few hours during the day. If you are on a tight schedule, try to check operating hours first.

BERIOZKAS

The *Beriozkas*, once the official hard currency outlets, are now in open competition with other shops and kiosks that are opening up constantly. For the traveler they are still well worth visiting for the occasional bargain and because, more impotantly, all their merchandise is genuine. One of the most popular Russian souvenir is the *matryoshka*, the painted set of nested dolls. *Khokhloma* lacquerware comes in the form of trays, cups, spoons, bowls and vases. Other buys are handicrafts, wood carvings, amber, fur hats, embroidered shawls and linens, lace, filigree jewelry, ceramics, samovars, balalaikas, painted eggs, caviar, tea and tea sets, vodka, books, records and *znachki* (small pins used for trading). Most *Beriozkas* are open from 9 am to 8 pm daily and close for an hour at lunch sometime between 12 and 3 pm. Your hotel also has small kiosks and post offices that sell foreign newspapers, magazines and books, postcards, stamps and pins. Recently, more Russian and Western-type stores have opened throughout the city selling food and souvenirs. See page 173 for *Beriozka* listings.

SHOPPING TIPS

Usually the procedure for purchasing an item in a local store involves several steps. First, locate the desired item and find out its price. Second, go to the the *kassa* (cashier's booth)and pay. Third, bring the receipt back to the salesgirl, who will wrap and hand over your purchase. Prices are usually posted, especially in food stores. If things get too mathematical for you to fathom, gesture to the salesgirl to write down the total for you. Many stores still use an abacus to tally. Know your exact bill; if you are even a few rubles off, you may have to return to the cashier to pay the discrepancy! Sometimes you will have to force your way to the counter. If you have to stand in a long line (a way of life for most of the population), take the opportunity to practice your Russian. If you have any questions, do not be afraid to ask—many people even know a few words of English and would be glad to help. If you see something you like, buy it! Most likely, it will not be there when you go back. Always bring along a small string or shopping bag; many of the stores and markets do not provide any, and you may end up having to put two kilos of strawberries in your pocket or purse!

THE MARKET

There are many popular open-air souvenir and flea markets in St Petersburg, the latest being the Klenovaya Alleya at Manezhnaya Square. Across from the circus building, the Architect Rossi laid out Klenovaya or Maple Alley on the south side of Czar Paul's military parade grounds. This area has now been turned into a market filled with everything from *matryoshka* dolls to icons and jewelry. Paintings by local artists are also on sale. See page 182 for a listing of markets.

Holidays and Festivals

OFFICIAL HOLIDAYS

January 1: New Year's Day. The last week in December is quite festive, culminating with New Year's Eve. Presents are given on New Year's Day.

January 7: A new official holiday celebrates **Russian Orthodox Christmas**. (The Orthodox Church still follows the old calendar, which differs from the Gregorian by 13 days.) Churches throughout the country hold services.

March 8: Women's Day. Established after the Second International Conference of Socialist Women in Copenhagen in 1910, women receive gifts and usually do not have to work! Even though socialism is out, celebrating women is still in!

March/April: Easter or Pashka. Traditional Russian Orthodox holiday.

May 1: May Day. Even though no longer celebrated as International Workers' Solidarity Day, this event, now known as Labor and Spring Holiday, retains the festive nature, with colorful parades through Moscow's Red Square and St Petersburg's Palace Square.

May 9: Victory Day. Parades are held at war memorials such as the Piskaryovskoye Cemetery in St Petersburg to celebrate V-E Day at the end of World War II in Europe.

June 12: Another new holiday, known as **Russian Independence Day**.

Lenin—Leader of the Russian Revolution

Lenin, founder of the first Soviet State, was born Vladimir Ilyich Ulyanov, on April 22, 1870. Vladimir, along with his five brothers and sisters, had a strict but pleasant childhood in the small town of Simbirsk (now Ulyanovsk) on the Volga River. On March 1, 1887, when Vladimir was 17, a group of students attempted to assassinate Czar Alexander III in St Petersburg. Vladimir's older brother, Alexander, was one of five students arrested. They were imprisoned in Peter and Paul Fortress in St Petersburg, and on May 8 were hung in the Fortress of Schlüsselburg (Kronstadt).

As a marked family of a revolutionary, the Ulyanovs left Simbirsk for Kazan, where Vladimir attended Kazan University. In December 1887, after the local papers reported the news of the student riots in Moscow, 99 Kazan students protested against the strict rules of their university. Ulyanov, one of them, was immediately expelled and exiled to the town of Kokushkino and kept under police surveillance. Here Vladimir began to study the works of Karl Marx (*Das Kapital*, and *The Communist Manifesto*) and Chernyshevsky (*What Is To Be Done?*). Thereupon, he decided to devote his life to the revolutionary struggle. Lenin wrote that 'my way in life was marked out for me by my brother'.

Since he was refused permission to enter another university, the young Ulyanov covered the four-year law course, independently, in a little over a year. He then journeyed to St Petersburg and passed the bar exam with honors. With his law degree, Ulyanov moved to the Asian town of Samara, where he defended the local peasants and secretly taught Marxist philosophy.

In 1893, he left again for St Petersburg, where he formed the revolutionary organization, the 'League of Struggle for the Emancipation of the Working Class'. At 24, in 1894, Vladimir Ulyanov published his first book, *What Are The Friends of the People?* During a secret meeting of the League of Struggle, Ulyanov decided to publish an underground newspaper called *The Workers' Cause*. That same day he was arrested by the police, along with hundreds of other people from the League. Ulyanov was exiled to Siberia, as was Nadezhda Konstantinovna Krupskaya. They were married in the small village of Shushenskoye on July 22, 1898.

While in exile, the League planned the first party newspaper, called *Iskra* (Spark), inspired by words from a Decembrist poem, 'A spark will kindle a flame'. After the Ulyanov's release, they settled in the town of Pskov outside St Petersburg. Since it was illegal to disseminate any print media criticizing the government, they eventually moved abroad. The first issues of *Iskra* were published in Leipzig, Germany. During these years abroad, Ulyanov wrote books on politics, economics and the revolutionary struggle. In December 1901, Vladimir Ulyanov began signing his writings with the name of Lenin.

In 1903, the Russian Party Congress secretly gathered in London. During this meeting, the Social Democratic Workers Party split into two factions: the Bolsheviks (Majority) and the Mensheviks (Minority). After the session, Lenin led the Bolsheviks to the grave of Karl Marx and said, 'Let us pledge to be faithful to his teachings. We shall never give up the struggle. Forward, comrades, only forward'.

By 1905, widespread unrest was sweeping across Russia. A popular May Day song was often sung: 'Be it the merry month of May. Grief be banished from our way. Freedom songs our joy convey. We shall go on strike today'. Workers at the Putilov factory in St Petersburg began a strike that triggered work stoppages at over 350 factories throughout the city. On Sunday, January 9, 1905, thousands of workers lined the streets of St Petersburg. In a peaceful protest, the crowd carried icons and portraits of the Czar. The procession walked toward the Winter Palace and congregated in Decembrist Square. The Palace Guards opened fire. More than 1,000 demonstrators were massacred in what is known today as 'Bloody Sunday'. Not long afterward, sailors manning the *Potemkin*, largest battleship in the Russian Navy, also protested against their miserable working conditions. In a mutiny headed by Afanasy Matyushenko, the sailors raised their own revolutionary red flag on June 14, 1905.

The Geneva newspapers carried the news of 'Bloody Sunday' and Lenin decided to return to St Petersburg. He wrote in his newspaper *Vperyod* (Forward): 'The uprising has begun force against force. The Civil War is blazing up. Long live the Revolution. Long live the Proletariat'. But it was still too dangerous for Lenin to remain in Russia. Two years later he left again for the West, and over the next ten years, lived in Finland, Sweden, France and Switzerland.

Accounts of a new Russian Revolution were published throughout the West in February, 1917. Lenin immediately took a train to Finland and on April 3 proceeded in an armored car to Petrograd. Today the train's engine is displayed at St Petersburg's Finland Station, where Lenin first arrived.

In Petrograd, Lenin lived on the banks of the Moika River and started up the newspaper *Pravda* (Truth), which was outlawed by the new Kerensky Provisional Government. Lenin was later forced into hiding outside the city on Lake Razliv. The hut and area where he hid out has been made into a museum. With his beard shaved off and wearing a wig, Lenin was known as Konstantin Ivanov.

On the grounds of the Smolny Cathedral, a finishing school served as headquarters for the Petrograd Workers Soviet, which organized the Red Guards. During the summer of 1917, more than 20,000 workers in Petrograd were armed and readied for a Bolshevik uprising. Lenin gave the command for attack from the Smolny on October 24, 1917. To signal the beginning of the Great October Socialist Revolution, the battleship *Aurora* fired a blank shot near the Hermitage. The Red Guards stormed the Winter Palace and almost immediately defeated the White Guards of the Provisional Government; the Moscow Kremlin was taken two days later.

On October 25th, the Second Congress of Soviets opened in the Smolny and Lenin was selected chairman of the first Soviet State; Trotsky was his Foreign Minister. Sverdlov, Stalin, Bobnov and Dzerzhinsky (later to head the Cheka, which authorized police to 'arrest and shoot immediately all members of counterrevolutionary organizations') were elected to the Revolutionary Military Committee. Lenin introduced a Decree on Land, proclaiming that all lands become State property. At the end of the Congress, all members stood and sang the *Internationale*, the Proletarian anthem: 'Arise ye prisoners of starvation. Arise ye wretched of the earth. For Justic thunders condemnation. A better world's in birth'. On March 11, 1918, Lenin moved the capital from Petrograd to Moscow. He lived in a room at the National Hotel across from Red Square. The Bolsheviks, known as the Communist Party, had their offices in the Kremlin.

During the last years of Lenin's life, the country was wracked by war and widespread famine. He implemented the NEP (New Economic Policy) that allowed foreign trade and investment, but he did not live long enough to bear witness to its effects. Lenin died, at the age of 54, on January 21, 1924. The cause of death was listed as cerebral sclerosis triggered, as stated in the official medical report, by 'excessive intellectual activity'. In three days a mausoleum was built for him on Red Square. Later, it was replaced by a mausoleum of red granite and marble. Today thousands still visit this mausoleum daily on Red Square to view his embalmed body and the changing of the guard. Soon after his death, the city of Petrograd's name was changed to Leningrad in his honor. From then until 1991 it bore his name.

FESTIVALS

February 23: Armed Forces Day (Because Russia still has a system of compulsory service, most men in Russia have spent two years in the army.)

First week in March: Maslenitsa, or Blini Day. This day stems from the Pagan tradition of making blini pancakes to honor the coming of spring; blini represent the sun. Each spring, there are festivals in the major cities and towns to celebrate the end of winter.

April 12: Cosmonaut's Day.

May 5 to 13: Festival of Moscow Stars.

June 6: Pushkin's Birthday. Poetry readings by Pushkin monuments.

The last Sunday in July is Navy Day. In St Petersburg, the fleet, including ships, submarines and sailors, is displayed about the city.

June 21 to July 11: White Nights Festival. While the sun hardly sets, many musical concerts, theatrical performances, street events, fireworks and other celebrations take place throughout Moscow, St Petersburg and the Golden Ring area.

August 19: Day of the Failed August, 1991 Coup. To mark the turn of Communism, and honor those who were killed.

September 8: Seige of Leningrad Day. This day marks the end of the 900-day seige of former Leningrad and includes special ceremonies at the Piskarovskoye Cemetery.

Sept 19: Moscow Day. A day for merry-making in the city.

November 7: A traditional holiday for nearly 75 years to commemorate the **Anniversary of the October Revolution** (on the old calendar, the revolution took place on Oct 25). No longer a state holiday, many Russians continue to celebrate not having to celebrate the 1917 Revolution anymore!

December 25-January 5: Russian Winter Festival. Events are held to celebrate the coming new year, especially in Moscow, St Petersburg, Novgorod, Vladimir and Suzdal, where troika rides, along with other traditional Russian folk customs, take place. Because the Soviet Union ceased to exist on December 21, 1991, Christmas week now offers another reason to celebrate a new beginning.

Many church holidays are celebrated by the Russian Orthodox Church, such as Easter, Christmas, Orthodox New Year (usually in January) and church name days.

Name Days: Many calendar dates have a corresponding name. Russians love to celebrate their own name day.

Food and Drink

Russian cooking is both tasty and filling, and in addition to the expected borsch and beef stroganov, it includes many delectable regional dishes from the other states, such as Uzbekistan, Georgia or the Ukraine.

The traditions of Russian cooking date back to the simple recipes of the peasantry, who made full use of the abundant supply of potatoes, cabbage, cucumbers, onions and bread to fill their hungry stomachs. For the cold northern winters, they would pickle the few available vegetables and preserve fruits to make jam. This somewhat bland diet was spiced up with sour cream, parsley, dill and other dried herbs. A popular old Russian saying is: *Shchi da kasha, Pishcha nasha*, 'Cabbage soup and porridge are our food'. The writer Nikolai Gogol painted a picture of the Russian peasant's kitchen: 'In the room was the old familiar friend found in every kitchen, namely a *samovar* and a three-cornered cupboard with cups and teapots, painted eggs hanging on red and blue ribbons in front of the icons, with flat cakes, horseradish and sour cream on the table along with bunches of dried fragrant herbs and a jug of *kvas*' (dark beer made from fermented black bread). Russians are still quite proud of these basic ingredients in their diet, which remain the staples of the Russian meal today. They will boast that there is no better bread (*khleb*) in the world than a freshly baked loaf of Russian black bread. Raisa Gorbachev presented Nancy Reagan with a cookbook containing hundreds of potato recipes!

Dining Out

The first point to remember is that most Russians consider eating out an expensive luxury and enjoy turning dinner into a leisurely evening-long experience. In the European fashion, different parties are often seated together at the same table—an excellent way to meet local people. If you are going out to a Russian restaurant, it is also advisable to make a reservation. The sign *Mect Het* may appear, meaning No Space Available. If so, stick your head in the door; often, if the proprietor notices a foreigner, he will miraculously find an empty table!

Most restaurants (in Cyrillic *pectopah*, pronounced 'restoran') are open from 11 am to 11 pm, and close for a few hours in the afternoon. Restaurants with music and dancing can be on the expensive side. Sometimes no liquor is served, but, in many Russian places, you can bring your own. Many of the newly opened co-op restaurants specialize in a regional cuisine—such as *shashlik*, shish kebab or other spicy dishes. Others may provide one choice as the 'plat du jour'. Even though there may not be a wide selection, the food is usually tasty and the meal served quickly in pleasant surroundings.

Since *perestroika*, more and more cafés have sprung up about town. Even though smaller than restaurants and with limited menus, they offer an adequate and quick meal. Look for the *zakusochnaya*, a snack-type bar serving hot and cold appetizers that often specialize in one dish, reflected in the name (see below): *Blinnaya* serves *blini*; *Pelmennaya, pelmeni*; *Pirozhkovnaya, pirozhki*; *Shashlichnaya, shashlik*; *Chainaya*, tea. Recently, Western fast-food chains have opened, such as McDonalds, Pizza Hut and even Baskin Robbins ice cream. Bars are found in all the major hotelswhere you will get Russian wines, champagne and cognac, along with espresso coffee, sandwiches and pastries. These are usually open until 2 am. If invited to a Russian home, expect a large welcome. The Russians are truly hospitable and usually prepare a spread. If you can, bring along a bottle of champagne or vodka—since these are harder for Russians to buy. A toast is usually followed by swigging down the entire shot of vodka—and then another toast!

On the Menu

The Russian menu is divided into four sections: *zakuski* (appetizers), *pervoye* (first course), *vtoroye* (second course), and *sladkoe* (dessert). The ordering is usually taken all at once, from appetizer to dessert. *Zakuski* are Russian-style *hors d'oeuvres* that include fish, cold meats, salads and marinated vegetables.

Ikra is caviar: *krasnaya* (red from salmon) and *chornaya* (black from sturgeon). The sturgeon is one of the oldest fish species known, dating back over 30 million years. Its lifespan is also one of the longest. No sturgeon is worth catching until it is at least seven years old, and *beluga* are not considered adult until after 20. The best is *zernistaya*, the fresh unpressed variety. The most expensive is the black *beluga*; another is *sevruga*. Caviar is usually available at Russian restaurants and can be bought in the *Beriozka* shops.

Caviar, in Russia, has long been considered a health food. Czar Nicholas II made his children eat the pressed *payusnaya* caviar every morning. Since they all hated the salty taste, their cook solved the problem by spreading it on black bread and adding banana slices. The caviar-banana sandwich became the breakfast rage for many aristocratic families. Russia is still the largest producer of caviar in the world, processing over 1,000 tons per year; 20 per cent of the catch is exported. The largest roe comes from the *beluga*, a dark grey caviar appreciated for its large grain and fineness of skin. Caviar from the *sevruga* is the smallest and most delicate tasting.

Many varieties of Russian soup are served, more often at lunch than dinner. *Borsch* is the traditional red beet soup made with beef and served with a spoonful of sour cream. *Solyanka* is a tomato-based soup with chunks of fish or meat and topped with diced olives and lemon. *Shchi* is a tasty cabbage soup. A soup made from pickled vegetables is *rasolnik*. *Okroshka* is a cold soup made from a *kvas* base.

Russian meals consist of meat (*mya'so*), chicken (*kur'iitsa*), or fish (*rii'ba*). *Bifshtek* is a small fried steak with onions and potatoes. Beef Stroganov is cooked in sour cream and served with fried potatoes. *Kutlyeta po Kiyevski* is chicken Kiev, stuffed with melted butter (cut slowly!); *Kutlyeta po Pajarski* is a chicken cutlet; *Tabak* is a slightly seasoned fried or grilled chicken. The fish served is usually salmon, sturgeon, herring or halibut.

Other dishes include *blini*, small pancakes with different fillings, *pelmeni*, boiled dumplings filled with meat and served with sour cream, and *pirozhki*, fried rolls with a meat filling.

Dessert includes such sweets as *vareniki*, sweet fruit dumplings topped with sugar, *tort* (cake), *ponchiki* (sugared donuts), or *morozhnoye* (ice cream).

Chai (tea) comes with every meal. It is always sweet; ask for *biz sak'hera*, for unsweetened tea. Many Russians stir in a spoonful of jam instead of sugar. Coffee is not served as often. Alcoholic drinks consist of *pivo* (beer), *kvas* (dark beer), *shampanskoye* (champagne), *vino* (wine) and vodka. Alcoholic drinks are ordered in grams; a small glass is 100 grams and a normal bottle consists of 750 grams or three quarters of a liter. The best wine comes from Georgia and the Crimea. There are both *krasnoye* (red) and *beloye* (white). The champagne is generally sweet. The best brandy comes from Armenia—*Armyanski konyak*. *Nalivka* is a fruit liqueur. Vodka is by far the favorite drink and comes in a number of varieties other than Stolichnaya, Moskovskaya or Russkaya. There is *limonnaya* (lemon vodka), *persovka* (with hot peppers), *zubrovka* (flavored with a special grass), *ryabinovka* (made from ash berries), *tminaya* (caraway flavor), *starka* (a smooth dark vodka), *ahotnichaya vodka* (hunter's vodka), and *zveroboy* (animal killer!). One of the strongest and most expensive is *Zolotoye Koltso*, the Golden Ring. Vodka can be most easily found in the *Beriozkas*, along with beer, champagne, wine and Western alcohols. A full list of cafes and restaurants can be found on page 165.

Inside a St Petersburg Restaurant

Peter and Paul Fortress

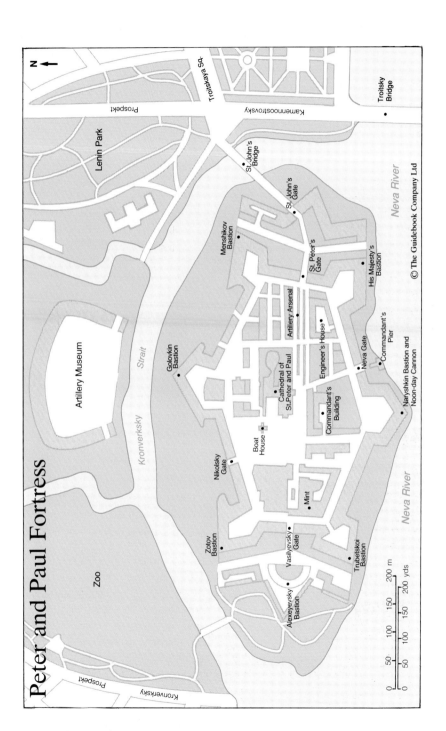

Kronverksky Prospekt

Zoo

Artillery Museum

Kronverksky

Strait

Lenin Park

Prospekt

Troitskaya Sq.

Kamennoostrovsky

St. John's
Bridge

St. John's
Gate

Menshikov
Bastion

Golovkin
Bastion

Nikolsky
Gate

Boat
House

Zotov
Bastion

Mint

Vasilyevsky
Gate

Alexeyevsky
Bastion

Trubetskoi
Bastion

Cathedral of
St. Peter and Paul

Artillery Arsenal

Commandant's
Building

Engineer's House

Commandant's
Pier

St. Peter's
Gate

His Majesty's
Bastion

Neva Gate

Naryshkin Bastion and
Noon-day Cannon

Neva River

Neva River

Troitsky
Bridge

© The Guidebook Company Ltd

N

0   50   100   150   200 m
0   50   100   150   200 yds

Sights

Peter and Paul Fortress

The origins of the city are traced to the Peter and Paul Fortress, Petropavlovskaya Krepost. Peter the Great was attracted to Zayachy Ostrov (Hare Island), situated between the right bank of the Neva and the Kronverk Strait, because of its small size and strategic position in the area. On May 16, 1703, the first foundation stone of the fortress, named after the apostles Peter and Paul, was laid by Peter himself. The fortress was designed to protect the city from the invading Swedes, and was built as an elongated hexagon with six bastions that traced the contours of the island. Over 20,000 workers were commissioned and, within only six months, the earthern ramparts were set in place. Work continued on the fortress, replacing the wooden buildings with brick and stone until its completion in 1725. The new walls were over 36 feet (12 meters) thick and 300 guns were installed. Soon after its completion, the fortress lost its military significance, and over the next 200 years it served instead as a political prison. In 1922, the fortress was opened as a museum. The museum is open from 11 am–5 pm but it is closed on Wednesdays.

Ironically, the first prisoner was Peter's son, Alexei, suspected of plotting against the czar. Peter supervised his son's torture and Alexei died here in 1718. (Alexei was buried by Peter beneath the staircase of the cathedral, so he would always be 'trampled'.) The history of the fortress is also closely connected with revolutionary movements. Catherine the Great locked up Alexander Radishchev, who criticized the autocracy and feudal system in his book *Voyages from St Petersburg to Moscow*. Later, in 1825, the Decembrists were placed in the Alexeyevsky Bastion, a special block for important prisoners. Five were executed on July 13, 1826, and hundreds of others were sentenced to hard labor in Siberia. Members of the Petrashevsky political movement, including Dostoevsky, were sent here in 1849, and sentenced to death. Only at the last minute did Nicholas I revoke the sentence. Nikolai Chernyshevsky wrote his influential novel, *What is To Be Done?*, while imprisoned here for two years in 1862. In the 1880s, many members of the Narodnaya Volya (Peoples Freedom Group) were placed in solitary-confinement cells in the Trubetskoi Bastion. In 1887, five prisoners were executed for the attempt on the life of Alexander III, including Lenin's brother, Alexander Ulyanov. The writer, Maxim Gorky, was incarcerated for writing revolutionary leaflets. During the October 1917 Revolution, when the fortress's last stronghold was captured by the Bolsheviks and the political prisoners set free, a red lantern was hung in the Naryshkin Bastion, signaling the battleship *Aurora* to fire the first shot of the Revolution. Everyday a blank cannon shot is fired from the Naryshkin Bastion at noon. This tradition actually began in the

18th century to let the townspeople know the time. The nearest Metro stop to the fortress is Gorkovskaya. The visitor's entrance to the fortress is at **St John's Gate**, on the east side of the island not far from Kamennoostrovsky (formerly Kirov) Prospekt. After crossing St John's Bridge, you come to **St Peter's Gate** (1718), the main entrance and oldest unchanged structure of the fort. Hanging over the archway is a double-headed eagle, the emblem of the Russian Empire, along with bas-reliefs of the Apostle Peter. The carver, Konrad Osner, gave the Apostle the features of the czar. Beyond the gate is His Majesty's Bastion, used as a dungeon for Peter's prisoners.

A straight path leads to **St Peter and Paul Cathedral**, built between 1712 and 1732 in the Dutch style by the architect, Trezzini. Peter the Great laid the cornerstone. The cathedral, with its long slender golden spire topped with an angel holding a cross, is the focal point of the square. The belfry used to be the tallest structure in the whole country. (Today the TV tower is the tallest structure in St Petersburg.)

Inside, the gilded wooden iconostasis was carved in 1722–26 and holds 43 icons. The cathedral is the burial place for over 30 czars and princes, including every czar from Peter I to Alexander III (except for Peter II). The sarcophagi of Alexander II and his wife took 17 years to carve from Altai jasper and Ural red quartz. Peter the Great himself chose his resting place to the right of the altar. In 1994 Queen Elizabeth of the United Kingdom paid a visit to her ancestors tombs here. This was the first visit by a monarch for 75 years.

Outside again, with your back facing the cathedral entrance, on the right is a small pavilion with a statue of the Goddess of Navigation. The **Boat House** was erected in 1761 to store a small boat that was built by Peter the Great. Today, this 'Grandfather of the Russian Fleet' is on display at the Central Naval Museum at 4 Birzhevaga Square on Vasilyevsky Island. Directly in front of the cathedral is the yellow-white building of the **Mint** (1800–1806). In 1724, Peter the Great transferred the Royal Mint from Moscow to St Petersburg. The first lever press in the world was used here in 1811. The Mint still produces special coins, medals and badges. Beyond the Mint are the Alexeyevsky, Zotov and Trubetskoi Bastions, where many of the revolutionaries were imprisoned. The latter houses an exhibit which traces the history of prisoners who stayed in the cells.

As you leave the Cathedral, on the left side is the stone Commandant's Building, built as the commander's headquarters and the interrogation center for prisoners. It now houses the **Museum of History of St Petersburg and Petrograd from 1703 to 1917**. Next door, the old Engineer's House is now the **Architectural Museum of St Petersburg**, displaying many original drawings and drafts of the city. Both are closed on Wednesday. Behind these stands the **Neva Gate**, once known as the 'Gate of Death', because prisoners were led through it to the execution spot. Now it leads to the beach area (with a spectacular view of the city) that is quite crowded in summer with sunbathers. The Walrus Club gathers here in Winter to swim between the ice floes of the Neva.

Across The Kronverk Strait

Exiting the fortress by way of St John's Bridge takes you back to Kamennoostrovsky Prospekt. To the right is the **Troitsky (formerly Kirov) Bridge**, with a splendid view of the fortress. A short walk down the Prospekt, to the left, leads to Metro stop, Gorkovskaya. The small path to the left of St John's Bridge circles around the Kronverk Strait. This path leads to a monument: a small obelisk, to the Decembrist revolutionaries, stands on the spot where Nicholas I executed the five leaders of the 1825 uprising. A witness account described the execution: 'The hangmen made them stand on a bench and put white canvas hoods over their heads. Then the bench was knocked from under their feet. Three men whose ropes had broken fell on the rough boards of the scaffold bruising themselves. One broke his leg. According to custom, in such circumstances, the execution had to be canceled. But in an hour, new ropes were brought and the execution carried through'.

Past the obelisk, on the right, is a large building that was once the artillery arsenal. Today it is the **Kronverk Artillery, Engineers and Signals Museum**, first formed by Peter the Great to display the history of Russian weaponry. It is open 11 am–5 pm, (closed on Mondays and Tuesdays). Behind the museum is Lenin Park, stretching from the Strait to Kronsversky (formerly Maxim Gorky) Prospekt, where the writer lived at no. 23 from 1914 to 1921. Inside the park is the Zoo (open daily 10 am–7 pm) and gardens, with over 1,000 animals, and the Planetarium. By the planetarium are the Baltiysky Dom Theater and the Music Hall.

Sergei Kirov (1886–1934), regional head of the Leningrad Party before he was murdered, lived not far from Leo Tolstoy Square. The house is now a museum, open 11 am–6 pm, (closed on Wednesdays). At no. 10 Kirov is Lenfilm Studios, founded in 1918.

Crossing Kamennoostravsky Prospekt and walking east along the Neva (in the opposite direction to the fortress), you come to Troitsky Square, formerly Revolution Square, where many of the first buildings of the city once stood. These included the Senate, Custom House and Troitsky Cathedral, where Peter was crowned Emperor in 1721. Today the square is a large garden. At the northern end of the square, at no. 4 Kuibishev, is a mansion (built in 1902 by the architect Gogen) formerly belonging to Matilda Kshesinskaya, a ballerina and mistress of Nicholas II before he married. It is open 10 am–5 pm daily (closed on Thursdays). Once the Museum of the October Revolution, it is now the Museum of the Political History of Russia. On Saturday evenings and every first and third Wednesday, concerts are held in the chamber music hall at 6 pm.

Continuing along Petrovskaya Embankment, you pass the two-ton granite figures of Shih-Tze, brought from Manchuria in 1907, poised on the steps by the Neva. In China, these sculptures, a cross between a lion and a frog, guarded the entrances to palaces. Behind them is the **Cottage of Peter the Great**, one of the oldest surviving buildings of the city. It was constructed in a mere three days in May 1703, out of pine logs painted to look like bricks. One room was a study and reception area and the other was used as a dining-room and bedroom. The largest door was five foot nine inches high—Peter stood at six foot seven! From here Peter directed the building of his fortress—with no stoves or chimneys, since Peter lived in the cottage only in summer. Once his summer palace was completed, Peter stopped living here altogether. In 1784, Catherine the Great encased the tiny house in stone to protect it. The cottage is now a museum, displaying his furniture, utensils and a small boat which Peter is supposed to have built himself.

A bronze bust of Peter can be found in the garden. The cottage is open 11 am–6 pm daily (closed on Tuesdays) between November 11 and April 30.

The beautiful building of the **Nakhimov Naval School**, at no. 4 is a short walk farther east, where young boys learn to carry on the traditions of the Russian fleet. The battleship **Aurora** is anchored in front of it. The cruiser originally fought during the Russo-Japanese War (1904–05). In October 1917, the sailors mutinied and joined in the Bolshevik Revolution. On the evening of October 24, following the orders of Lenin and the Military Revolutionary Committee, the *Aurora* sailed up the Neva and at 9.45 pm fired a blank shot to signal the storming of the Winter Palace. In 1948, it was moored by the Navy School and later opened as a museum. Various displays include the gun that fired the legendary shot, and the radio room where Lenin announced the overthrow of the Provisional Government to the citizens of Russia . The battleship is open 10.30 am to 4 pm, closed Mondays and Fridays. In front of the *Aurora* are a number of kiosks.

The **St Petersburg Hotel** can be reached by crossing the bridge over the Bolshaya Neva. Here you can have a quick coffee, buffet lunch or dinner (for rubles) at the cafeteria-type restaurant on the ground floor.

Kirov Islands

The northernmost islands on the Petrogradskaya side of the Neva (the right bank), the Kirov, are made up of a number of small islands: the Krestovsky, Yelagin and Stone. Stone Island Bridge leads from the end of Kamennoostrovsky Prospekt to Workers Island, a popular summer resort area in the days of Peter. Paul I erected the beautiful yellow Stone Island Palace on the eastern part of the island. Today it is filled with holiday centers and sanitoriums. Yelagin Island was owned in the late 18th century by a wealthy aristocrat of the same name. A century later, it became the summer residence of the czars. In 1822, Carlo Rossi built the elegant Yelagin Palace (open 10 am–6 pm, Wednesday–Sunday) for Alexander I. The Kirov Recreation Park takes up most of the island; festive carnivals are held there during the White Nights.

The largest island in the group, Krestovsky, houses two stadiums, the Dynamo and the 80,000-seat Kirov. At the end of the island is a Buddhist temple, designed by a Tibetan monk. Nearby is the place where Alexander Pushkin fought his duel; a small obelisk marks the spot where he was mortally wounded. The main attraction is Victory Park (built in 1945 after WW II), with artificial lakes and swimming pools. Leningrad poet Anna Akhmatova wrote: 'Early in the morning, the people of Leningrad went out. In huge crowds to the seashore, and each of them planted a tree up on that strip of land, marshy, deserted. In Memory of that Great Victory Day'. The Metro line (line #2), runs out in this direction.

The Strelka of Vasilyevsky Island

Vasilyevsky is the largest island in the Neva Delta, encompassing over 4,000 acres. At the island's eastern tip, known as the *Strelka* (arrow or spit of land), the Neva is at its widest and branches into the two channels of the Bolshaya and Malaya Neva. The Palace and Birzhevoy Bridges span the Bolshaya Neva to the left bank and the Malaya to the Petrogradskaya side. At first Peter chose to build his future city, modeled after Venice, on Vasilyevsky Island. But when the Neva froze over in winter, the island was cut off from the rest of Russia. By the mid-18th century, it was decided to develop the administrative and cultural centers instead on the left bank of the Neva. However, many of the original canals are still present on the island, whose streets are laid out as numbered lines (where canals were planned) and crossed by three major *prospekts*.

After Peter and Paul Fortress was completed, vessels docked along the Strelka. The Exchange Hall was the first wooden building on the Strelka, where merchants and visiting tradesmen gathered. By the end of the century, a stone building was erected to house the new Stock Exchange. Thousands of piles were driven into the riverbed to serve as the foundation for a granite embankment with steps leading to the Neva flanked on each side by two large stone globes. This area served as the main port of the city from 1733 to 1855, before it was switched to the lower left bank of the Neva. Designed by architect Thomas de Thomon, the Stock Exchange, with 44 white Doric columns and the sea-god Neptune in a chariot harnessed to sea horses over the main entrance, took five years to complete. This building, at 4 Birzhevaya Square, serves as a stock exchange and the **Central Naval Museum**, open 10.30 am–5.30 pm, (closed on Mondays and Tuesdays). Peter originally opened this museum in the Admiralty in 1709 to store models and blueprints of Russian ships. His collection numbered over 1,500 models and the museum contains a half million items on the history of the Russian fleet.

Birzhevaya Square lies in front of the Exchange. The dark red **Rostral Columns**, 96 feet (32 meters) high, stand on either side of the square. These were also built by de Thomon from 1805 to 1810. The Romans erected columns adorned with the prows of enemy ships, or rostres, after naval victories. These rostral columns are decorated with

Cadets on board the cruiser Aurora

figures symbolizing the victories of the Russian fleet. Around the base of the columns are four allegorical figures, representing the Neva, Volga, Dnieper and Volkhov rivers. The columns also acted as a lighthouse; at dusk hemp-oil was lit in the bronze bowls at the top. Nowadays, gas torches are used, but only during festivals. This area is one of the most beautiful spots in all of St Petersburg, offering a large panoramic view of the city. Imagine the days when the whole area was filled with ships and sailboats. The Frenchman, Alexandre Dumas, was quite captivated with the area on his first visit over a century ago: 'I really don't know whether there is any view in the whole world which can be compared with the panorama which unfolded before my eyes'.

Two gray-green warehouses, built between 1826 and 1832, stand on either side of the Exchange. The northern warehouse is now the Central Soil Science Museum and the southern is the **Zoological Institute and Museum**, which has a collection of over 40,000 animal species, including a 44,000 year-old stuffed mammoth, (both open 11 am–5 pm and closed on Mondays and Fridays).

The eight-columned **Customs House** (1829–32) along the embankment of the Malaya Neva, at no. 4 Makarova, is topped with mounted copper statues of Mercury (Commerce), Neptune (Navigation) and Ceres (Fertility). The cupola was used as an observation point to signal arriving trade ships. It is now the **Museum of Russian Literature**, open 11 am–5 pm, Wednesday–Sunday, generally known as the Pushkin House. In 1905, the Museum purchased Pushkin's library. Other rooms contain exhibits devoted to famous Russian writers such as Lermontov, Gogol, Chekhov, Dostoevsky, Gorky, Blok, Turgenev and Tolstoy.

The light green and white **Kunstkammer** (1718–34), with its distinctive domed tower, is located at the beginning of Universitetskaya Naberezhnaya, the University Embankment, which extends west along the Bolshaya Neva. Nearly every building in this district is a monument of 18th-century architecture. Kunstkammer, stemming from the German words *kunst* (art) and *kammer* (chamber), was the first Russian museum open to the public. Legend has it that Peter the Great, while walking along the embankment, noticed two pine trees, entwined around each other's trunks. The czar decided to cut down the trees and build a museum on the spot to house 'rarities, curiosities and monsters'. The tree was also in the museum. In order to attract visitors, admission was free and a glass of vodka was offered at the entrance. The building became known as the 'cradle of Russian science' and was the seat of the Academy of Sciences, founded by Peter in 1724. The famed scientist, Mikhail Lomonosov, worked here from 1741 to 1765. Today the Kunstkammer is made up of the **Ethnographical Institute and Peter the Great Museum** and the **Museum of Mikhail Lomonosov**. In the museum's tower (at the top of the building), the first Russian astronomical observatory was installed. The large globe (nine feet/three meters in diameter) had a model of the heavens in its interior. Twelve people could fit inside, where a mechanism was regulated to create the motion of the night sky, a forerunner of the planetarium. Soon, the Kunstkammer became too small and a new building was constructed next to it for the Academy of Sciences, by the architect, Giacomo Quarenghi, from 1783 to 1788. A statue of Mikhail Lomonosov stands outside the Academy. The museums are open 11 am–5 pm (closed on Fridays and Saturdays).

Peter commissioned the architect, Trezzini, to build the Twelve Collegiums (1722–42) next to the Kunstkammer (along Mendeleyev Prospekt) for his future Senate and Ministries. After 1819, it became part of St Petersburg University. Many prominent writers and scholars studied here; Lenin passed his bar examinations and received a degree in law. Some of the teachers were the renowned scientists, Popov and Pavlov, and Dmitri Mendeleyev (Periodic Law and Tables) worked here for 25 years; the apartment where he lived at no. 7/9 is now a museum, open 10 am–5 pm, closed weekends. The red and white buildings are now part of St Petersburg University, which has more than 20,000 students. Higher education is free in Russia and most students receive a state stipend.

Adjacent to the University at no. 15 is the yellow baroque-style **Menshikov Palace**, open 10.30 am–4.30 pm (closed Mondays). Menshikov was the first governor of St Petersburg. Peter the Great presented his close friend with the whole of Vasilyevsky Island in 1707. This Palace of Prince Alexander Menshikov, built between 1710 and 1714, was the first stone and residential structure on the island. It was the most luxurious building in St Petersburg and known as the Ambassadorial Palace. After the death of Peter the Great, the building was given to the First Cadet Corps as their Military College. The restored palace is now part of the Hermitage Museum and exhibits collections of 18th-century Russian culture.

The next building along the embankment, at no. 17, is the **Academy of Arts** (1764–88). The former Academy of the Three Most Noble Arts (painting, sculpture and architecture) was founded in 1857 and many of Russia's renowned artists and architects studied here. It is now a museum that depicts the history of Russian art and architecture; open 11 am–5 pm, (closed on Mondays and Tuesdays). The largest art school in the world is also here, the Repin Institute of Painting, Sculpture and Architecture.

In front of the Academy, two pink granite **Egyptian Sphinxes** flank the stairway leading down to the water. These 3,000-year-old statues were discovered in the early 19th century during an archaeological excavation on the site of ancient Thebes.

The Lieutenant Schmidt Bridge (a hero of the 1905 Revolution) separates the University Embankment from the Lieutenant Schmidt Embankment. The former Annunciation and Nikolaevsky Bridge (1842–50) was the first permanent bridge across the Neva and is the last bridge crossing the Neva before it flows into the Gulf of Finland. During the White Nights season, it is quite lovely to watch the bridges of the city open at 2 am from this vantage point. The Kirov Cultural Palace is also found here. The rest of the island is largely residential and industrial. The Metro stop closest to the Strelka is Vasiloevstrovkaya.

The Pribaltiiskaya Hotel is at the western end of the island, not far from Metro stop Primorskaya (Maritime). After shopping in the large *Beriozka*, watch a sunset over the Gulf from the embankment behind the hotel. A few minutes down the road from the hotel is the International Seaman's Club, near the Morskaya Vokzal (Marine Terminal), where most cruiseboats dock. The Olympia Ship, a Swedish hotel and restaurant, offers good meals for foreign currency. Marine Glory Square is in front with permanent glass pavilions that house international exhibitions. The Dekabristov (Decembrist) Island lies farther to the north.

For the next 200 miles (320 kilometers), this section of the Gulf of Finland off Vasilyevsky Island is known as Cyclone Road. West to east, traveling cyclones create what is known as the 'long wave'. Originating in the Gulf during severe storms, it then rolls toward St Petersburg. Propelled by high winds, it enters into the narrow banks of the Neva with the speed of a freight train. The city has experienced over 300 floods in its 300-hundred-year history. An 18-mile (29-kilometer) barrier has been built across a section of the Gulf to control the flooding. Much controversy surrounds the barrier, since many scientists believe that it is changing the ecological balance of the area.

The Palace Square

Palace Square was the heart of Russia for over two centuries and is one of the most striking architectural ensembles in the world. It was not only the parade ground for the czar's Winter Palace, but a symbol of the revolutionary struggle as well. The square was, in fact, the site of three revolutions: The Decembrists first held an uprising near here in 1825. On Sunday, January 9, 1905 over 100,000 people marched to Palace Square to protest intolerable working conditions. The demonstration began peacefully as the families carried icons and pictures of the czar. But Nicholas II's troops opened fire on the crowd, and thousands were killed in the event known as 'Bloody Sunday'. After the massacre, massive strikes ensued. In October of the same year, the ' St Petersburg Soviet of Workers' Deputies' was formed. Twelve years later, in February 1917, the Kerensky Government overthrew the autocracy and in October, the Red Guards stormed through Palace Square to capture the Winter Palace from the Provisional Government.

In 1819, Carlo Rossi was commissioned to design the square. The government bought up all the residential houses and reconstructed the area into the Ministries of Foreign Affairs and Finance, and the General Staff Headquarters of the Russian Army. These two large yellow buildings curve around the southern end of the Square and are linked by the **Triumphal Arch** (actually two arches), whose themes of soldiers and armor commemorate the victories of the War of 1812. It is crowned by the 16-ton Winged Glory in a chariot led by six horses, which everyone believed would collapse the arch. On opening day, Rossi declared: 'If it should fall, I will fall with it'. He climbed to the top of the arch as the scaffolding was removed.

As you enter Palace Square from Bolshaya Morskaya (Herzen) Street, an unforgettable panorama (of the palace and square) unfolds. The Alexander Column stands in the middle of the square, symbolizing the defeat of Napoleon in 1812. Nicholas I had it erected in memory of Alexander I. The 700-ton piece of granite took three years to be extracted from the Karelian Isthmus and brought down by a system of barges to the city. Architect Auguste Montferrand supervised the polishing in 1830, and by 1834 the 143-foot-high (47.5-meter) column was erected by 2,500 men using an elaborate system of pulleys. The statue of the angel (whose face resembles Alexander I) holding a cross was carved by sculptor Boris Orlovsky. The Guard's Headquarters (to the right of the Column facing the Palace) was built by Bryullov (1837–43) and now serves as an administrative building.

(Following pages) The Hermitage viewed from Peter and Paul Fortress

The main architectural wonder of the Square is the **Winter Palace**, standing along the banks of the Neva. This masterpiece by Rastrelli was commissioned by the Czarina Elizabeth, daughter of Peter, who, fond of the baroque style, desired a lavish Palace decorated with columns, stucco and sculptures. It was built from 1754 to 1762, as Rastrelli remarked, 'solely for the glory of all Russia'. The Palace remained the czars' official residence until the February 1917 Revolution. The magnificent Palace extends over 20 acres and the total perimeter measures over a mile (2 kilometers)! There are 1,057 rooms (not one identical), 1,945 windows, 1,886 doors and 117 staircases. The royal family's staff consisted of over 1,000 servants. At 600 feet (200 meters) long and 66 feet (22 meters) high, it was the largest building in all St Petersburg. After the 1837 fire destroyed a major portion of the Palace, architects Bryullov and Stasov restored the interior along the lines of Russian Classicism, but preserved Rastrelli's light and graceful baroque exterior. The blue-green walls are adorned with 176 sculpted figures. The interior was finished with marble, malachite, jasper, semi-precious stones, polished woods, gilded moldings and crystal chandeliers. In 1844, Nicholas I passed a decree (in force until 1905) stating that all buildings in the city (except churches) had to be at least six feet (two meters) lower than the Winter Palace. During World War II, the Winter Palace was marked on German maps as 'Bombing Objective number 9'. Today, the Winter Palace houses the **Hermitage Museum**. The largest museum in the country, the Hermitage, houses close to 2,800,000 exhibited items, seen by more than three million people annually. It contains one of the largest and most valuable collections of art in the world, dating from antiquity to the present.

Peter the Great began the city's first art collection after visiting Europe. In 1719, Peter I purchased Rembrandt's *David's Farewell to Jonathan*, a statue of Aphrodite (*Venus of Taurida*), and started a museum of Russian antiquities (now on display in the Hermitage's Siberian collection).

In 1764, Catherine the Great created the **Hermitage** (a French word meaning 'secluded spot') in the Winter Palace for a place to house 225 Dutch and Flemish paintings she had purchased in Berlin. Her ambassadors were often sent to European countries in search of art; in 1769, she purchased the entire collection of Count de Bruhl of Dresden for 180,000 rubles. The Hermitage numbered almost 4,000 paintings at the time of her death. Subsequent czars continued to expand the collection: Alexander I bought the entire picture gallery of Josephine, wife of Napoleon, and Nicholas I even purchased pictures from Napoleon's stepdaughter. Until 1852, the Hermitage was only open to members of the royal family and aristocratic friends. Catherine the Great wrote in a letter to one of her close friends that 'all this is admired by mice and myself'. A small list of rules, written by Catherine, hung by the Hermitage's entrance: 'Make merry, but do not spoil, break or gnaw anything. Eat with pleasure, but drink with measure, so you will be able to find your feet when you go out the door'. In 1852, Nicholas I opened the Hermitage on certain days as a public museum (but still closed to common people), and put it under the administrative direction of curators. After the l917 Revolution, the Hermitage was opened full-time to the whole public.

The Hermitage occupies several other buildings in addition to the Winter Palace. The **Little Hermitage** housed Catherine's original collection in a small building next to the Palace; it was constructed by Vallin de la Mothe in l764–67. Stakenschneider's Pavilion Hall is decked with white marble columns, 28 chandeliers, the four 'Fountains of Tears' and the Peacock Clock. The royal family would stroll in the 'hanging gardens', along with peasants and peacocks in the summer. In winter, snow mounds were built for sledding. The **Old Hermitage** (or Large Hermitage) was built right next to it to provide space for Catherine's growing collections. The **Hermitage Theater**, Catherine's private theater, is linked with the Old Hermitage by a small bridge that spreads across the Winter Ditch canal. The theater was built by Quarenghi in l787 and modeled after the amphitheaters of Pompeii. The **New Hermitage** (l839–52), located behind the Old Hermitage, houses additional works of art. Its main entrance off Millionaya (formerly Khalturina) Street is composed of the 10 large and powerful **Statues of Atlas**. They were carved by Terebenyer from blocks of granite.

The Hermitage collections span a millennia of art and culture. It is said that if a visitor spent only a half minute at each exhibit, it would take nine years to view them all! A map of the layout can be purchased inside, from which you can select places of interest. Particularly impressive are the Ambassadorial Staircase (at the Neva entrance), Gallery of the War of l812, the Royal Suites, Throne Room of Peter the Great, Golden Room, Vatican Room, Malachite Room and Hall of St George. Where the Imperial Throne once stood, in St George Hall, now hangs an enormous mosaic map of the former Soviet Union covered with 45,000 semi-precious stones. Moscow is marked by a ruby star and St Petersburg is written in letters of alexandrite. The 19-ton Kolyvan Vase was made from Altai jasper and took 14 years to carve. An entire wall in the Hermitage was knocked down to bring it inside.

Other exhibits delineate the history of Russian culture on the first floor; primeval art (over 400,000 objects) is covered on the ground floor; oriental art and culture (a quarter-million pieces) from Egypt, Babylon, Byzantium, Middle East, Japan, China and India, occupy the second and ground floors; antique culture and art from Greece, Italy and Rome are also on the ground floor. Over 650,000 items in the collection of the art of Western Europe are found on the first and second floors. This includes paintings by da Vinci, Raphael, Titian, El Greco, Rubens, Rembrandt, and a fine Impressionist collection by Monet, Lautrec, Van Gogh and Picasso. In addition are numerous displays of sculpture, tapestries, china, jewelry, furniture, rare coins and handicrafts. A recommended book to buy at the Hermitage store is *Saved for Humanity*, tracing the history of the museum (with pictures and available in English, German and Russian). The museum is open from 10.30 am–6 pm (closed on Mondays). Entrance tickets are sold at kiosks out-

The many rooms of The Hermitage

side the Winter Palace. Or book a tour through the Intourist desk at your hotel.

Leaving the Hermitage through Palace Square to the left and past the Guard's Head-quarters brings you through the Choristers' Passage and across a wide bridge known as Pevchesky Most (Singers Bridge). This bridge crosses the lovely **Moika Canal** and leads to the former Imperial Choristers' Capella (1831), now the Glinka Academy Capella. At no. 12 Moika, to the left of the Capella, is the Pushkin Museum, where the poet lived from October 1836 until his death in January 1837. A statue of Pushkin stands in the courtyard. The rooms have all been preserved and contain his personal belongings and manuscripts. The study is arranged in the exact order it was left after Pushkin died on the divan from a wound he received in a duel. Even the clock is set to the moment of his death, 2.45 am. The next room displays the clothes worn during the duel and his death mask. Since Pushkin is still one of the most popular figures in Russia, museum tickets are often sold out; it may be necessary to buy them a few days in advance. The museum is open 10.30 am–6 pm (closed on Tuesdays).

The Area of Senate Square

Walking west of the Winter Palace along the Neva, you come to another chief architec-tural monument of the city, the **Admiralty**, recognizable by its long golden spire, topped by a golden frigate, the symbol of St Petersburg. The best views of the building are from its southern end. A beautiful fountain stands in the middle of Alexandrovsky Garden surrounded by busts of Glinka, Gogol and Lermontov. In 1704, Peter the Great ordered a second small outpost constructed on the left bank of the Neva and opposite the main part of town. This shipyard was later referred to as the Admiralty. Over 10,000 peasants and engineers were employed to work on the Russian naval fleet. By the end of the 18th century, the Navy had its headquarters here. Whenever the Neva waters rose during a severe storm, a lantern was lit in the spire to warn of coming floods. In 1738, the main building was rebuilt by the architect, Ivan Korobov, who replaced the wooden tower with a golden spire. From 1806 to 1823, the building was again redesigned by Zakharov, an architectural professor at the St Petersburg Academy. The spire was heightened to 218 feet (72.5 meters) and decorated with 56 mythological figures and 350 ornamenta-tions based on the glory of the Russian fleet. The scene over the main-entrance archway depicts Neptune handing over his trident to Peter the Great, a symbol of Peter's mastery of the sea. In 1860, many of the statues were taken down when the Orthodox Church demanded the 'pagan' statues removed. Today the Admiralty houses the Dzerzhinsky Naval School.

Across the street from the Admiralty at no. 6 Admiralty Avenue is the building known as the All Russia Extraordinary Commission for Struggle Against Counter-Revolution and Sabotage, the *VeCheKa*. Felix Dzerzhinsky, the first chairman of the Cheka Police Force (forerunner of the KGB), had his office here. His best remembered words were that a member of the Cheka 'must have clean hands, a warm heart and a cold head'. A memorial museum, dedicated to Dzerzhinsky, has been here since 1974.

Next to the Admiralty, situated right along the Neva, is the infamous Senate Square, formerly known as Decembrists' and Peter Square. In 1925, to mark the 100-year anniversary of the Decembrist uprising, the area was renamed Decembrists' Square. (In 1992, its name reverted to Senate.) After the Russian victory in the 'Patriotic War of 1812' and the introduction of principles from the French Enlightenment, both the nobility and peasants wanted an end to the monarchy and serfdom. An opportune moment for insurrection came on November 19, 1825, when Czar Alexander I suddenly died. A secret revolutionary society, consisting mainly of noblemen, gathered over 3,000 soldiers and sailors who refused to swear allegiance to the new czar, Nicholas I. The members compiled the 'Manifesto to the Russian People', which they hoped the Senate would approve. (What they did not know was that the Senate had already proclaimed their loyalty to Nicholas.) They decided to lead an uprising of the people in Senate Square on December 14, 1825 and from there, to capture the Winter Palace and Peter and Paul Fortress. But Nicholas I discovered the plan and surrounded the square with armed guards. The Decembrists marched to an empty Senate and, moreover, Prince Trubetskoi, who was elected to lead the insurrection, never showed up! Tens of thousands of people joined the march and prevented the guards from advancing on the main parties. But Nicholas I then ordered his guards to open direct fire on the crowd. Hundreds were killed and mass arrests followed. In addition, over 100 people were sentenced to serve 30 years in penal servitute. Five leaders of the rebellion were hanged in Peter and Paul Fortress. Others received such sentences as having to run a gauntlet of a thousand soldiers 12 times, amounting to 12,000 blows by rod. Even though the 1825 revolution was unsuccessful, 'the roar of cannon on Senate Square awakened a whole generation', observed the revolutionary writer, Alexander Herzen.

In 1768, Catherine the Great commissioned the sculptor, Etienne Falconet, to build a monument to Peter the Great. For 12 years, Falconet worked 'to create an alive, vibrant and passionate spirit'. He successfully designed a rider on a rearing horse, crushing a serpent under its feet—just as Peter reared St Petersburg. Instead of a molded pedestal, Falconet wanted to place his monument atop natural stone. A suitable rock was found about six miles (10 kilometers) from the city. It had been split by lightning and was known as Thunder Rock. Peter the Great was said to have often climbed the rock to view his emerging city. With the help of levers, the 1,600-ton rock was raised on a platform of logs and rolled to the sea on a system of copper balls; it took a year to get it to St Petersburg. The rock bears the outlines of crashing waves. Marie Collot, Falconet's pupil

and future wife, sculpted the head, and the Russian sculptor, Gordeyev, the snake. The bronze inscription on the base, written in Russian and Latin, reads: 'To Peter I from Catherine II, 1782', the date the monument was unveiled. The monument to Peter came to be known as **The Bronze Horseman**, after the popular poem by Pushkin. The nearby yellow-white buildings linked by an arch were built in the 1830s by Carlo Rossi. This ensemble was used as the Senate, Supreme Court and Holy Synod before the Revolution. Today they house the Historical Archives. Take a stroll down the small Galernaya (formerly Krasnaya) Ulitsa, that lies beyond the arch; this was the area of the galley shipyards. The two Ionic columns, standing at the start of the next boulevard, bear the goddesses of Glory. These monuments commemorate the valor of Russia's Horse Guards during the war against Napoleon. The building that looks like an ancient Roman temple, is the Horse Guard Manège, where the czar's horseguards were trained. Today it is used as an exhibit hall for the Union of Artists.

St Isaac's Square

The whole southern end of Senate Square is framed by the grand silhouette of **St Isaac's Cathedral**. In 1710, the first wooden church of St Isaac was built by Peter, who was born on the day which celebrated the sainthood of Isaac of Dalmatia; it was replaced in 1729 by one of stone. At that time, the church was situated nearer to the banks of the Neva, and it eventually began to crack and sink. It was decided in 1768 to build another church farther away from the riverbank. But at its completion in 1802, the church was not deemed grand enough for the growing magnificence of the capital. After the War of 1812, Czar Alexander I announced a competition for the best design of a new St Isaacs. The young architect, Montferrand, presented an elaborate album filled with 24 different variations, from Chinese to Gothic, for the czar to choose from. Montferrand was selected for the monumental task in 1818, and the czar also assigned the architects, Stasov, Rossi and the Mikhailov brothers, to help with the engineering.

The cathedral took 40 years to build. In the first year alone, 11,000 serfs drove 25,000 wooden planks into the soft soil to set a foundation. Each of the 112 polished granite columns, weighing 130 tons, had to be raised by a system of pulleys. The system was so perfected that the monolithic columns were eventually installed in a mere 45 minutes. The entire building weighs over 300,000 tons. The three domes give the cathedral a total height of 305 feet (101.5 meters). An observation deck along the upper colonnade (562 steps to climb) provides a magnificent view of the city. The State spared no expense—the cathedral cost 10 times more than the Winter Palace. Nearly a 100 kilos of pure gold were used to gild the dome, which, in good weather, is visible 25 miles (40

St Isaac's Dome

Siege of Leningrad

'It's now the fifth month since the enemy has tried to kill our will to live, break our spirit and destroy our faith in victory...But we know that victory will come. We will achieve it and Leningrad will once again be warm and light and even gay'.

Olga Berggolts, *Leningrad Poet*

For 900 days between 1941 and l944, Leningrad was cut off from the rest of the Soviet Union and the world by German forces. During this harsh period of World War II, the whole city was linked to the outside world only by air drops and one dangerous ice road, 'The Road of Life' (opened only in winter), that was laid across the frozen waters of Lake Ladoga.

The invading Nazis were determined to completely destroy Leningrad, and Hitler's goal was to starve and bombard the city until it surrendered. The directive issued to German command on September 29, 1941 stated: 'The Führer has ordered the city of   St Petersburg to be wiped off the face of the earth...It is proposed to establish a tight blockade of the city and, by shelling it with artillery of all calibres and incessant bombing, level it to the ground'. Hitler was so certain of immediate victory that he even printed up invitations to a celebration party to be held in the center of the city at the Hotel Astoria.

But the Germans did not plan on the strong resistance and incredible resilience of the Leningrad people. For almost three years, the Nazis tried to penetrate the city. All totaled, over 100,000 high-explosive bombs and 150,000 shells were dropped on the city. The suffering was immense: almost one million people starved to death. At one point, only 125 grams (four ounces) of bread were allocated to each inhabitant per day. The winters were severe with no heat or electricity. There are many stories, for example, of mothers collecting the crumbs off streets or scraping the paste off wallpaper and boiling it to feed their hungry children. Tanya Savicheva, an 11-year-old girl who lived on Vasilyevsky Island, kept a diary that chronicled the deaths of her entire family. It ended with the words: 'The Savichevs died. They all died. I remained alone'. Tanya was later evacuated from Leningrad, but died on July 1, l944.

Damage to the city was extensive. More than half of the 18th-and 19th-century buildings classified as historical monuments were destroyed; over 30 bombs struck the Hermitage alone. Within one month of the German invasion in June l941, over one million works of art were packed up by the Hermitage staff and sent by train to Sverdlovsk in the Urals for safekeeping. Other works of art and architecture that could not be evacuated were buried or secretly stored elsewhere within the city. Over 2,000 staff members and art scholars lived in 12 underground air-raid shelters beneath the Hermitage in order to protect the museum and its treasures. Boris Piotrovsky, the Hermitage's former director, lived in one of these shelters and headed the fire brigade. He noted that 'In the life of besieged Leningrad a notable peculiarity manifested itself—an uncommon spiritual strength and power of endurance...to battle and save the art treasures created over the millennia by the genius of humanity'. Architect Alexander Nikolsky, who also lived in an air-raid shelter, sketched the city during the entire blockade. His pencil and charcoal drawings can be seen today in the Hermitage Department of Prints and Drawings. and Drawings.

The city's outskirts were the worst hit. The palaces of Peter the Great, Catherine II, and Elizabeth I were almost completely demolished. Peter's Palace of Petrodvorets was put to use as a Nazi stable. The Germans sawed up the famous Samson Fountain for wood and took rugs and tapestries into the trenches.

The Soviet author, Vera Inber, was in Leningrad during the Seige. She wrote the narrative poem 'Pulkovo Meridian' about the Pulkovo Astronomical Observatory outside Leningrad, where many scientists were killed when it was struck by an enemy bomb.

Dmitri Shostakovich's The Seventh Symphony was composed in Leningrad during the siege and broadcast from the city around the world on August 9, 1942. Shostakovich was a member of the fire-defense unit housed in the Leningrad Conservatory. During bomb attacks, Shostakovich would hurriedly write the Russian letters 'BT,' which stood for air-raid, on his score before running to his post on the roof of the conservatory.

On January 27, 1944, Leningraders heard the salute of 324 guns to celebrate the complete victory over German troops. Even though most of the buildings, museums, and palaces have now been restored, the citizens of St Petersburg will never forget the siege, during which every fourth person in the city was killed. May 9th, a city holiday, is celebrated as Liberation Day. School children take turns standing guard at cemeteries.

Over a half million of the people who died between 1941 and 1943 are buried in mass graves at Piskaryovskoye Cemetery outside St Petersburg. Inside the pavilion is a museum dedicated to the Siege of Leningrad. Outside, the Statue of the Motherland stands over an eternal flame. At the base of the monument are inscribed words by Olga Berggolts. The end of the inscription reads: 'Let no one forget. Let nothing be forgotten'.

kilometers) away. The interior is faced with 14 different kinds of marble, and 43 other types of stone and minerals. Inside at the western portico is a bust of Montferrand, made from each type of marble. (Montferrand died one month after the completion of the cathedral. He had asked to be buried within the walls, but the Czar, Alexander II, refused. Instead, Montferrand was buried in Paris.) It can hold 14,000 people and is filled with over 400 sculptures, paintings and mosaics by the best Russian and European masters of the 19th century. Twenty-two artists decorated the iconostasis, ceilings and walls. The altar's huge stained-glass window is surrounded by frescoes and Bryullov painted the frescoes in the ceiling of the main dome. A St Petersburg newspaper wrote that the cathedral was 'a pantheon of Russian art, as artists have left monuments to their genius in it'. On May 29, 1858, St Isaac's was inaugurated with much pomp and celebration as the main cathedral of St Petersburg. In 1931, it was opened by the government as a museum, now open 11 am–6 pm daily, except on Wednesdays.

St Isaac's Square, in front of the cathedral, was originally a market-place in the 1830s. At its center stands the bronze statue of Nicholas I, constructed by Montferrand and Clodt in 1856–59. The czar, who loved horses and military exploits (nicknamed 'Nicholas the Stick'), is portrayed in a cavalry uniform wearing a helmet with an eagle. His horse rests only on two points. The bas-reliefs around the pedestal depict the events of Nicholas' turbulent rule. One of them shows Nicholas I addressing his staff after the Decembrist uprising. The four figures at each corner represent Faith, Wisdom, Justice and Might, and depict the faces of Nicholas' wife and three daughters, who commissioned the statue.

The two buildings on each side of the monument were built between 1844–53 and now house the Institutes of the Lenin Academy of Agricultural Sciences. Behind the monument is the **Blue Bridge** (1818), broadest in the city. The structure, even though it appears as a continuation of the square, is actually a bridge over the Moika River. There was a slave market here before the abolition of serfdom in 1861. It is painted blue on the sides facing the water. Many of St Petersburg's bridges were named after the color they were painted; up river are the Green and Red bridges. On one side of the bridge is an obelisk crowned by a trident. Five bronze bands indicate the level of the water during the city's worst floods. The Leningrad poet, Vera Inber, wrote of this place:

'Here in the city, on Rastrelli's marble
Or on plain brick, we see from time to time
A mark: 'The water-level reached this line'
And we can only look at it and marvel'.

Beyond the bridge stands the former Mariinsky Palace. It was built in 1839–44 for Maria, the daughter of Nicholas I. In 1894, it was turned into the State Council of the Russian Empire. The artist, Repin, painted the Centennial Gala of the Council in 1901,

Looking east to Saint Nicholas Cathedral

entitled *The Solemn Meeting of the State Council*; it can be viewed at the Russian Museum. In 1917, the Palace was the residence of the Provisional Government. It now houses the St Petersburg City Assembly (the city parliament). The gray and orange seven-story **Astoria Hotel**, on the west side of the square, was built in 1910, one of the grandest hotels in the city. Hitler even sent out engraved invitations for a banquet to be held at the Astoria on November 7, 1942, as soon as he captured the city. Of course, this never took place. The hotel has been remodeled and is a very popular place to stay. In front of it is the Lobanov-Rostovsky Mansion. Montferrand built this for the Russian diplomat between 1817 and 1820. Pushkin mentioned the marble lions in front of the house in the *Bronze Horseman*, when the hero climbed one of them to escape the flood. The mansion is referred to as the 'House with Lions'.

On the other side of the square stands Myatlev's House. Built in 1760 for the poet by Rinaldi, it is one of the oldest structures on the square. Behind the house is the **Museum of Musical Instruments**, with one of the largest collections (3,000) of musical instruments in the world. Some of the items on display are the grand pianos of Rimsky-Korsakov, Glinka and Rubenstein. It is open on Wednesday, Friday, and Sunday.

In the area is the Intourist Building, originally built in 1910 to accommodate the German Embassy. The newly created museum dedicated to the writer Nabokov, who lived in the area, is behind the Intourist building. At no. 57 Dekabristov Street is the **Alexander Blok Museum**, where the writer lived. It is open 11 am–5 pm (closed Wednesdays). At no. 4 Pochtamtsky Lane is the **Popov Central Communication Mu-**

seum, which traces the history of communications in the former USSR; open noon–6 pm, closed on Monday. At no. 9 Pochtamtskaya Street is the General Post Office (1782–89), with the Clock of the World mounted on its archway. Dostoyevsky lived at no. 23 Malaya Morskaya (Gogol) Street before his imprisonment at Peter and Paul Fortress. Here he wrote *Netochka Nezvanova* and *The White Nights*.

Field of Mars

A short walk east from the Hermitage, along Millionnaya ('Millionaire's Row') brings you to the **Marble Palace**. In 1785, Catherine the Great commissioned Antonio Rinaldi to build a palace for her favorite, Count Grigory Orlov. But Orlov died before its completion, and it was turned over to a grand-duke. This was the only building in St Petersburg faced both inside and outside with marble—32 different kinds. In 1937, the Marble Palace opened as the Leningrad Branch of the Central Lenin Museum, with over 10,000 exhibits in 34 rooms relating to Lenin's life and work. In the former Leningrad alone, over 250 places were associated with Lenin. (In a small garden at the main entrance stood an armored car with the inscription, 'Enemy of Capital'. It was removed to the Artillery Museum in 1992.) After the February 1917 Revolution, Lenin returned to St Petersburg from exile in Europe in this armored car and, upon his arrival at the Finland Station on April 3, delivered a speech from the turret proclaiming, 'Long live the Socialist Revolution!' On February 22, 1924, the Central Committee declared that 'all that is truly great and heroic in the proletariat—a fearless mind, a will of iron—unbending, persistent and able to surmount all obstacles, a revolutionary passion that moves mountains, boundless faith in the creative energies of the masses—all this found splendid embodiment in Lenin whose name has become the symbol of the new world from East to West, North to South'. After the 1991 failed coup, the Lenin Museum was removed from the Marble Palace which now, as a branch of the Russian Museum, houses the National Portrait Gallery.

Right in front of the Troitsky (formerly Kirov) Bridge is **Suvorov Square**, with the statue of the Russian Generalissimus, Alexander Suvorov, depicted as the God of War. The square opens to one of the most beautiful places in St Petersburg, the Field of Mars. Around 1710, Peter the Great drained the marshy field and held parades after military victories. The festivities ended in fireworks (known as 'amusement lights'), so the square was called **Poteshnoye Polye** (Amusement Field). By the end of the 18th century, the area was used as a routine drill field, which destroyed the grasses; for a while the field was nicknamed the ' St Petersburg Sahara'. When, in 1801, the monument to Field Marshal Suvorov, depicted as Mars, was placed here (moved to its present location, Suvorov Square, in 1818), the area became known as **Marsovo Polye** (Field of Mars). The 30-acre

(12-hectare) field is bordered on the west by the Barracks of the Pavlovsky Regiment, the first among the czar's armies to take the side of the people during the February 1917 Revolution. It is now the St Petersburg Energy Commission. The southern side is bordered by the Moika River and Ekaterininsky (formerly Griboyedov) Canal, and the eastern by the Lebyazhiya Kanavka (Swan Canal).

The **Memorial to the Fighters of the Revolution** stands in the center. On March 23, 1917, 180 heroes of the February uprising were buried here in mass graves. The next day, the first granite stone was laid in the monument foundation, which was unveiled in 1920. On each of the eight stone blocks are words by the writer, Anatoly Lunacharsky. One reads: 'Not victims, but heroes, lie beneath these stones. Not grief, but envy, is aroused by your fate in the hearts of all your grateful descendants'. During the 40th anniversary of the Revolution in 1957, the eternal flame was lit, in memory of those killed during the revolutions.

The eastern side of the Field opens up on the lovely **Letny Sad** (Summer Garden). The main entrance to the garden is from the Neva-Kutuzov embankment. A beautiful black and golden grille (1770–84 by Yuri Felten) fences it. The open railing, decorated with 36 granite columns and pinkish urns, is one of the finest examples of wrought-iron work in the world. The Summer Garden, the city's oldest, was designed by Leblond in Franco-Dutch style in 1704. Peter the Great desired to create a garden more exquisite than Versailles. On 25 acres of land, he planted trees and had hothouses, aviaries, grottos and sculptures placed within. Some of the original statues remain, such as Peace and Abundance, the busts of John Sobiesky (a Polish king), Christina (a Swedish queen), the Roman Empress, Agrippina, and Cupid and Psyche. The Swan Canal dug on the western side was filled with swans and had a tiny boat for Peter's favorite dwarf jester. The garden also had many fountains, depicting characters from Aesop's *Fables*. The water for the fountains was drained from a river on its east side; the river was called **Fontanka**, from the Russian *fontan* (fountain). Pipes made from hollowed logs ran from the Fontanka to a city pool, from which a one-mile (1.6-kilometers) pipeline brought water to the gardens. The Fontanka formed the southern border of the city in the mid-18th century. At this time, the first stone bridge was built where the Fontanka flows into the Neva. It is still known as **Prachechny Most** (Laundry Bridge) because it was located near the Royal Laundry. The gardens received their name from the many festivals that Peter the Great loved to hold in summer; the area became the center of social life in St Petersburg.

Many of the fountains, pavilions and statues were destroyed during the 1777 and 1824 floods. The Summer Garden was open only to nobility until, in the mid-19th century, Nicholas I issued a decree, stating that it would be 'open for promenading to all military men and decently dressed people. Ordinary people, such as *muzhiks* (peasants) shall not be allowed to walk through the garden'. After the Revolution, the Garden was opened fully to the public.

After the garden was designed, Peter had his **Letny Dvorets** (Summer Palace) built at the northern end by the Neva. After its completion in 1714 by Trezzini, Peter moved from his cottage into the Summer Palace. The modest stone building was decorated with 29 terracotta figures and a weather vane of St George slaying the dragon. Peter lived on the ground floor and his wife, Catherine, on the second. In 1974, it was opened as a museum. The Palace is open 11 am–6 pm (closed on Tuesdays and from November 11–April 30).

Behind the Summer Palace is an interesting bronze Monument to Ivan Krylov, the popular Russian fablist, by the sculptor, Clodt, and a playground for children with subjects from Krylov's fables. Nearer to the fountain are the **Chainy Domik** (Tea House), built in 1827 by Ludwig Charlemagne, and Coffee House, which is known as 'Rossi's Pavilion', built by Rossi in 1826; recitals are now held here. Walking south toward the Moika River, you come upon the Porphyry Vase, a gift to Nicholas I from the Swedish King, Karl Johann.

Engineer's (Mikhailovsky) Castle

Crossing the Moika and continuing along the banks of the Fontanka leads to the **Mikhailovsky Castle**, built in 1797–1800 by the architects, Bazhenov and Brenna, for Czar Paul I. Paul did not like his mother Catherine the Great's residence in the Winter Palace and, fearing attempts on his life, he ordered the castle constructed as an impregnable fortress. The Mikhailovsky Castle (the archangel, Michael, was Paul's patron saint) was bordered in the north by the Moika, and the east by the Fontanka; two artificial canals, the Resurrection and Church, were dug on the other sides, creating a small island. Drawbridges, protected by cannons, were raised at 9 pm when the czar went to bed. In spite of all this, Paul was strangled 40 days after he moved in on March 11, 1801, by one of his own guards. Today the Engineer's Castle is part of the Russian Museum, and houses a walk-through history of Russia. Open daily 10 am–6 pm; closed Tuesdays.

In 1822, after a military engineering school was opened, the place became known as Engineer's Castle. Dostoevsky went to school here from 1837 to 1843 (from age 16), and later lived in 17 different residences throughout the city. It is now a scientific and naval library and a branch of the Russian Museum. In front of the castle's main entrance is a Rastrelli statue of Peter the Great, erected in 1800. The inscription at its base, 'To great-grandfather from great-grandson', was ordered by Paul I.

Not far from the Mikhailovsky Castle, along the Fontanka (at no. 3) is the **St Petersburg Circus**. The circular building of the circus was constructed in 1877 by Kenel, making it one of the oldest permanent circus buildings in the world. During the intense revolutionary years, some of Russia's finest artists, such as Chekhov, Gorky, Eisenstein

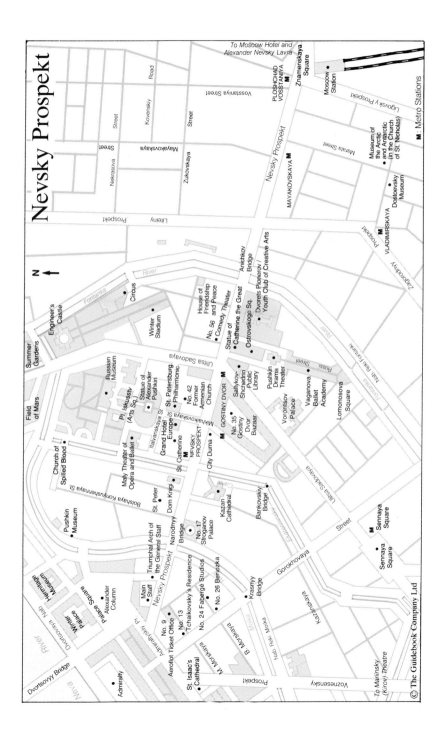

Nevsky Prospekt

To Moscow Hotel and
Alexander Nevsky Lavra

N

M : Metro Stations

© The Guidebook Company Ltd

A Cultural Extravaganza

*In the season of 1903-4 Petersburg witnessed concerts in the grand manner.
I am speaking of the strange, never-to-be surpassed madness of the concerts
of Hoffmann and Kubelik in the Nobility Hall during Lent. I can recall no other
musical experiences, not even the premiere of Scriabin's Prometheus, that
might be compared with these Lenten orgies in the white-columned hall. The
concerts would reach a kind of rage, a fury. This was no musical dilettantism:
there was something threatening and even dangerous that rose up out of
enormous depths, a kind of craving for movement; a mute prehistorical
malaise was exuded by the peculiar, the almost flagellant zeal of the
halberdiers in Mikhaylovsky Square, and it whetted the Petersburg of that day
like a knife. In the dim light of the gas lamps the many entrances of the Nobility
Hall were beset by a veritable siege. Gendarmes on prancing horses, lending
to the atmosphere of the square the mood of a civil disturbance, made clicking
noises with their tongues and shouted as they closed ranks to guard the main
entry. The sprung carriages with dim lanterns slipped into the glistening circle
and arranged themselves in an impressive black gypsy camp. The cabbies
dared not deliver their fares right to the door; one paid them while approaching, and then they made off rapidly to escape the wrath of the police. Through
the triple chains the Petersburger made his way like a feverish little trout to
the marble ice-hole of the vestibule whence he disappeared into the luminous
frosty building, draped with silk and velvet.*

*The orchestra seats and the places behind them were filled in the customary
order, but the spacious balconies to which the side entrances gave access were
filled in bunches, like baskets, with clusters of humanity. The Nobility Hall
inside is wide, stocky, and almost square. The stage itself takes up nearly half
the area. The gallery swelters in a July heat. The air is filled with a ceaseless
humming like that of cicadas over the steppe.*

Osip Mandelstam, The Noise of Time

and Stanislavsky, focused their attention on the circus, so much so that the Soviet government decided not to abolish it. Inside there is also the Museum of Circus History and Variety Art (established in 1928), with over 100,000 circus-related items (closed on Saturdays and Sundays). The circus has daily performances, except on Thursdays.

At no. 34 Fontanka is the **Anna Akhmatova Apartment Museum**. The famous St Petersburg poet lived here by the former Sheremetyev Palace for many years. The entrance is off the main street around the back; follow signs for *myzeu*, museum. It is open from 10 am–6 pm (but closed on Mondays). Closest Metro is Vladimirskaya. The **Anna Akhmatova Museum** is at 67/4 Stachek per. Open 10 am to 6 pm; closed weekends.

Nevsky Prospekt

In the words of Nikolai Gogol: 'There is nothing finer than the Nevsky Prospekt...In what does it not shine, this street that is the beauty of the capital'. Nevsky Prospekt, which locals refer to as Nevsky, is the main thoroughfare of the city and the center of business and commercial life. A stroll down part of it, during any time of day, is a must, for no other street like it exists anywhere in the world. It is a busy, bustling area, filled with department stores, shops, cinemas, restaurants, museums, art studios, cathedrals, mansions, theaters, libraries and cafés. The Nevsky is made even more interesting and beautiful by the stunning architectural ensembles that line the three-mile-long (4.8-kilometer) route that stretches from the **Admiralty** to **Alexander Nevsky Monastery**. As an architectural showcase, it also brims with history; you can find the spot where Pushkin met his second on the day of his fatal duel, where Dostoevsky gave readings of his works, and where Liszt and Wagner premiered their music.

Shortly after the Admiralty was completed, a track was cut through the thick forest, linking it with the road to Novgorod and Moscow. This main stretch of the city was known as the Great Perspective Road. The road took on the name of Neva Perspectiva in 1738, when it was linked to another small road that ran to Alexander Nevsky Monastery. In 1783, the route was renamed Nevsky Prospekt, the wide, straight road from the Neva to the Nevsky. Peter the Great had elegant stone houses built along the Nevsky and ordered food sold in the streets by vendors dressed in white aprons. The first buildings went up between the Admiralty and the Fontanka Canal. The area, nicknamed 'St Petersburg City', was a fashionable place to live, and it became the center for banks, stores and even insurance offices. The architects desired to create a strong and imposing central district and constructed the buildings out of granite and stone brought in from Sweden.

Beginning at the Admiralty (where the street is at its narrowest—75 feet/25 meters), walk along to no. 9 Nevsky. On the corner you will find Vavelberg's House which, originally a bank, is now the **Aeroflot** ticket office. The large stone house was built in 1912 by

the architect, Peretyatkovich, to resemble the Doge's Palace in Venice and the Medici in Florence. At no. 10 Malaya Morskaya is the 'Queen of Spades' residence, the house of the old countess on whom Pushkin based his story of the same name. Here the Nevsky is intersected by Ulitsa Malaya Morskaya (Gogol Street), where the writer lived at no. 17 from 1833 to 1836. Here Gogol wrote *Taras Bulba*, *The Inspector General* and the first chapters of *Dead Souls*. At no. 13 Malaya Morskaya (Gogol), Tchaikovsky lived up until his death in 1895.

The next intersection on the Nevsky is Ulitsa Bolshaya Morskaya (Herzen Street); Herzen lived at no. 25 for a year in 1840. The main telephone and telegraph center is on the left by the Triumphal Arch of the General Staff. Fabergé had its main studios at no. 24; *Beriozkas* are now at no. 26 and no. 38. The architect, Carlo Rossi, laid out the street along the 'Pulkovo Meridian' (which was on the meridian on old Russian maps) so that, at noon, the buildings cast no shadows on the street.

The oldest buildings are at no. 8 and 10 Nevsky. Built between 1760 and 1780, they are now exhibition halls for work by St Petersburg artists. The house at no. 14 (built in 1939) is a school. A pale blue rectangular plaque on the wall still reads: 'Citizens! In the event of artillery fire, this side of the street is the most dangerous!' The House with Columns at no. 15 was built in 1768 as a stage site for one of Russia's first professional theaters. Later a small studio, where Falconet modeled **The Bronze Horseman**, was connected to the theater. It is now the **Barrikada Movie Cinema** with cafés and shops. The building at no. 18 was known as Kotomin's House (1812–16), after the original owner. Pushkin often frequented the confectioner's shop that used to be in the bottom story; he lived nearby at no. 12 Moika. It was here on January 27, 1837, that Pushkin met up with his second on the way to his fatal duel with George D'Anthès. The shop is now the **Literaturnoye Café**, a popular spot to eat that offers piano and violin music. Outside the café, you can have your portrait drawn by one of the numerous artists.

The section on the left side of the Nevsky beyond the Moika River was once reserved for churches of non-Orthodox faiths. Now a library, the Dutch Church at no. 20 was built in 1837 by Jacquot. The central part functioned as a church and the wings housed the Dutch Mission. Opposite at no. 17 is the baroque **Stroganov Palace**, built by Rastrelli in 1754. The Stroganov family owned and developed vast amounts of land in Siberia and their coat-of-arms, depicting two sables and a bear, lies over the gateway arch. The palace, a branch of the Russian Museum, open 10 am–6 pm; closed Tuesdays. At 22–224 Nevsky is the Romanesque-style **Peter and Paul Lutheran Church** (1838).

Across the street from the church is the large, majestic, semi-circular colonnade of the **Cathedral of Our Lady of Kazan**. The Kazanski Sobor was named after the famous icon of Our Lady of Kazan that used to be here. It is on view at the Russian Museum. The architect, Voronikhin, faced two challenges in 1801. First, Czar Paul I wished the cathedral modeled after St Peter's in Rome, and second, the Orthodox Church required that the altar must face eastwards, which would have had one side of the cathedral facing

(Preceding pages) Bank Bridge, Ekaterininsky Canal

A Simple Life

Even at those hours when the grey Petersburg sky is completely overcast and the whole population of clerks have dined and eaten their fill, each as best he can, according to the salary he receives and his personal tastes; when they are all resting after the scratching of pens and the bustle of office, their own necessary work and other people's, and all the tasks that an overzealous man voluntarily sets himself even beyond what is necessary; when the clerks are hastening to devote what is left of their time to pleasure; some more enterprising are flying to the theatre, others to the street to spend their leisure staring at women's hats, some spend the evening paying compliments to some attractive girl, the star of a little official circle, while some—and this is the most frequent of all—go simply to a fellow clerk's apartment on the third or fourth storey, two little rooms with a hall or kitchen, with some pretensions to style, with a lamp or some such article that has cost many sacrifices of dinners and excursions—at the time when all clerks are scattered about the apartment of their friends, playing a stormy game of whist, sipping tea out of glasses, eating cheap biscuits, sucking in smoke from long pipes, telling, as the cards are dealt, some scandal that has floated down from higher circles, a pleasure which the Russian can never by any possibility deny himself, or, when there is nothing better to talk about, repeating the everlasting anecdote of the commanding officer who was told that the tail had been cut off the horse on the Falconet monument—in short, even when everyone was eagerly seeking entertainment, Akaky Akakievich did not indulge in any amusement. No one could say that they had ever seen him at an evening party. After working to his heart's content, he would go to bed, smiling at the thought of the next day and wandering what God would send him to copy. So flowed on the peaceful life of a man who knew how to be content with his fate on a salary of four hundred roubles, and so perhaps it would have flowed on to extreme old age, had it not been for the various disasters strewn along the road of life.

Nikolai Gogol, The Overcoat,
translated by Constance Garnett

Kamenny Bridge, Ekaterininsky Canal

the Nevsky. Voronikhin devised 96 Corinthian columns to fan out toward the Nevsky. The bronze Doors of Paradise, which were replicas of the 15th-century Baptisery doors in Florence, opened on the Nevsky side. The structure took 10 years to build and, at that time, was the third largest cathedral in the world. The brick walls are faced with statues and biblical reliefs made from Pudostsky stone, named after the village where it was quarried. The stone was so soft when dug out that it was cut with a saw. It later hardened like rock when exposed to air. In niches around the columns are statues of Alexander Nevsky, Prince Vladimir, St John the Baptist and the Apostle Andrew. The interior was decorated by the outstanding painters Bryullov, Borovikovksy and Kiprensky. There are 56 pink granite columns and polished marble and red-stone mosaic floors. Field Marshall Mikhail Kutuzov is buried in the northern chapel. The general stopped to pray at the spot where he is now buried before going off to the War of 1812. Many trophies from this war, like banners and keys to captured fortresses, hang around his crypt. In 1837, the two statues of Kutuzov and Barclay de Tolly were put up in the front garden.

At the main entrance to the cathedral, to the right off Plekhanov Street, is a small square surrounded by a beautiful wrought-iron grille, called 'Voronikhin's Railing'. In 1876, the first workers' demonstration took place in front, with speeches by the Marxist, Georgi Plekhanov, (after whom the street is named). A square and fountain were later added to prevent further demonstrations. But the area remains to this day a popular spot for gatherings and, since *perestroika*, political and religious demonstrations as well. Today the cathedral is the **Museum of the History of Religion** (open 11 am–5 pm, Sunday 2 pm–6 pm (closed on Wednesdays). The nearest Metro to the cathedral is in Nevsky Prospekt.

A short walk down the **Ekaterininsky** (formerly **Griboyedov**) **Canal** (located to the left behind the cathedral) spans the lovely footbridge of **Bankovski Most** (Bank Bridge), adorned with winged lion-griffins. At the time it was built in 1800, the bridge led to the National Bank; according to Greek mythology, griffins stood guard over gold. On the other side of Nevsky, also on the Griboyedov canal, is **Dom Knigi**, (House of Books). This polished granite building topped by its distinguishing glass sphere and globe, was originally built by Susor in 1907 for the American Singer Company. The first two floors now make up one of the largest bookstores in the country. Posters, calendars and postcards are sold on the second floor.

The Kazansky Bridge crosses the canal and was built by Illarion Kutuzov, the father of the military leader. Down the canal to the left stands the 17th-century Russian-style building (modeled on St Basil's in Moscow) known as the **Savior's Church of Spilled Blood**. Spasa Na Krovi was erected on the spot where Czar Alexander II was assassinated in 1881 by a member of the revolutionary group, People's Will. Alexander III ordered architect Alfred Parland, to build the altar where the former czar's blood fell on the cobblestones. The next building over the bridge at no. 30 was that of the Philharmonic Society, where Wagner, Liszt and Strauss performed. Today it is the Hall of the Glinka Maly Philharmonic. The Catholic Church of St Catherine, built from 1763 to 1783 in baroque-classical design by Vallin de la Mothe, is at no. 32 – 4 Nevsky. The former Armenian Church, built by Felten in 1780, is at no. 42.

Right across the street at no. 35 is the **Gostiny Dvor Department Store**. Visiting merchants used to put up guest houses, *gostiniye dvori*, which served as their resident places of business. From 1761 to 1785, the architect, Vallin de la Mothe, built a long series of open two-tiered arcades, where merchants had their booths. Today the two-story yellow department store, with over 200 shops, is a popular place for shopping. The small building that stands between the Hall and Gostiny Dvor was built as the Portico, and now holds the Central City Theater Booking Office. The art nouveau **Grand Hotel Europe** is on the corner of Nevsky and Mikhailovsky. Built in the 1870s, it has been renovated by a Russian-Swedish joint venture. It has many antiques including one of Catherine the Great's carriages (available for guests). The hotel has a number of bars, restaurants and an American Express office.

On the next corner, is the Shostakovich Philharmonic Society's Great Hall, built in 1839 by Jacquot for the Club of the Nobility. The St Petersburg Philharmonic Society was founded in 1802. The works of many Russian composers, such as Glinka, Rachmaninov, Rimsky-Korsakov and Tchaikovsky, were first heard at the Society. Wagner was the official conductor during the 1863 season. The Philharmonic Symphony Orchestra performs world-wide. The Philharmonic was named after Dmitri Shostakovich in 1976. Shostakovich lived in Leningrad during the 900-day seige of Leningrad. In July 1941, he began to write his *Seventh Symphony*, while a member of an air-defense unit. Hitler boasted that Leningrad would fall by August 9, 1942. On this day, the *Seventh Symphony*, conducted by Karl Eliasberg, was played in the Philharmonic and broadcast throughout the world. 'I dedicate my *Seventh Symphony* to our struggle with fascism, to our forth-coming victory over the enemy, and to my native city, Leningrad'.

The square in front of the Philharmonic is called **Ploshchad Iskusstv** (Square of Arts). In the mid-18th century, Carlo Rossi designed the square and the areas in between the Ekaterinsky Canal, the Moika River and Sadovaya Ulitsa (Garden Street); Garden Street leads past the Winter Stadium and Manège Square to the Engineer's Castle and Field of Mars. The center of the square is dominated by the **Statue of Alexander Pushkin**, sculpted by Mikhail Anikushin in 1957. To the right of the Philharmonic, along Italyanskaya (formerly Rakov) Street, is the Theater of Musical Comedy, the only theater in the city that stayed open during the seige. Next to it is the Komissarzhevskaya Drama Theater. Headed by Russian actress, Vera Komissarzhevskaya, from 1904 to 1906, the company staged plays (including Gorky's) around the political mood of the times.

Behind the square on Engineer's Street stands the majestic eight-columned building of the **Russian Museum**, second largest museum of art in the city. Carlo Rossi built this palace (1819–1827) for Mikhail, youngest son of Paul I; it was called the Mikhailovsky Palace. A splendid wrought-iron fence (embossed by the double-headed eagle) separates the palace from the square. The courtyard allowed carriages to drive up to the front por-tico, where a granite staircase, lined with two bronze lions, still leads to the front door. The Hall of White Columns was so admired by the czar that he ordered a wooden model made for King George IV of England. Rubenstein opened the city's first music school in the hall in 1862. The Mikhailovsky Gardens are situated behind the museum. In 1898, Alexander III set up the Russian Museum inside the palace. The 1,000-year history of Russian art is represented by over 300,000 works of art in the museum's 130 halls (open 10 am–6 pm, closed Tuesday). To the right of the museum is the **Museum of Ethno-graphy** (open 10 am–5 pm, closed Monday). The nearest Metro is Gostiny Dvor.

The statue of Pushkin gestures to the building in the square known as the **Mussorgsky Maly Theater of Opera and Ballet**. Built in 1833 by Bryullov, it was known as the Mikhailovsky Theater, and housed a permanent French troupe. Today it is 'the laboratory of opera and ballet', presenting 360 performances a year in a daily alternating repertory of opera and ballet. Subsidized by the government, it employs 800 people, including an orchestra of 100 and a chorus of 65. It is the second most popular theater (next to the Mariinsky) in St Petersburg. The **Brodsky Museum-Flat**, is next to the Maly; open 11 am-7 pm, closed on Sundays, Mondays and Tuesdays.

Continuing down the Nevsky, the Russian National Library stands on the corner of Nevsky and Garden streets. Built in 1801 by Yegor Sokolov, it opened in 1814 as the Imperial Public Library. In 1832, Carlo Rossi built further additions. The statue of Minerva, Goddess of Wisdom, stands atop the building. It is one of the largest libraries in the world—over 25 million books! A reading room is inside, but no books are allowed to be checked out.

The library faces **Aleksandrisky Square**. Up until 1992 it was known as Ostrovsky Square, after the playwright, Alexander Ostrovsky. A **Statue of Catherine the Great** graces the center; Catherine, dressed in a long flowing robe, stands on a high rounded pedestal that portrays the prominent personalities of the time: Potemkin, Suvorov, Rumyantsev and Derzhavin, to name a few. Along the left side are two classical pavilions, designed by Rossi, in the Garden of Rest.

Behind the square is the **Aleksandrisky Theater** (or Pushkin Drama Theater), a veritable temple to the arts. Flanked by Corinthian columns, the niches are adorned with the Muses of Dance, Tragedy, History and Music. The chariot of Apollo, patron of the arts, stands atop the front facade. The yellow building, erected by Rossi in 1828, was first known as the Aleksandrisky Theater (after Alexandra, the wife of Nicholas I), and housed Russia's first permanent theater group. Today, as the oldest drama theater in Russia, it has a varied repertoire of classical and modern plays. Behind the theater is the **Museum of Theatrical Art**, at no. 6 Ostrovsky Square, exhibiting the history of Russian drama and musical theater. It is open 11 am–6 pm, Wednesdays 1 pm–6 pm, Saturdays 11 am–4 pm (closed Tuesday). Also here is the Lunacharsky National Library, with more than 350,000 volumes.

The famous **Rossi Street** (named after the architect) stretches from Aleksandrisky Square to Lomonosov Square. The street has perfect proportions: 22 meters wide, the buildings are 22 meters high and the length is 10 times the width. The world-renowned **Vagonova Academy of Ballet** is the first building on the left. Twelve boys and 12 girls (children of court servants) were the city's first ballet students, attending a school started by the Empress Anna in the same year, 1768, that she founded the St Petersburg Imperial Ballet. The choreography school now bears the name of Agrippina Vagonova, who taught here 1921–51. Some of the Imperial Ballet and Vagonova pupils have been Pavlova, Ulanova, Petipa, Nijinsky, Fokine and Balanchine. Over 2,000 hopefuls apply to the school each year, about 100 are chosen. The school's 500 pupils hope to go on to a professional ballet company such as the Mariinsky. A museum inside the school to the left contains many magical displays, for example Pavlova's ballet shoes and Nijinsky's costumes. Posters and pictures trace the history of ballet from Diaghliev to Baryshnikov who, along with Natalia Makarova, attended the Vagonova School. (The museum is closed to the general public—but if you express an interest in ballet, you may get in.) A

The Petition of January 9, 1905

A Most Humble and Loyal Address of the Workers of St Petersburg Intended for Presentation to HIS MAJESTY on Sunday at two o'clock on the Winter Palace Square.

SIRE:

We, the workers and inhabitants of St Petersburg, of various estates, our wives, our children, and our aged, helpless parents, come to Thee, O SIRE, to seek justice and protection. We are impoverished; we are oppressed, overburdened with excessive toil, contemptuously treated. We are not even recognised as human beings, but are treated like slaves who must suffer their bitter fate in silence and without complaint. And we have suffered, but even so we are being further pushed into the slough of poverty, arbitrariness, and ignorance. We are suffocating in despotism and lawlessness. O SIRE, we have reached that frightful moment when death is better than the prolongation of our unbearable sufferings.

Hence, we stopped work and told our employers that we will not resume work until our demands are fulfilled. We did not ask much; we sought only that without which there is no life for us but hard labor and eternal suffering. Our first request was that our employers agree to discuss our needs with us. But even this we were refused. We were prohibited even from speaking of our needs, since no such right is given us by law. The following requests were also deemed to be outside of the law: the reduction of the work day to eight hours; our manual participation in determining the rates for our work and in the settlement of grievancs that might arise between us and the lower managerial staff; to raise the minimum daily wages for unskilled workers, and for women as well, to one ruble; to abolish overtime work; to give our sick better medical attention without insults; and to arrange our workshops so that we might work there without encountering death from murderous drafts, rain, and snow.

According to our employers and managers, our demands turned out to be illegal, our every request a crime, and our desire to improve our conditions an insolence, insulting to them. O SIRE, there are more than 300,000 of us but we are human beings in appearance only, for we, with the rest of the Russian people, do not possess a single human right, not even the right to speak, think, gather, discuss our needs, and take steps to improve our conditions. We are enslaved, enslaved under the patronage and with the aid of Thy officials. Anyone of us who dares to raise his voice in defense of the working class and the people is thrown into jail or exiled. Kindheartedness is punished as a crime. To feel sorry for a worker as a downtrodden, maltreated human being bereft of his rights is to commit a heinous crime! The workers and the peasants are delivered into the hands of the bureaucratic administration, comprised of embezzlers of public funds and robbers, who not only care nothing for the needs of the people, but flagrantly abuse them. The bureaucratic administration brought the country to the brink of ruin, involved her in a humiliating war, and is leading Russia closer and closer to disaster. We, the workers and people, have no voice whatsoever in the spending of huge sums collected from us in taxes. We do not even know how the money, collected from the impoverished people, is spent. The people are deprived of the opportunity to express their wishes and demands, to participate in the establishment of taxes and public spending. The workers are deprived of the oppportunity to organize their unions in order to defend their interests.

O SIRE, is this in accordance with God's laws, by the grace of which Thou reignest? Is it possible to live under such laws? Would it not be preferable for all of us, the toiling people of Russia, to die? Let the capitalists-exploiters of the working class and officials, the embezzlers and plunderers of the Russian people, live and enjoy their lives.

Translated by Walter Sablinsky

few documentary films have been made about the school, such as *The Children of Rossi Street*. The National Geographic Special, *Voices of Leningrad*, available in video rental stores, includes a segment about the Vagonova.

Back on the *prospekt* in the corner building across the street is the impressive Yeliseyev's, once one of the most luxuriant food stores in St Petersburg. Today, even though the food supplies have dwindled, it is well worth seeing the interior of the store. The Puppet Theater, started in 1918, is at no. 52 Nevsky. The Comedy Theater, founded in 1929, is at no. 56. At the corner of Nevsky and the Fontanka River is the House of Friendship and Peace. A former residence, built in the 1790s, it is now a society that promotes friendship and cultural relations with over 500 organizations in 30 countries.

The area around the Fontanka River (the old southern border of the city) was first developed by an engineer team headed by Mikhail Anichkov, who built the first bridge (still named after him) here in 1715 across the Fontanka. In 1841, a stone bridge with four towers replaced the wooden structure. Peter Klodt cast the tamed-horse sculptures a century ago and today they give the bridge its distinguishing mark. During World War II, the sculptures were buried in the Palace of Young Pioneers across the street. The **Anichkov Bridge** is a popular hang out, and boats to the left on the Fontanka leave frequently for a city tour of the canals and waterways. A kiosk by the dock provides time departures and tickets (sold in rubles only).

The first palace built on the Nevsky was named after Anichkov. Empress Elizabeth (Peter's daughter) commissioned the architects, Dmitriyev and Zemtsov, to build a palace on the spot where she stayed on the eve of her coronation. In 1751, Elizabeth gave the Anichkov Palace to her favorite, Count Alexei Razumovsky. Later, Catherine the Great gave it to her own favorite, Count Grigory Potemkin, who frequently held elaborate balls here. After that it was a part of His Majesty's Cabinet. Since 1937, it has been the **Dvorets Pionerov** (Palace of Young Pioneers). The Young Pioneers was a communist organization for children from ages 9 to 14, who wore distinguishing orange silk scarves to mark their membership. Nearly 15,000 children in the city voluntarily participated in some 600 youth clubs (roughly equivalent to our scouting organizations). At no. 41 Nevsky is a mansion built in the 1840s by the architect, Stackenschneider, for a prince by the name of Beloselsky-Belozersky. Formerly the Communist Party headquarters, it now houses art exhibits; chamber music concerts are held in the Mirror Hall on Fridays at 7 pm and Sundays at 3 pm. The Gostiny Dvor/Nevsky Prospekt Metro station brings you right out on Nevsky Prospekt by the department store and Dom Knigi.

Following the Nevsky a bit farther you come to **Ploshchad Znamenskaya**, formerly **Vosstaniya** (Uprising) **Square**. It was so named when troops of the czar refused to shoot a group of unarmed demonstrators during the February 1917 uprising. One of the interesting buildings on the Square is **Moskovsky Vokzal** (Moscow Train Station). It was built by the architect, Thon, in 1847. The St Petersburg-Moscow railway line opened on

November 1, 1851. A smaller version of this station in Moscow is appropriately named the Leningrad Station. The word *vokzal* is used for a station and now St Petersburg has five major train *vokzals* in the city: Moscow, Finland, Warsaw, Baltic and Vitebsky. The latter was known as 'Czarskoye Selo', the station connecting Russia's first railroad line, built in 1837, to the czar's summer residence in Pavlovsk. The Hotel Oktyabrskaya dates from the 1890s. The Metro stop, Ploshchad Vosstaniya/Mayakovskaya, is near the Square. The Mayakovskaya exit lets you out at about 100 Nevsky and Marata Street.

A few blocks down Marata Street from Nevsky is the Marata Banya complex; open 7 am–11 pm, closed on Mondays and Tuesdays. At no. 24 Marata is the **Museum of the Arctic and Antarctic** (in the Church of St Nicholas). It is open 10 am–5 pm (closed on Mondays and Tuesdays). The **Nekrasov Home Museum** is nearby at 36 Liteiny Prospekt, displaying the writer's works; open 11 am–5 pm, Thursday 1 pm–7 pm (closed on Tuesdays and weekends).

The modern Moscow Hotel (with restaurants and a *Beriozka*) stands at the end of Nevsky Prospekt on Alexander Nevsky Square. Across the street is the **Alexander Nevsky Lavra**, the oldest monastery in St Petersburg. Peter the Great founded the monastery, southeast of the city, in 1710 and dedicated it to the Holy Trinity and military leader, Alexander Nevsky, Prince of Novgorod, who won a major victory on the Neva against the Swedes in 1240. In Russia, the name *lavra* was applied to a large monastery. Before the Revolution, there were four prestigious *lavra* in the country. The Alexander Nevsky was in St Petersburg; another was the Trinity-St Sergius Monastery in the Golden Ring town of Zagorsk. The Blagoveshchevsky Sobor (Annunciation Church) is the oldest church in the Lavra, built by Trezzini in 1720. It now houses the **Museum of Urban Sculpture**; open 11 am–3 pm, closed on Thursdays.

The Troitsky Sobor (Holy Trinity Cathedral) is the main church of the complex. The Church of Alexander Nevsky is also here. In 1723, the remains of Alexander Nevsky were brought to the Cathedral. The sarcophagus, cast from 1.5 tons of silver, is now at the Hermitage. Peter the Great buried his sister, Natalie, in the Lazarevskoye Cemetery (to the left of the main entrance), St Petersburg's oldest cemetery. To the right of the main entrance is the Tikhvinskoye Cemetery. Here are the carved gravestones of many of Russia's greatest figures such as Tchaikovsky, Glinka, Rimsky-Korsakov, Mussorgsky, Stasov, Clodt and Dostoevsky. Another entrance is across the street from the Moscow Hotel. The cemeteries are closed on Thursday and Saturday. The cathedral holds services, and on Alexander Nevsky Day, September 11–12, huge processions take place. Near the monastery is the Theological Seminary, re-established in 1946, which trains 440 students for the clergy. About 100 women are taught to be teachers or choir conductors. Four cathedrals and over 20 churches currently perform services in St Petersburg. The Alexander Nevsky Bridge, largest bridge in the city, crosses the Neva from the monastery. The Metro stop, Ploshchad Aleksandra Nevskovo, brings you right to the Moscow Hotel and the Monastery complex.

Finland Station

The **Finland Railway Station** is located on the right bank of the Neva, a little east of where the cruiser, *Aurora,* is docked. It is also a short walk from the **Aleksandrovsky (Liteiny) Most** on the Petrogradskaya side, with its beautiful railings filled with mermaids and anchors. The station, behind a towering monument to Lenin, dates back to 1870; from here Lenin secretly left from Petrograd for Finland in August 1917, after he was forced into hiding by the Provisional Government. A few months later he was brought back via the same locomotive to direct the October uprising. This locomotive, engine

Statue of Alexander Pushkin in the Square of Arts

no. 293, is on display behind a glass pavilion in the back of the station by the platform area. A brass plate on the locomotive bears the inscription: 'The government of Finland presented this locomotive to the government of the USSR in commemoration of journeys over Finnish territory made by Lenin in troubled times. June 13, 1957'.

The monument to Lenin stands in Lenin Square. After the February 1917 Revolution overthrew the czarist monarchy, Lenin returned to Petrograd from his place of exile in Switzerland on April 3, 1917. He gave a speech to the masses from the turret of a car. Originally the Lenin monument was erected on the spot where he gave the speech. But during the construction of the square, the statue, portraying Lenin standing on the car's turret addressing the crowd with an outstretched hand, was moved closer to the Neva embankment, where it stands today. It was unveiled on November 7, 1926. Metro stop, Ploshchad Lenina, lets out at Finland Station.

The Aleksandrovsky Most in front of the station leads to Shpalernaya Street and the Taurida Palace at no. 47. The street was once named after journalist Ivan Voinov who

(Above) Nevsky Prospekt, (top) Pushkin Theater

was killed in this street on July 6, 1917. The palace was built by Ivan Starov in 1789 for Prince Grigory Potemkin—a gift from Catherine the Great. Potemkin was Commander-In-Chief of the Russian Army in the Crimea during the Turkish wars. The peninsula there was called Taurida, and Potemkin was given the title, Prince of Taurida. One party Potemkin held in the palace used 140,000 lamps and 20,000 candles. After both he and Catherine the Great died, the new Emperor Paul I (who disliked his mother, Catherine, and her favorites), converted the palace into a riding house and stables. It was later renovated and became the seat of the State Duma in 1906. On February 27, 1917, the left wing of the palace held the first session of the Petrograd Soviet of Workers.

Behind the gardens is the **Museum to Alexander Suvorov**, the great 18th-century Russian military leader; open 11 am–6 pm, closed on Wednesdays. Across the street from the front of the palace is the **Kikin Palace**. Built in 1714 and one of the oldest buildings in the city, it belonged to the Boyar Kikin, who plotted, along with Peter's son, Alexei, to assassinate Peter the Great. After Kikin was put to death, Peter turned the palace into Russia's first natural science museum. The collections were later moved to the Kunstkammer on Vasilyevsky Island. Today the yellow-white palace is a children's music school. The closest Metro stop is Chernyshevskaya.

The Smolny

Catherine set up the Institute for Young Noble Ladies in the Smolny Convent, Russia's first school for the daughters of nobility. Today the Church of the Resurrection and the former convent is the concert and exhibition hall. In the years 1806–08, Quarenghi erected additional buildings for the Smolny Institute to the right of the convent. In August, 1917, the closed Institute became the headquarters for the Petrograd Bolshevik Party and the Military Revolutionary Committee. On October 25, 1917, Lenin arrived at the Smolny and gave the command for the storming of the Winter Palace. On October 26, the Second All-Russia Congress of Soviets gathered in the Smolny's Assembly Hall to elect Lenin the leader of the world's first 'Socialist Government of Workers and Peasants', and to adopt Lenin's Decrees on Peace and Land. John Reed wrote in his book *Ten Days That Shook the World* that Lenin was 'unimpressive, to be the idol for a mob, loved and revered as perhaps few leaders in history have been. A leader purely by virtue of intellect; colorless, humorless, uncompromising and detached, without picturesque idiosyncrasies—but with the power of explaining profound ideas in simple terms...he combined shrewdness with the greatest intellectual audacity'. Lenin lived at the Smolny for 124 days before transferring the capital to Moscow. Today the places in the Smolny where Lenin lived are part of the Lenin Museum. The rest of the building houses the mayor's office.

Theater Square

In the southwest part of the city along Glinka and Decembrists Prospekts lies **Teatral-naya Ploshchad** (Theater Square). This section of land was once the location for St Petersburg carnivals and fairs. In the 18th century, it was known as *Ploshchad Karusel* (Merry-Go-Round Square). A wooden theater was built here and later, in 1783, it was replaced by the Bolshoi Stone Theater, with over 2,000 seats. In 1803, the drama troupe moved to the Alexandrinsky Theater and the opera and ballet remained at the Bolshoi. In 1860, Albert Kavos completed the Mariinsky Theater (which replaced the Bolshoi), named after Maria, the wife of Alexander II. It was named the **Kirov Theater**, after a prominent Communist leader in 1935 and renamed Mariinsky in 1992. The five-tiered theater is decorated with blue velvet chairs, gilded stucco, ceiling paintings and chandeliers.

In the 19th century, St Petersburg was the musical capital of Russia. At the Mariinsky Theater, premiers of opera and ballet were staged by Russia's most famous composers, dancers and singers. Under Petipa, Ivanov and Fokine, Russian ballet took on world-wide recognition. The Fyodor Chalyapin Memorial Room, named after the great singer, is open during performances. At no. 26 Grafftio Street the Chalyapin Memorial Museum has chamber music September–May on Thursdays at 7 pm. The museum is open 11 am–6 pm, Wednesday–Sunday. The closest Metro stop is Petrogradskaya. The Mariinsky Theatre of Opera and Ballet continues to stage some of the world's finest ballets and operas; its companies tour many countries throughout the world.

Opposite the Mariinsky stands the **Rimsky-Korsakov State Conservatory**, Russia's first advanced school of music. The founder of the Conservatory was the composer, Anton Rubenstein. Some of the graduates include Tchaikovsky, Prokofiev and Shostakovich. On either side of the Conservatory stand the monuments to Mikhail Glinka and Rimsky-Korsakov. The Rimsky-Korsakov Museum is at 28 Zagorodny Prospekt. It is open from 11 am–6 pm Wednesday–Sunday. The nearest Metro station is Vladimirskaya. Further down Decembrists Street, past the Mariinsky, is a synagogue.

A walk down Glinka Street leads to the Nikolsky Marine Cathedral (also functioning), built in 1753–62 by Chevakinsky in honor of St Nicholas, the protector of seamen. Naval officers once lived in the area, thus the full name of Nikolsky Morskoi (Marine). Standing at the intersection of the Ekaterininsky and Kryukov canals, the blue and white church combines the old Russian five-dome tradition with the baroque. A lovely carved wooden iconostasis is inside and a four-tiered belltower stands by itself in the gardens. It has daily church services.

Up Glinka Street in the opposite direction, the narrow *Potseluyev Most* (Bridge of Kisses) crosses the Moika River. To its right, the second building from the corner at no. 94 is the Yusupov Palace, now the **Teachers' Club**. There, also, is the **Rasputin Memorial Room** and **Restaurant Rasputin**. The last owner of the palace was the wealthy Prince

Overdressed

He was so badly dressed that even a man accustomed to shabbiness would have been ashamed to be seen in the street in such rags. In that quarter of the town, however, scarcely any shortcoming in dress would have created surprise. Owing to the proximity of the Hay Market, the number of establishments of bad character, the preponderance of the trading and working-class population crowded the streets and alleys in the heart of Petersburg, types so various were to be seen in the streets that no figure, however queer, would have caused surprise. But there was such accumulated bitterness and contempt in the young man's heart that, in spite of all the fastidiousness of youth, he minded his rags least of all in the street. It was a different matter when he met with acquaintances or with former fellow students, whom, indeed, he disliked meeting any time.

And yet when a drunken man who, for some reason, was being taken somewhere in a huge wagon dragged by a heavy dray horse, suddenly shouted at him as he drove past: 'Hey there, German hatter!' bawling at the top of his voice and pointing at him—the young man stopped suddenly and clutched tremulously at his hat. It was a tall round hat from Zimmerman's, but completely worn out, rusty with age, all torn and bespattered, brimless and bent on one side in a most unseemly fashion. Not shame, however, but quite another feeling akin to terror had overtaken him.

'I knew it,' he muttered in confusion, 'I thought so! That's the worst of all! Why, a stupid thing like this, the most trivial detail might spoil the whole plan. Yes, my hat is too noticeable...It looks adsurd and that makes it noticeable...With my rags I ought to wear a cap, any sort of old pancake, but not this grotesque thing. Nobody wears such a hat, it would be noticed a mile off, it would be remembered...What matters is that people would remember it, and that would give them a clue. For this business one should be as little conspicuous as possible...Trifles, trifles are what matter! Why it's just such trifles that always ruin everything...'

Fyodor Dostoevsky, Crime and Punishment,
translated by Constance Garnett

Yusupov, who was responsible for the assassination of Grigory Rasputin (the priest who exerted much influence in the court of Nicholas II) in 1916. Rasputin was first given poisoned cakes in the palace's basement, set up to look like a study. Nothing happened—the sugar in the cakes was thought to have neutralized the poison. Then the conspirators started shooting at Rasputin, and continued to do so as he ran from the house. Finally, they threw Rasputin's body through a hole in the ice of the river. Later, after his body was found floating under the ice downstream, an autopsy showed that Rasputin had water in his lungs, proving he had still been alive after all the attempts to kill him. Yusupov later fled Russia. The Palace is open 12 pm–7 pm, Saturdays 11 am–4 pm (closed Sundays and Mondays). Nearest Metro Sennaya Ploshchad.

Continuing along Glinka toward the Neva, a number of brick buildings are situated on a small triangular island. These were the storehouses for ship timber during the time of Peter the Great. Man-made canals created the small island known as Novaya Gollandiya (New Holland). The New Admiralty Canal, dug in 1717, connected the island with the Admiralty. Konnogvardeysky (formerly Trade Union) Boulevard was laid partly along the route of the old Admiralty canal.

The last square before the Neva is known as Annunciation Square, formerly Truda Square. Between 1853 and 1861, a palace for the oldest son of Nicholas I was built by Stakenschneider near the square. In 1895, it was turned into the Xenia Institute for Noble Ladies, named after Xenia, the daughter of Alexander III. In 1919, it was again turned over to the Trade Union Regional Council and renamed the **Palace of Labor**. At no. 44 Red Fleet Embankment is the branch of **Museum of the History of St Petersburg**, open 11 am–5 pm (closed on Wednesdays) in the former Rumyantsev Mansion.

Moscow Avenue

Moskovsky Prospekt runs for nearly 10 miles (16 kilometers) in a straight line from **Sennaya** (formerly Peace Square) to the airport. The avenue follows the line known as the Pulkovo Meridian (zero on old Russian maps) that led to the Pulkovo Astronomical Observatory. The square was known, in Czarist times, as *Sennaya Ploshchad*, a place used for public punishment of serfs. The area was the residence of many of Dostoevsky's characters—including *Crime and Punishment*'s Sophia Marmeladova. On **Grazhdanskaya Ulitsa** (Citizen's Prospekt) is the Raskolnikov House, from whose basement Raskolnikov stole the murder axe. The **Dostoevsky Home Museum** is at 5/2 Kuznechny Pereulok, open 10.30 am–5 pm (closed Mondays). The nearest station is at Vladimirskaya/Chernyshenskaya. A little past the Fontanka River is the **Moscow Triumphal Gate**, built in 1834–38 by Vassily Stasov to commemorate the Russian victories during the Russo-Turkish War of 1828–29. It was the largest cast-iron structure in the world in the mid-

Russian Ballet

The first *balli*, or *balletti*, originated in Italy during the Renaissance, when dance became an important social function in court life. Men would entertain at court festivities in routines combining music, dancing, singing and acting; women, on the other hand, were forbidden to dance openly in public. By the late 15th century, it was the vogue for court entertainment to be combined with banquets—each course was accompanied by a new scene in the story. Menus still list the *entrées* as they did five centuries ago. The French soon copied the Italians by staging their own *ballets de cour*. Their courts brought in Italian dancing masters, and many outstanding French painters and poets collaborated in the elaborate displays. These staged spectacles were set up to glorify the power and the wealth of the monarchy.

King Louis XIV of France was an avid dancer himself and was to take the part of the sun in the *Ballet de la Nuit*. Later in life, when Louis could no longer dance, he established the first *Académie Royale de Musique* (now the Paris Opera), a dancing school was added that set the foundation of classical ballet.

As the Italians invented the idea of the *balli* as a combination of all the arts, the French developed this new vision of dance into a professional school, the *danse d'école*. A style of classical dancing was born with its own vocabulary of individual steps, the five positions of the feet (fashioned from court ballroom dance moves) and synchronized group movements. French terminology is still used today.

This form of ballet-dance was first staged in Russia in 1672 by a German ensemble in Moscow for Tsar Alexei I. The theatrical performance, lasting 10 hours, was based on the Bible's Book of Esther. Alexei's daughter, Sophia (the future regent), was very fond of dancing herself and composed comedy ballets, such as *Russalki* ('The Mermaids'). Sophia's half-brother, Peter the Great, encouraged Western dance and later, as tsar, brought in many French, English and Polish companies for lavish productions in his new city of Sankt Pietersburkh. Later the Petersburg Imperial Ballet was founded in 1738.

During the reigns of Elizabeth (1741–61) and Catherine the Great (1762–96), many French and Italian masters took up residence in St Petersburg and Moscow. By the turn of the century, St Petersburg was approaching the peak of its cosmopolitan fame. It had four separate opera houses with permanent companies, all fully supported by the tsarinas and tsars. While ballet grew in popularity and artistic importance in Russia, it declined throughout the rest of Europe.

One of the most influential characters of the early Russian ballet scene was the Frenchman Charles Didelot, who arrived in Russia in 1801. He taught at the Petersburg Imperial Ballet School for more than 25 years and wove French classical and Russian folk themes through the new romantic style of the times. He was the first to translate Pushkin's poems, *The Prisoner of the Caucasus* and *Ruslan and Ludmilla,* into the physical world of ballet. Under his direction, the ballet was made into a *grand* spectacle, incorporating the entire *corps de ballet,* costumes, scenery, and even special effects—dancers were fitted with mobile wings and live pigeons flew across the stage.

Another of St Peterburg's well-known dancers was the Frenchman Marius Petipa, who came to Russia in 1847. Petipa was the master of the grand spectacle and produced an original ballet for the opening of each new season. During his 56-year career on the Russian stage, Petipa choreographed over 60 ballets for the Imperial Ballet, highlighting solos within each performance. In the early 1890s, this grand master worked almost exclusively with Tchaikovsky, choreographing *Sleeping Beauty, The Nutcracker,* and *Swan Lake.* It was Petipa, who brought the Imperial Ballet to the pinnacle of the ballet world.

All the St Petersburg ballets premiered at the Mariinsky Theater . Built by Albert Kavos in 1860, it was named after Maria, wife of Tsar Alexander II. In 1935, it was renamed the Kirov, after the prominent Communist leader under Stalin; but in 1992 the original name was restored . The Mariinsky remains one of the most respected names in the ballet world. It is situated in St Petersburg along Glinka and Decembrists streets on Teatralnaya Ploshchad ('Theater Square'). This section of land was once the location for St Petersburg carnivals and fairs. (In the 18th century, it was known as Ploshcad Karusel, 'Merry-Go-Round Square.') This gorgeous 1700 seater, five-tiered theater is decorated with blue velvet, guilded stucco, ceiling paintings, and chandeliers.

By the end of the 19th century, the Mariinsky Theater had almost 200 permanently employed dancers, graded in rank. Each graduate of the Imperial Ballet School was placed into the corps de ballet; only a few rose to *coryphée, sujet, prima ballerina,* and lastly *prima absoluta* (or, for a man, soloist to the tsar). They were employed by the tsar for 20 years and retired with full pensions. Ballet dancers were often invited to court banquets, and favorites received many luxurious presents from admirers and the royal family themselves. Nicholas II bestowed large gifts of diamonds and emeralds upon his jewel *danseur,* Kschessinska which she often wore during performances.

As the spirit of revolution hung in the air, the Imperial Ballet's conventional classical style plunged into decline. It was the St Petersburg artistic entrepreneur

(Following pages) Mariinsky (Kirov) Ballet dancers

Sergei Diaghilev (1872–1929), who revived the stagnating Imperial Ballet with the individual and innovative style of the *Ballets Russes*.

Diaghilev brought Russia's best dancers, choreographers, musicians, and artists together to create some of the most stunning spectacles that the world had ever known. His dancers were Pavlova, Karsavina and Nijinsky; his choreographers Fokine, Massine, Nijinskaya (Nijinsky's sister) and later Balanchine; musicians Tchaikovsky, Chopin, Stravinsky and Rimsky-Korsakov; and artists Benois, Bakst, Goncharova and even Picasso. During the first season abroad in Paris in 1909, the repertoire of the *Ballets Russes* consisted of Borodin's *Polovtsian Dances from Prince Igor*, Chopin's *Les Sylphides* and *The Banquet*, with music by Tchaikovsky, Mussorgsky and Rimsky-Korsakov. The programs were designed by the French writer Jean Cocteau and posters painted by Moscow artist Valentin Serov. Even Erik Satie joined the group of musicians. In the center of all this furor were two of the most magnificent dancers of the 20th century, Anna Pavlova and Vaslav Nijinsky.

Born the illegitimate daughter of a poor laundress, Pavlova did not seem destined for the stage. But in 1891, at the age of 10, this petite dark-eyed beauty was accepted into the Petersburg Imperial Ballet School. When she graduated in 1899, the stunning performer leaped right into solo roles in the Mariinsky Theater . Anna then left to dance with the *Ballets Russes*; after her first performance in Paris, a French critic exuberantly claimed 'she is to dance what Racine is to poetry, Poussin to painting, Gluck to music'. Pavlova was known for her dynamic short solos, filled with an endless cascade of jumps and pirouettes as in *The Dying Swan* and *The Dragonfly*.

Nijinsky was heralded as the greatest male dancer of his day—dancing was in his blood. For generations his family worked as dancers, acrobats, and circus performers. Vaslav was born in Kiev, Russia, in 1888, where his Polish parents were performing. When he was 11, his mother enrolled him in the Petersburg Imperial Ballet School, where he studied for eight years. His graduation performance so impressed the *prima absoluta* ballerina Mathilde Kschessinska that he immediately began his career at the Mariinsky Theater as a principal soloist.

His full genius emerged at the *Ballets Russes*' 1909 Paris debut. One spectator felt that 'his was the victory of breath over weight, the possession of body by the soul'. In 1911, Nijinsky was fired from the Imperial Ballet for not wearing the required little pair of trunks over his tights when he danced *Giselle;* this did not go over well with the Dowager Empress, who witnessed with crimson face the entire performance. His range in roles was astonishing. Everywhere he went, Nijinsky captured the hearts and adoration of the critics and audiences. One American critic noted, 'few of us can view the art of Nijinsky without emotion . . . he completely erased the memory of all male dancers that I had previously seen'.

Nijinsky danced with Pavlova in *Cleopatra* and as the ethereal spirit in *Le Spectre de la Rose*. Jean Cocteau, who saw his first performance in Paris, exclaimed that Nijinsky's jumps 'were so poignant, so contrary to all the laws of flight and balance, following so high and curved a trajectory, that I shall never again smell a rose without this unerasable phantom appearing before me'. Fokine choreographed up a storm of innovative and dynamic ballets and stressed strong male dancing; Nijinsky danced in almost all his creations, including *Le Pavillon d'Armide, Sheherazade, The Firebird, Narcisse, Daphnis and Chloe,* and *Le Dieu Bleu* ('The Blue Clown'). In his diary, Nijinsky wrote 'I am beginning to understand God. Art, love, nature are only an infinitesimal part of God's spirit. I wanted to recapture it and give it to the public . . . . If they felt it, then I am reflecting Him. 'He saw himself as a clown of God'. The world, in turn, would regard him as '*Le Dieu de la Danse*'.

His first choreographic work, *L'Après Midi d'un Faune*, was performed in 1912. Even though only eight minutes long, it managed to cause a scandal that rocked even Paris. With his natural faunlike eyes, waxed pointed ears and horns, and dressed only in tights with a curly golden wig, Nijinsky danced around seven lively nymphs. At the end of the ballet, each nymph fled as she dropped her veil. During this flight of passage, he caught up with each nymph and swept down under her in one convulsive, erotic movement. The audience gasped audibly.

A year later, Nijinsky's *Le Sacre du Printemps*, performed on May 29, 1913, stopped just short of causing a riot in Paris; even the composer, Igor Stravinsky, had to flee the theater. The story of the ballet weaves around the ritual of the pagan rites of spring. The dancers' movements were not traditional gentle swayings and graceful turns, but asymmetrical rhythms and gestures, twists and jerks. By the time the first act was completed, many spectators were already hissing and screaming; the music was barely audible over the cries of emotional insults.

Nijinsky gave his last dance in Switzerland in 1919, at the age of 31, 10 years after his first performance. By then he had already embarked on his voyage into madness; his memory became a blank. Prophesying in his diary, he had written, 'people will leave me alone, calling me a mad clown'. Nijinsky lived out the rest of his days in an asylum; his body died in 1950.

On the night of 15 March 1917, the day Tsar Nicholas II abdicated the throne to the provisional government, *Sleeping Beauty* was performed at the Mariinsky Theater in St Petersburg.

19th century. The gate decorated with the Winged Victory, Glory, and Plenty once marked the end of the city, where a road toll was collected. The closest Metro stop is Moskovskiye Vorota.

Farther along the prospekt on the left side is the Gothic Chesma Palace and Church. Catherine the Great commissioned Felten to build it. It was named Chesma in 1770, after the Russian victory over the Turkish fleet at Chesma Bay. The Chesma Museum houses displays on the naval battle at Chesma. It is open 10 am– 5 pm, closed on Mondays and Tuesdays. Next comes Moscow Square, whose whole eastern side is lined by the former House of Soviets, with a Statue of Lenin at the center. Not far away is *Ploshchad Pobedy* (Victory Square). The **Monument to the Heroes of the Defense of Leningrad** (unveiled on May 9, 1975, 30 years after the victory) is the Square's focal point. The sculptured group, called The Victors, look out to where the front once ran. Pink granite steps lead down to an obelisk that stands inside a circle symbolizing the breaking of the Blockade ring. An Eternal Flame is lit at the base. The ground floor serves as a **Museum for the Seige of Leningrad**, open 10 am–6 pm, closed on Wednesdays. Closest Metro stop is Moskovskaya. The Green Belt of Glory is a memorial complex that stretches 145 miles (230 kilometers) along the front line of 1941–44. Not far from the Baltic railway station, at Metro stop Narvskaya, is **Narvskaya (formerly Stachek) Square** with the **Narva Triumphal Gate** marking the victorious outcome of the War of 1812. Returning troops passed through this gate.

Piskarovskoye Memorial Cemetery lies to the north of St Petersburg; open 10 am–6 pm daily. Here are the common graves, marked only by year of burial from 1941–44, of over a half million Leningraders who died during the 900-day seige. The central path of the cemetery leads to the **Statue of the Mother Country**, holding a wreath of oak leaves, the symbol of eternal glory. Two museum pavilions are on either side of the entrance, where one realizes the horrors that faced the citizens of this city. The cemetery register is open at a page with the entries: 'February, 1942: 18th—3,241 bodies; 19th—5,569; 20th—10,043'. Another display shows a picture of 11-year old Tanya Sevicheya and pages from her diary: 'Granny died today. Mama died today. The Savichevs have died. Everybody died. Only Tanya is alive'. Tanya later died after she was evacuated from the city.

The memorial Seige of Leningrad day is held every year on September 8.

A chapel in the Alexander Nevsky Monastery

Vicinity of St Petersburg

If you have time, go on a few excursions outside St Petersburg. Daytrips to Peter the Great's Summer Palace on the Gulf of Finland or to the towns of Czarskoye Selo and Pavlovsk are recommended.

Petrokrepost or Schlüsselburg

Peter's Fortress, Petrokrepost, on a small island near the southwestern shore of Lake Ladoga, was founded by Slavs in 1323 to protect the trade waterways linking Novgorod with the Baltic. At that time, the small outpost was known as Oreshek (Nut). When Peter the Great captured the tiny fortress in 1702 from the Swedes (they took control of the lands in the 17th century), he renamed it Schlüsselburg, the Key Fortress. The town of Schlüsselburg sprang up along the left bank of the Neva, where it flows out of the lake. After the Northern War ended in 1721, Peter converted the fortress into a prison. He had members of his family imprisoned here and many Russian revolutionaries suffered similar fates. On May 8, 1887, Lenin's brother, Alexander Ulyanov, along with four others who attempted to assassinate Czar Alexander III, were hung in the prison yard. The German name of Schlüsselburg was changed to Petrokrepost in 1944 during World War II. If you would like to visit Schlüsselburg, and it is not part of your tour, check at your hotel's travel desk; Intourist offers daily bus trips there or you can reach it by car along the M18 highway in about 45 minutes.

Kronstadt

When Peter the Great began to build St Petersburg in 1703, the Northern War (1700–21) with the Swedes was in its early stages. To protect the sea approaches to his city, Peter built the Kronstadt Fortress, which also contained his shipyards, on the island of Kotlin in the Gulf of Finland in 1704. Monuments on the island are linked to the history of the Russian fleet. Intourist offers bus excursions to Kronstadt from St Petersburg. In summer, a hydrofoil leaves daily from St Petersburg's Tuchkov Bridge every 45 minutes from 7 am–9 pm. For the rest of the year, you must take the elektrichka from Finland station to Gorskaya on the Karelian Isthmus, and then the hourly bus to Kronstadt. A ferry also leaves from Oranienbaum. At Petrodvorets, take a local bus to Oranienbaum or a train from St Petersburg's Baltic station to Oranienbaum and a ferry to Kronstadt. Notice the

29-kilometer 'barrier', built across a section of the Gulf of Finland to control the floods (over 300 in St Petersburg's history). Tidal waves get swept inland during severe storms. In 1824, the water level rose four meters, killing 569 people.

Petrodvorets

While Peter the Great was supervising the building of the Kronstadt fortress, he stayed in a small lodge on the southern shore of the Gulf of Finland. After Russia defeated the Swedes in the Battle of Poltava in 1709, Peter decided to build his summer residence, Peterhof, so that it not only commemorated the victory over Sweden (and of gaining access to the Baltic), but also the might of the Russian empire. Peterhof was designed to resemble the French Palace of Versailles.

Architects were summoned from around the world: Rastrelli, Le Blond, Braunstein, Michetti and the Russian, Zemtsov. Over 4,000 peasants and soldiers were brought in to dig the canals, gardens and parks in the marshy area. Soil, building materials and tens of thousands of trees were brought in by barge. Peter helped to draft the layout of all the gardens and fountains. The fountains were built by Vasily Tuvolkov, Russia's first hydraulics engineer. Over 12 miles (20 kilometers) of canals were constructed in a way so that 30,000 liters (7,500 gallons) of water flowed under its own pressure (without the aid of a single pump) to 144 fountains.

The great **Cascade Fountain** in front of the palace has 17 waterfalls, 142 water jets, 66 fountains (including the two cup fountains on either side), 29 bas reliefs, and 39 gilded statues, including the famous Samson—the Russians won the Battle of Poltava on St Samson's Day. The five-ton Samson, surrounded by eight dolphins, is wrestling open the jaws of a lion, from which a jet of water shoots over 20 meters into the air.

Approaching the back of the palace from Red Avenue, the first fountain is known as the **Mezheumny**, with a dragon in the center pool. The **Neptune Fountain** was brought to Russia from Nüremberg, Germany. Square Ponds are right by the walls of the palace in the Upper Park.

The northeast path leading to **Alexander Park** takes you by the Gothic Court chapel (with 43 saints along the outer walls), the **Cottage** (built in 1829 by Adam Menelaws, who designed it to resemble an aristocratic Englishman's cottage), and the **Farm**. This was also built by Menelaws as a storage house, but was later turned into a small summer palace by Alexander II. Following the path back around to the palace, you will come upon the **Conservatory**, used as a greenhouse. Nearby is the **Triton Fountain**, which shows Neptune's son wrestling with a sea monster. **Chess Hill**, with a checkerboard design, contains some of the best waterfalls, cascading over bronzed dragons. The two

(Following pages) Bell Tower near St Nicholas' Cathedral

Roman Fountains (modeled after those at the Cathedral of St Peter in Rome) stand at the bottom of the hill and were designed by Karl Blank. Following the path around to the right of the palace brings you to the Pyramid Fountain. Peter the Great designed this water pyramid, made up of seven tiers and 505 jets. A circular seat is positioned under the Little Umbrella Fountain. If you are tempted to have a short rest on the bench under the umbrella, be ready to scramble—as 164 jets spray out water as soon as anyone sits down! As you scamper away, you will approach the Little Oak Fountain, which has dozens of hidden jets (as do the artificial tulips) that spray as any weight approaches the oak tree. When you run off to the nearby bench to catch your breath, you will now get drenched by 41 more jets! Beware of the three fir trees!

Approaching Monplaisir, the Sun Fountain shoots out from a rectangular pond as 16 golden dolphins swim around shiny disks. Jets of water sprinkle out from the center column, creating the golden rays of the sun. The Adam and Eve fountains (the statues were done by the Venetian sculpturer Bonazza) stand on either side of the path leading to the Gulf from the Palace.

While the Grand Palace was under construction, Peter designed and lived in the smaller Dutch-style villa that he called Monplaisir (My Pleasure), right on the Gulf of Finland on the eastern side of the lower park. Even after the larger palace was completed, Peter preferred to stay here while he visited Peterhof. Today it houses a small collection of 17th- and 18th-century European paintings. The two-story house, by the water on the western side of the lower park, is known as the Château de Marly, built in 1714 in Louis XIV style—Peter visited a French king's hunting lodge in Marly. Behind it flows the Golden Hill Cascade. The other quaint two-story structure is known as the Hermitage Pavilion. It was built by Johann Friedrich Braunstein. The retreat was surrounded by a moat and had a drawbridge that could be raised to further isolate the guests. The first floor consisted of one room with a large dining room table that could be lifted from or lowered to servants on the ground floor; the guests placed a note on the table, rang a bell, and the table would shortly reappear with the orders. The Lion Cascade Fountains stand in front of the Hermitage. Inside are over 100 paintings by 18th-century European artists.

The original palace was built between 1714 and 1724, designed in the baroque and classical styles. It stands on a hill in the center of the Peterhof complex and overlooks the parks and gardens. Rastrelli enlarged it (1747–54) for Empress Elizabeth. After Peter's death, the palace passed on to subsequent czars. It was declared a museum after the revolution. During World War II, the name Peterhof was changed to Petrodvorets, Peter's Palace. The palace is three stories high and attached by wings that contain the galleries. The central part contains the Exhibition Rooms, Peter the Great's Oak Study and the Royal Bedchamber. The rooms have magnificent parquet floors, gilded ceilings, crystal chandeliers, and are filled with exquisite *objets d'art* from around the world. The **Crimson Room** has furniture by Chippendale; the walls of the oak study are covered by the portraits of the Empress Elizabeth, Catherine the Great and Alexander I; the **Partridge Chamber**, so named for the silk ornamental partridges that covered the walls, is filled with French silk-upholstered furniture, porcelain and clocks.

The **Portrait Gallery**, in the central hall of the palace, is filled with portraits by such painters as Pietro Rotari (the whole collection was acquired by Catherine the Great) and serves as an interesting catalog of period costumes. The **White Dining Hall**, used for State dinners, is decorated in the classical style with white molded figures on the walls and a crystal and amethyst chandelier. The table is ceremoniously laid out for 30 people with 196 pieces of English porcelain. Rastrelli built the adjacent **Throne Room** for official receptions. A portrait of Catherine the Great on horseback hangs over Peter's first throne.

The **Chesma Room** commemorated the battles between the Russian and Turkish fleets in Chesma Bay in the Aegean Sea. The German artist, Hackert, was commissioned to paint the victorious pictures in the room. Count Orlov (a squadron commander at Chesma) checked the artist's sketches and was dissatisfied with one that depicted an exploding ship. Hackert mentioned that he had never seen one. Orlov ordered a 60-cannon Russian frigate, anchored off the coast of Italy, to be packed with gunpowder. Hackert had to journey to Italy to see the ship exploding. The rest of the palace is joined by numerous galleries and studies. At the east end is a Rastrelli rococo chapel with a single gilded cupola. The **Benois Museum**, in the house of the maids of honor in the large palace, exhibits the famous set designer's work. It also includes works by several generations of the Benois family; open 11am–6 pm (closed Monday).

Hitler invaded Russia on June 22, 1941. When, on September 23, 1941, the Nazis reached Peterhof, many of the art pieces and statues had still not been evacuated. The German Army spent 900 days here and destroyed the complex. Monplaisir was an artillery site, used to shell Leningrad. The Germans cut down 15,000 trees for firewood, used tapestries in the trenches, plundered over 34,000 works of art, and made off with priceless objects, including the Samson statue, which were never recovered. After the war, massive restoration work began, and on June 17, 1945, the fountains flowed once again. The head of the Hermitage, Joseph Orbelli, who lived in the Hermitage during the seige, remarked: 'Even during our worst suffering, we knew that the day would come when once again the beautiful fountains of Petrodvorets would begin to spray and the statues of the park flash their golden gleam in the sunlight'. There are black-and-white photographs on display in the Exhibition Room that show the extensive damage to the palace.

Leningrad poet, Olga Bergholts, after visiting Peterhof after the siege, wrote:

The gardens and rooms of Peter The Great's Palace, Petrodvorets

'Again from the black dust, from the place
of death and ashes, will arise the garden as before.
So it will be. I firmly believe in miracles.
You gave me that belief, my Leningrad'.

GETTING THERE

The Upper and Lower parks and gardens cover about 300 acres (121 hectares), stretching around the palace to the Gulf of Finland. When it is warm and clear, it is wonderful to have a picnic (bring food) on the grounds or beach, stroll in the gardens and spend the entire day. Daily tour buses run (20 miles/32 kilometers) from St Petersburg, and Intourist offers group excursions (check at the hotel service desk). An electric train also leaves from the Baltic station to the stop, Novy Peterhof (35 minutes).

A much more interesting way to get there is by hydrofoil, known as the **Rocket**. This jets across the Gulf of Finland to the palace grounds in about 30 minutes. Catch one at the dock right across from the Hermitage (also opposite the statue of Peter the Great)— the hydrofoils run about every 20 minutes (May through September) and cost very little each way. (Intourist also offers daily group excursions. Inquire at your hotel.) Get there early to buy the ticket, since there tend to be long lines. Besides your boat ticket, you will also be issued a separate ticket to get into the palace grounds. Do not lose it—you need to show it when you enter the complex from the dock.

Typical of the Russian love of paper, this ticket will not admit you into the palace itself! Buy *this* ticket (for a few *rubles*) at the small kiosk at the end of the dock. The palace is a good 10-minute walk from the docks; if you do not have an entrance ticket, you must walk all the way back! Also, it is a good idea to buy your return ticket as soon as you arrive at Petrodvorets. If you wait til the last minute on a crowded day, all tickets for the time you want to return may be sold out. The return-ticket kiosks are to your left across the bridge as you get off the dock. A boat number will be stamped on the back of your ticket. When on the dock, look for your boat number posted on signs. The palace grounds are open daily from 9 am–10 pm; the palace itself from 11 am–6 pm (and the fountains operate from May–September). The Grand Palace is closed on Monday and the last Tuesday of each month. Monplasir and the Hermitage are closed on Wednesday and the last Thursday of each month. The Chateau de Marly is closed on Tuesday and the last Wednesday of each month. In June, during the White Nights, many festivals are held the palace grounds. It is wise to bring your own food. For overnight stays, try the hostel next to the Benois Wing.

Lomonosov or Oranienbaum

Known until recently as Lomonosov, **Oranienbaum** is situated only six miles (10 kilometers) west of Petrodvorets. Peter the Great gave the lands to his close friend, Prince Alexander Menschikov, to develop. Menschikov was the first governor-general of St Petersburg and supervised the building of the nearby Kronstadt Fortress. He turned the estate into his summer residence. Since he planted orange trees in the lower parks and grew them in hothouses, Menschikov named his residence *Oranienbaum*, German for 'orange trees'. The estate served as the country residence for later czars. Peter III and Catherine the Great expanded the buildings and grounds in the style of the times.

In 1948, the name was changed to Lomonosov after the great Russian scientist, who had a glasswork factory nearby.

The estate escaped major shelling during the war and is beautifully preserved. The two-story Grand Palace (1725, by architects Fontane and Shedel) stands atop a hill overlooking parks and gardens that were originally designed by Antonio Rinaldi, who also built the two pleasure pavilions, the **Chinese Palace** and **Katalnaya Gorka**, (Sliding Hill). Visitors could glide on sleds along a wooden path from the third story of the pavilion and ride down through the lower parks. Oranienbaum became the center of masqued balls and parties that entertained Russian royalty and foreign diplomats. The estate is now a museum (the buildings are closed October–April, and some on Tuesdays) and can be reached by bus, car, or by the train leaving from St Petersburg's Baltic Station every half hour. From the train station head for the green-domed Orthodox Church. There is also a ferry from Kronstadt or a local bus from Petrodvorets. Bring your own food.

Pushkin (Czarskoye Selo)

The town of **Czarskoye Selo**, meaning the Czar's Village, is 15.5 miles (25 kilometers) south of St Petersburg. After the Revolution, the named was changed to **Detskoye Selo** (Children's Village), and many of the town's buildings became schools. The poet, Pushkin, studied at the Lyceum (1811–17). In 1937, to commemorate the 100-year anniversary of Pushkin's death, the town was renamed **Pushkin**.

Peter the Great won the region between the Neva and the Gulf of Finland during the Northern War. He later presented these lands to his wife Catherine I who built parks and gardens and the **Yekaterininsky Dvorets**, Catherine's Palace. In 1752, the Empress Elizabeth commissioned Rastrelli to renovate the palace. The beautiful baroque building stretches 900 feet (300 meters) and is lavishly decorated.

(Following pages) The Great Cascade, Petrodvorets

Catherine the Great built additions to the palace. During her reign, many renowned architects, such as Cameron, Rinaldi and Quarenghi, worked in the neo-classical style on the palace. Many exhibition halls, Cameron's **Green Dining Room** and **Chinese Blue Room** are breathtaking. The walls of the **Blue Room** are decorated with Chinese blue silk and the Empress Elizabeth is portrayed as Flora, Goddess of Flowers. The white marble staircase leading into the palace was built in 1860 by Monighetti. On the inside walking tour, you pass through Rastrelli's **Cavalier Dining Room** and **Great Hall**. Peter the Great presented 248 personal guards to a Prussian king and in return received panels of amber. Rastrelli built the **Amber Room** using those panels in 1755.

During WW II, the Nazis made off with the panels, which were never found. The **Picture Hall** stretches the entire width of the building; of the 130 French, Flemish and Italian canvasses that were here before the war, 117 were evacuated and can be seen today. The palace chapel was begun by Rastrelli and completed by Stasov. The northeast section of the palace, in the chapel wing, contains the **Pushkin Museum**, made up of 27 halls, displaying his personal belongings and manuscripts.

The Lyceum is linked to the Palace by an archway. It was originally built by Catherine the Great as the school for her grandsons and was expanded in 1811 for the children of the aristocracy. The classrooms were on the second floor and the dormitory on the third. The Lyceum's first open class consisted of 30 boys between 11 and 14. One of these students was Alexander Pushkin. The Lyceum is now a museum and the classrooms and laboratories are kept as they were during Pushkin's time. A room in the dormitory reads, 'Door no. 14 Alexander Pushkin'. Pushkin read aloud his poem 'Recollections of Czarskoye Selo' on June 9, 1817, in the school's Assembly hall. The statue of Pushkin outside was sculpted by Robert Bach in 1900. The church (1734–47) next to the Lyceum is the oldest building in the town.

Catherine's parks consisted of three types: the French one was filled with statues and pavilions, the English had more trees and shrubs, and the Italian contained more sculpted gardens. The grounds stretch over 1,400 acres (567 hectares). Rastrelli built the Orlov column in the middle of the lake as a monument to the victory at the Battle of Chesma.

The Hermitage structure was built between 1744 and 1756 to entertain the guests. No servants were allowed on the second floor. The guests wrote requests on slates; the tables were lowered and raised with the appropriate drink and dishes, including some like elk lips and nightingale tongues! The adjacent fish canal provided seafood for the royal banquets. The upper bath house was used by the royal family and the lower by the visitors. Other buildings on the estate include the Admiralty (with a boat collection), the Grotto (once decorated with over 250,000 shells), the Cameron Gallery, the Hanging Gardens, the Agate Rooms, the Granite Terrace, Marble Bridge (made from Siberian marble), Turkish Baths (resembling a mosque) and the Milkmaid Fountain (built in 1816 by

Sokolov from a fable by La Fontaine). Pushkin wrote a poem based on the fable about the sad girl who holds a piece of her milk jug that lies broken at her feet. The Alexander Palace was built by Catherine the Great (1792–96 by Quarenghi) for her grandson, the future Alexander I. Nicholas II lived here after the 1905 revolution in St Petersburg.

An easy way to the town is by the frequent train from St Petersburg's Vitebsky Station (Pushkinskaya Metro stop). Get off the train at Detskoye Selo and take a local bus to Czarskoye Selo or a taxi to Catherine's Palace. Otherwise, walk the 15 minutes from the station. The Palace is open 11 am–6 pm (closed on Tuesdays). The Lyceum is also closed on Tuesdays, and some of the museums on Mondays or Wednesdays, so it is best to visit Thursday–Sunday. If you need to stay overnight, try the **Fedorovsky Gorodok Hostel** north of the Alexander Palace or the **Architect's House** at 2 Puschina St, tel 466–6459.

Pavlovsk

The flamboyant court life of Czarskoye Selo scared away most of the wildlife, so the royal family went into the nearby area of **Pavlovskoye** (about two miles/four kilometers away) to hunt. Two wooden hunting lodges were known as 'Krik' and 'Krak'. In 1777, Catherine the Great presented the villages, along with the serfs, to her son, Pavel (Paul), whose first son, Alexander, had just been born. The village was renamed Pavlovsk when Paul became czar. The Scottish architect, Cameron, began building the palace in the 1780s and Paul turned it into his official summer residence. Pavlovsk Park was created by Pietro Gonzaga (who lived here from 1803 to 1838) and covers over 3,750 acres (1,500 hectares), making it one of the largest landscaped parks in the world, with designs such as the Valley of the Ponds and the White Birchtree. Cameron also designed the Pavilion of Three Graces, the Temple of Friendship (1782) and the Apollo Colonnade (1783). Other structures include the Twelve Paths (and 12 bronze statues), Pavilion of the Monument to My Parents (of Paul I's wife), and the Mausoleum of Paul I (the murdered czar is buried in the Peter and Paul Fortress).

The palace and grounds were virtually destroyed during the war, but have been beautifully restored. Pavlovsk is 19 miles (30 kilometers) south of St Petersburg. You can take a bus tour (check at Intourist) combining both Czarskoye Selo and Pavlovsk in the same day. You can also get there in about 35 minutes by electric train from St Petersburg's Vitebsk station (Pushinskaya Metro stop). Drivers should leave the car by the wooden bridge and walk to the palace (open from 10.30 am–5.30 pm, closed Friday and first Monday of each month. On Thursdays, entrance to the palace is restricted to the first floor. It is an enjoyable excursion all season long. There is boating in the summer and skiing, ice skating and *troika* rides in the winter. Concerts are held every Saturday and Sunday in the Greek Hall of the Palace.

The Old Guard

An old man of eighty-four attracted my attention in the Mikhailovsky gardens. He brandished a sabre-shaped walking-stick as he strode down the paths, his war medals dangled in ranks at his chest, and his features showed bellicose above a mist of white beard. He looked like God the Father peering over a cloud.

'I'm an Old Bolshevik,' he announced to me. 'One of the original Revolutionaries!'

A ghost from the twenties, he still exulted in the people's common ownership. He patted the tree trunks possessively as he marched by and frequently said 'This is my tree, and this is my tree.'

In 1907 he had become a revoluionary, and had been sent in chains to Siberia. But a fellow-prisoner, he said, had concealed a file in the lapel of his coat, and together they had cut through the manacles and fled back to Leningrad. Those were the days when Siberian exiles and prisoners—Trotsky, Stalin and Bakunin among them—escaped from Siberia with laughable ease and slipped over frontiers with the freedom of stray cats.

Then the old man had joined the Revolution and fought for the three years against the Whites. He settled into a military stride as he spoke of it, and thrust out his beard like a torpedo, while all the time his gaze flashed and fulminated over the gardens. 'Get off the grass, comrade!' he bellowed. A young mother, seated on the sward beside her pram, looked up in bewilderment. 'Get off our motherland's grass!'

He embodied the intrusive precepts of early Communism, whose zealots were encouraged to scrutinize, shrivel and denounce each other. He was the self-proclaimed guardian and persecutor of all about him, and he entered the 1980s with the anachronism of a mastodon. Farther on a girl was leaning in the fork of one of his precious trees. 'Keep away from there!' he roared. 'Can't you see you're stopping it grow? Get off!' She gaped at him, said nothing, did not move. He marched on unperturbed. He even anathematized a mousing cat. 'What are you looking for, comrade? Leave nature alone!' He did not seem to mind or notice that nobody obeyed him.

We rested under a clump of acacias. 'When I was a boy,' he said, 'I saw these trees planted.' He pointed to the largest of them, which bifurcated into a gnarled arm. 'That tree was no taller than a little lamp-post then. The garden was private, of course, but as a boy I often squeezed in over the railings. The tsar and tsaritsa used to walk here in the summer.' His voice dwindled from an alsatian growl to purring reminiscence. 'Once, while I was hiding in the shrubs, I saw them myself...What were they like? It's hard to recall exactly. But she was a beautiful woman, I remember. She had her hand on his arm. And he seemed very large and handsome, and...' But he never finished. The lurking commissar in him erupted again. 'What are you doing, comrade?' Beneath us, a man was raking weeds out of an ornamental pond. 'How can you weed a lake?'

The gardener looked up stoically. 'I'm at work.'

Work. The magic syllable.

Immediately, as if some benedictory hand had passed its grace across the old man's brow, his expression changed to a look of benign redress. 'Fine,' he murmered, 'work.' For him the word had the potency of 'revolution' or 'collective'. The mousing cat, too, had been at work, I thought, but had been unable to voice this watchword.

Before we parted he said: 'I'll give you my address, not the real one. That's secret. You see,' he repeated, 'I'm one of the Old Bolsheviks.'

I wondered then if he were not deranged. He scribbled out his address on the back of a newspaper, in enormous handwriting. It was only as he was leaving me that I realized from his age that the history he had given me was nonsense. The tsars did not send lone boys of eleven to Siberia.

'How old did you say you were?' I asked. For he looked timeless.

'I know what you're thinking,' he answered. His eyes twinkled at me collusively. 'You Estonians, you're a clever lot. You're thinking that I can't have been sent to Siberia aged eleven. But actually I'm ninety-four...'—and he strode away through the trees.

Colin Thubron, Among the Russians

Gatchina

The village of **Gatchina**, 45 kilometers southwest of St Petersburg, was first mentioned in 15th century chronicles. In the early 18th century, Peter the Great presented his sister, Natalia, with a farm in the area. Later, Catherine the Great gave the villages as a present to her lover Count Orlov; he had a castle built by Rinaldi in 1781. Paul I (Catherine's son) later took control of the lands and redesigned the palace into a medieval castle. Being a paranoid czar (he was later murdered), Paul had the architect Brenna build a moat with a drawbridge, sentry boxes, toll-gates and a fortress around the castle. Gatchina Park surrounds White Lake.

Behind Long Island is Silver Lake, which never freezes over. The first Russian submarine was tested here in 1879. At the end of the lake there is a lovely little Temple to Venus on the Island of Love. The Castle and grounds, badly damaged during WW II, have not yet been totally restored. But it is a lovely place to walk around and here one can really take notice of the havoc caused by German shelling to Leningrad and the environs during WW II. From St Petersburg's Baltic Station, trains take an hour to Gatchina. The palace (open 11 am–6 pm, closed Monday and first Tuesday of the month) is a short walk from the station.

Razliv

St Petersburg and its environs have over 300 places connected with the life of Lenin. To hide from the Provisional Government in 1917, Lenin came to the village of Razliv, 22 miles (35 kilometers) northwest of the city on the Karelian Isthmus near the former Finnish border. Agents were searching everywhere for him and advertised a reward of 200,000 rubles in gold. Shaving off his trademark beard and wearing a wig, he ventured out in the darkness of night from the Finland railroad station to the village, and stayed in a barn owned by the Yemelyanov family. The barn is now the **Sarai Museum**, housing some of the things Lenin used (open 11 am–5 pm, closed Wednesday). A few days later Nikolai Yemelyanov rowed Lenin across Lake Razliv and built a hut out of hay for a more secretive shelter. By the lake, Lenin lived and wrote articles in a *shalash*, or thatched hut. The **Shalash Museum**, near the hut, is open 11 am–5 pm, closed Wednesday. There are bus tours to Razliv (check at Intourist) and it is easy to reach by car. In summer, a tourist boat takes visitors across the lake. You can also get there by electric train (toward Sestroretsk) from the Finland station.

Samson Fountain, Petrodvorets

Repino

The road from Razliv along the Karelian Isthmus leads to Repino and the town of Sestroretsk about 20 miles (32 kilometers) northwest of St Petersburg. Repino is a small town in the resort area once known as Kurnosovo. It now bears the name of the celebrated painter, Ilya Repin (1844–1930), who bought a cottage in the settlement in 1899 and made it his permanent residence. All his friends and students gathered there every Wednesday and Repin painted the rest of the week. Repin named his estate **The Penates**, after the Roman gods of home and well-being. Repin is buried on the grounds. The Penates burned down during World War II, but was totally reconstructed and is now a museum, displaying Repin's art and personal belongings. His grave lies on the grounds atop a hill. The house, containing his studio, is at 411 Primorskoye Shosse (open 10 am–6 pm, groups after 4 pm, closed Tuesday). Get there by tour bus (Intourist) or car. Electric trains from Finland station in the direction of Vyborg also stop at Repino. From the station head towards the sea.

Novgorod

If there is time a visit to Novgorod and Pskov is highly recommended, Novgorod is about a three-hour drive (190 km) south of St Petersburg. Going by car is the easiest way, otherwise take a bus from St Petersburg; go to the Obvodny Canal Emb no. 26, bus station no. 2. Buses leave for Novgorod about every two hours. The bus and train stations are next to each other in the northwestern part of Novgorod. From here take bus no. 20; it goes by the western wall of the kremlin in the town's center. From St Petersburg's Moscow station, trains run only in the evenings, Monday to Saturday; the only good time to take the train is early Sunday morning.

Novgorod is one of the oldest towns in all of Russia, founded almost 1,200 years ago. The first Varangian leader, Rurik, settled here. The shores of the Ilmen Lake. The town served as the main northern trading center between the Varangians and the Greeks. As it grew, it became known as Novgorod the Great. The city was one of the few places that escaped the Mongol occupation; in the 12th century, while other areas of the country were totally destroyed, there were over 200 churches here. The golden age of Novgorod lay between the 12th and 15th centuries, when the wealthy nobles built the fantastic Kremlin and Byzantine churches, including the **Churches of Ss Boris and Gleb, St Theodore and of the Transfiguration** which still remain. The city remained a center for tade and religion well into the 16th century. When Novgorod refused to give up its independence, it is said that Ivan the Terrible built a wall around the town, preventing anyone from leaving. Then Ivan, after the population still refused his subjugation, had thousands of people tortured and killed in front of him.

The old town is divided through its center by the River Volkhov. The right side is known as the Commercial side where the merchants lived and the markets were held. The left bank Sofia side is the area of the kremlin and fortress; the prince once governed from within these walls. Novgorod is an excellent example of an old Russian town with its ancient architecture (over 30 old churches remain), paintings (icons, frescos and mosaics) and history (birchbark manuscripts).

The original wall of the kremlin was laid in about 1000 AD. At this time, it was still common practice in Russian towns to lay the first stone over a living child, thought to bring prosperity to the future town. The most famous structure inside the kremlin is the five-domed **Cathedral of St Sophia** (1045–50). The son of Yaroslavl the Wise modeled it after the great cathedral in Kiev, which his father had built.

The **Museum of History, Architecture and Art** is the largest building inside the Kremlin; it was built as administative offices in the 1800s. It is located south of the cathedral. The museum has 35 halls and over 8,000 exhibitions. To the west of the Cathedral is the 15th-century **Clock Tower**, whose bell was carried away by the father of Ivan the Terrible. Alongside the tower is the **Faceted Chamber** and on the other side of the Cathedral is **St Sophia's Belfry**. The **Millennium Monument** was erected in 1862 to commemorate the 1000th anniversary of Rurik's arrival in Novgorod.

Across the river on the Commercial side, remains part of a 17th-century arcade which boasted 1500 stalls in its heyday. Behind it is **Yaroslavl's Court** and one of the largest surviving churches, **Church of St Nicholas**, built in 1113. Take a no. 7 bus 3km south to the **Yurev Monastery** and the **Open Air Museum of Wooden Architecture**.

If you want to stay in Novgorod make reservations in St Petersburg through HOFA, tel 311–4586, 5–25 Tavricheskaya St. The most centrally located is the Hotel Volkhov at 24 Nekraskov St, tel (816) 75939, no luxuries but inexpensive. The Intourist Hotel with a restaurant at 16 Dmitrevsky St, (tel 75089) is moderately priced. The best place in town is the four-star Beresta Palace and restaurant on Studenchesky St, (tel 34747).

Pskov

Pskov is a few hours farther southwest of Novgorod. Another of Russia's most ancient towns, it was first mentioned in a chronicle in 903. Pskov began as a small outpost of Novgorod and later grew into a commercial center and developed its own school of icon painting. It is still filled with many beautiful churches and icons. Ivan the Terrible tried to annex Pskov, but the town resisted for many years before being subjugated. Rimsky-Korsakov later wrote an opera based on the uprisings called *The Maid of Pskov*. Nicholas II abdicated the throne while in his train at the Pskov station on March 15, 1917.

Code of the Empress Catherine

At the entrance of one hall, I found behind a green curtain the social rules of the Hermitage, for the use of those intimate friends admitted by the Czarina into the asylum of Imperial Liberty.

I will transcribe, verbatim, this charter, granted to social intimacy by the caprice of the sovereign of the once enchanted place: it was copied for me in my presence:-

RULES TO BE OBSERVED ON ENTERING.

ARTICLE I
On entering, the title and rank must be put off, as well as the hat and sword.

ARTICLE II
Prentensions founded on the prerogatives of birth, pride, or other sentiments of a like nature, must also be left at the door.

ARTICLE III
Be merry; nevertheless, break nothing and spoil nothing.

ARTICLE IV
Sit, stand, walk, do whatever you please, without caring for anyone.

ARTICLE V
Speak with moderation, and not too often, in order to avoid being troublesome to others.

ARTICLE VI
Argue without anger and without warmth.

ARTICLE VII
Banish sighs and yawns, that you may not communicate ennui, or be a nuisance to anyone.

ARTICLE VIII
Innocent games, proposed by any members of the society, must be accepted by the others.

ARTICLE IX
Eat slowly and with appetite; drink with moderation, that each may walk steadily as he goes out.

ARTICLE X
Leave all quarrels at the door; what enters at one ear must go out at the other before passing the threshold of the Hermitage.

'If any member violates the above rules, for each fault witnessed by two persons, he must drink a glass of fresh water (ladies not excepted); furthermore, he must read aloud a page of the Telemachiad (a poem by Trediakofsky). Whoever fails during one evening in three of these articles, must learn by heart six lines of the Telemachiad. He who fails in the tenth article must never more re-enter the Hermitage.

Marquis Astolphe Louis Leonard de Custine, Russia, 1854-5

Practical Information

Useful Addresses and Telephone Numbers

EMERGENCY SERVICES

Fire	01
Police	02
Ambulance	03
Gas Leaks	04
Car accidents	234–2646/2652

MONEY/CREDIT CARDS
See Facts for the Traveler section, page 50.

TELEPHONE INFORMATION

Exact time	08
Weather	001
Directory Enquiries	009
(about subscribers only)	
Address of St Petersburg	061
resident (must know name and birth date)	

EXPRESS MAIL/POST
If you need quick postal service, there are a number of options available:
DHL, 57 Nevsky Prospekt, in Nevsky Palace Hotel. Some hotels have pick-up service.
Federal Express, 3 Mayakovskaya Street, tel. 279–1287, open Mon–Fri 9 am–4 pm.
LEMS, express mail by Russian Postal Service, tel. 311–2346. Average delivery
time: 4 days to US, 3 days to Europe.
United Parcel Service, 31 Saltykova Shchedrina, tel. 312–2915 or 275–4405.
TNT Express Worldwide, 50 Liteiny Prospekt, tel. 273–6007 or 272-5886, fax 272–
9051. Pick-up service available.

MEDICAL
Most hotels have a resident nurse or doctor.
American Medical Center, a 24-hour service, is at 77 Fontanka Embankment, tel. 119–
6101. English, German and Finnish spoken.
St Petersburg Polyclinic, 22 Moskovsky Prospekt, tel. 292–6272, 24-hour tel. 110–1102.
Open 9 am–9 pm; Saturday 9 am–3 pm. It has a **Western Pharmacy**, tel. 110–1744.
Open 9 am–8 pm; closed Saturday and Sunday.

DENTAL
Central Dental Clinic, 46 Nevsky Prospekt, tel. 311–8328 or 110–5054.
Dental Center, at 13 10-ya Sovyetskaya Street, tel. 274–6480, is open 24 hours.
Dental Polyclinic, Vasilyevsky Island, at 12 21-ya Liniya, tel. 213–7551. Nights 213–
5550. Open 8 am–9 pm. Imported equipment, English spoken.
Nordmed, 12/15 Tverskaya Street, tel. 110–0654. Evenings and weekends 110–0401.
Open 9 am–5.30 pm; Thursday 9 am–8 pm.. English and German spoken.

Russian Embassies and Consulates

■ IN THE US
Washington DC
Russian Embassy
1115-25 16th Street NW, Washington DC,
20036 tel. (202) 628-7551/7554
Visa Consular Office
1825 Phelps Place NW, Washington DC,
20009 tel. (202) 332-1513

New York City
Russian Consulate-General
9 E 91st Street, New York, NY 10020 tel.
(212) 348-6772
San Francisco
2790 Green Street, San Francisco, CA
94123 tel. (415) 202-9800, fax 929-0306

■ IN THE UK
Russian Embassy
18 Kensington Place, London W8 4QP
tel. (071) 229-6412 or 727-6888
Russian Visa Consulate
5 Kensington Place Gardens, London W8
4QP tel. (071) 229-3215/3216

■ IN CANADA
Russian Embassy
285 Charlott Street, Ottowa, ONT K1N
8T5 tel. (613) 235-4341

■ IN AUSTRALIA
Russian Embassy
78 Canberra Avenue, Griffith, ACT 2603
tel. (06) 295-9474, fax 295-1847
Russian Cosulate
7-9 Fullerton Street, Woollahra, NSW
2025 tel. (02) 326-1188, fax 327-5065

Consulates

Australia, Moscow tel. (8) 095-246-5011/
5016.
Bulgaria, 27 Ryleeva Street, tel. 273-7347.
Canada, Moscow tel. (8) 095-241-5882/
5070.
China, Vasilyevsky Island, 12 3-ya Liniya,
tel. 218-1721.
Cuba, 37 Ryleeva Street, tel. 272-5303.
Czech and Slovak Republics, 5 Tverskaya
Street, tel. 271-0459.
Denmark, 13 Bolshaya Alleya, Stone Is-
land, tel. 234-3755.
Estonia, 14 Bolshaya Monetnaya, tel. 333-
5548.
Finland, 71 Chaikovskaya Street, tel. 272-
4256, 273-7321/4331.
France, 15 Moika Embankment, tel. 314-
1443, 312-1130.
Germany, 39 Furshtatskaya (Petra
Lavrova) Street, tel. 273-5598/5731.
Hungary, 15 Marata Street, tel. 312-6458/
6753.
Italy, 10 Teatralnaya Square, tel. 312-
3217/2896.
Japan, 29 Moika Embankment, tel. 314-
1418/1434.
Mongolia, 11 Seperny, tel. 272-2688.
Poland, 5 Sovyetskaya Street, tel. 274-
4170/4351.
Sweden, Vasilyevsky Island, 11 10-ya
Liniya, tel. 218-3526/3527.
United Kingdom, 5 Proletarsky Diktatury
Square, tel. 119-6036. (In Moscow tel. (8)
095-231-8511.)
United States, 15 Furshtatskaya (Petra
Lavrova) Street, tel. 274-8235/8568/
8689. Moscow tel. 095-252-2451-59;
when closed, call 230-2001/2610.

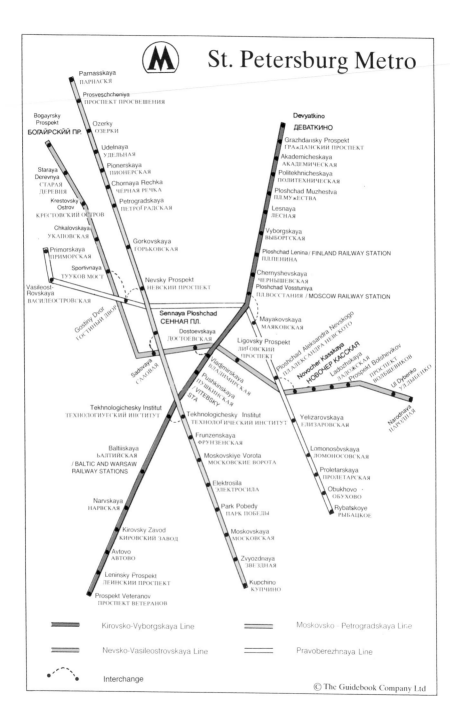

St. Petersburg Metro

Parnasskaya
ПАРНАСКЯ

Prosveshcheniya
ПРОСПЕКТ ПРОСВЕЩЕНИЯ

Bogayrsky
Prospekt
БОГАЙРСКЙЙ ПР.

Ozerky
ОЗЕРКИ

Devyatkino
ДЕВАТКИНО

Udelnaya
УДЕЛЬНАЯ

Grazhdansky Prospekt
ГРАЖДАНСКИЙ ПРОСПЕКТ

Staraya
Derevnya
СТАРАЯ
ДЕРЕВНЯ

Pionerskaya
ПИОНЕРСКАЯ

Akademicheskaya
АКАДЕМИЧЕСКАЯ

Chornaya Rechka
ЧЁРНАЯ РЕЧКА

Politekhnicheskaya
ПОЛИТЕХНИЧЕСКАЯ

Krestovsky
Ostrov
КРЕСТОВСКИЙ ОСТРОВ

Petrogradskaya
ПЕТРОГРАДСКАЯ

Ploshchad Muzhestva
ПЛ.МУжЕСТВА

Chkalovskaya
УКАПОВСКАЯ

Lesnaya
ЛЕСНАЯ

Gorkovskaya
ГОРЬКОВСКАЯ

Vyborgskaya
ВЫБОРГСКАЯ

Primorskaya
ПРИМОРСКАЯ

Sportivnaya
ТУУКОВ МОСТ

Ploschad Lenina / FINLAND RAILWAY STATION
ПЛ.ПЕНИНА

Vasileost-
Rovskaya
ВАСИЛЕОСТРОВСКАЯ

Nevsky Prospekt
НЕВСКИЙ ПРОСПЕКТ

Chernyshevskaya
ЧЕРНЫШЕВСКАЯ

Ploshchad Vosstuniya
ПЛ.ВОССТАНИЯ / MOSCOW RAILWAY STATION

Gostiny Dvor
ГОСТИНЫЙ ДВОР

Sennaya Ploshchad
СЕННАЯ ПЛ.

Mayakovskaya
МАЯКОВСКАЯ

Dostoevskaya
ДОСТОЕВСКАЯ

Ploshchad Aleksandra Nevskogo
ПЛ.АЛЕКСАНДРА НЕВСКОГО

Ligovsky Prospekt
ЛИГОВСКИЙ
ПРОСПЕКТ

Novocher Kasskaya
НОВОЧЕР КАССКАЯ

Ladozhskaya
ЛАДОЖСКАЯ

Prospekt Bolshevikov
ПРОСПЕКТ
ВОЛЬШЕВИКОВ

Sadovaya
САДОВАЯ

Vladimirskaya
ВЛАДИМИРСКАЯ

Pushkinskaya
ПУШКИНСКАЯ
/ VITEBSKY
STA

Ul.Dybenko
УЛ.ДЫБЕНКО

Tekhnologichesky Institut
ТЕХНОЛОГИУЕСКИЙ ИНСТИТУТ

Tekhnologichesky Institut
ТЕХНОЛОГИЧЕСКИЙ ИНСТИТУТ

Yelizarovskaya
ЕЛИЗАРОВСКАЯ

Narodnaya
НАРОДНАЯ

Frunzenskaya
ФРУНЗЕНСКАЯ

Baltiiskaya
БАЛТИЙСКАЯ
/ BALTIC AND WARSAW
RAILWAY STATIONS

Moskovskiye Vorota
МОСКОВСКИЕ ВОРОТА

Lomonosovskaya
ЛОМОНОСОВСКАЯ

Elektrosila
ЭЛЕКТРОСИЛА

Proletarskaya
ПРОЛЕТАРСКАЯ

Narvskaya
НАРВСКАЯ

Park Pobedy
ПАРК ПОБЕДЫ

Obukhovo
ОБУХОВО

Kirovsky Zavod
КИРОВСКИЙ ЗАВОД

Moskovskaya
МОСКОВСКАЯ

Rybatskoye
РЫБАЦКОЕ

Avtovo
АВТОВО

Zvyozdnaya
ЗВЕЗДНАЯ

Leninsky Prospekt
ЛЕИНСКИЙ ПРОСПЕКТ

Kupchino
КУПЧИНО

Prospekt Veteranov
ПРОСПЕКТ ВЕТЕРАНОВ

───── Kirovsko-Vyborgskaya Line

═════ Moskovsko - Petrogradskaya Line

═════ Nevsko-Vasileostrovskaya Line

═════ Pravoberezhnaya Line

Interchange

© The Guidebook Company Ltd

AIRLINES

Phone numbers for Pulkovo ll (International).

Austrian, see SAS.

Aeroflot, corner of Nevsky (no. 7) and Malaya Morskaya Sts, tel. 104-3822. Other offices at 47 Dzerzhinskaya Street and 5 Aprelskaya St. Information tel. 293-9031. Tickets 311-8072/8093. International arrival/departures tel. 314-6943. Domestic arrivals/departures tel. 293-9021. Intl. tel. 310-4581.

Air France (c/o KLM), airport tel. 104-3433.

Balkan Airlines, 36 Bolshaya Morskaya St, tel. 315-5030/5019. Airport tel. 104-3436.

British Airways (c/o Delta), 36 Bolshaya Morskaya St, tel. 311-5820. (Moscow, tel. 095-253-2482/2492). Airport tel. 104-3438 (3 Weekly direct flights to London.)

CSA (Czech-Slovakia Airlines), 36 Bolshaya Morskaya St, tel. 315-5264/5259. Airport tel.104-3430.

Delta, 36 Bolshaya Morskaya St, tel. 311-5820. Airport tel. 104-3438. (Two weekly flights to the US.) Moscow tel. 095-253-2658/2659.

Finnair, 19 Malaya Morskaya St, tel. 315-9736. Airport tel. 104-3439, fax 312-0459. (Daily flights to Helsinki.) Moscow tel. 095-292-8788.

KLM, airport tel. 104-3440/3441. Moscow tel. 095-253-2150/2151.

LOT (Polish Airlines), airport tel. 104-3437.

Lufthansa, 7 Voznesensky (Mayorova) Prospket, tel. 314-4979/5917, fax 312-3129. Airport tel. 104-3432.

SAS (Austrian-Swissair), 57 Nevsky Prospekt, tel. 314-5086.

AIRPORTS

Pulkovo II, (International flights), tel. 104-3444. Intourist 104-3329. International flights 293-9911.

Pulkovo I, (Domestic flights), tel. 293-9021/9031. An express bus from Bolshaya Morskaya Street (no. 13) goes to the airport. Also from Metro Moskovskaya, bus 39 or a taxi can get you here.

Rzhevka, (Flights to NW Russia), tel. 227-8562 or 527-5208.

RAILWAYS

Baltic Station (Baltiisky Vokzal), 120 Obvodov Kanal. Metro Baltiiskaya. (Trains include to/from Petrodvorets and Lomonosov.)

Finland Staton (Finlyansky Vokzal), 6 Lenina Square. Metro Ploshchad Lenina. (Trains include to/from Repino and Finland.)

Moscow Station (Moskovsky Vokzal), 2 Znamenskaya (Vosstaniya) Square. Metro Ploshchad Vosstaniya. (Trains include to/from Moscow, points north and south.)

Warsaw Station (Varshavsky Vokzal), 118 Obvodov Kanal. Metro Baltiiskaya. (Trains include to/from Warsaw, Eastern Europe, Berlin, Pskov and Lvov.)

Vitebsk Station (Vityebsky Vokzal), 52 Zagorodny Prospekt. Metro Pushkinskaya. (Trains include to/from Pushkin and Pavlovsk, points south to Belarus and Ukraine.)

Accommodation

Most foreigners stay in Russian Intourist or foreign-operated hotels, which have restaurants, cafés, *Beriozkas* (shopping), post offices, money exchanges, and usually nightly entertainment; most of these hotels need to be prebooked. Bed and breakfast and youth hostel opportunities now exist, and also should be arranged in advance. Some agencies rent apartments or space with families as homestays. The **Deluxe hotels** usually charge more than **$200 per person**, the **expensive** more than **$100**, and the **moderate** still cost upwards of **$50**. Most or all of the facilities are charged in hard currency; some restaurants and bars will take rubles; check first to find out if they take hard currency, credit cards or rubles. **Hostels, bed and breakfasts, homestays and campgrounds** charge from **$15 to $85 per day**. Prices vary according to season and occupancy (single or double). Check with a travel agency that deals with Russian travel; they should have price lists and locations. You may need proof of a hotel reservation to get your Russian tourist visa. Travel agencies can also secure your visas and hotel reservations.

DE LUXE

Grand Hotel Europe, 1/7 Mikhailovsky Street (right off Nevsky), is the former Evropeiskaya Hotel , reopened in December 1991, tel. 119–6666. To make reservations, (US) tel. 800–The Omni, (England) tel. 71–937–8033, fax 329–6001; nearest Metro station Nevsky Prospekt. It has 301 rooms, four restaurants, three bars and shops, a health club, billiard room, business center, AMEX office, and club and dance hall. The Sadko Restaurant next door (for rubles) is one of the city's most popular hang-outs.
Nevsky Palace Hotel, 57 Nevsky Prospekt, tel. 311–6366, fax 113–1470, 850–1501. Or reservations via Marco Polo Hotels and Resorts. Rivals the Grand Hotel Europe having 287 rooms, restaurants, bars, fitness and business centers, a sauna and pool—and a central location. Nearest Metro station Nevsky Prospekt.

EXPENSIVE

Astoria, 39 Bolshaya Morskaya Street, is located by St Issac's Cathedral, tel. (Block A) 210–5010, (Block B) 210–5020, fax 315–9668; nearest Metro station Nevsky Prospekt. One of St Petersberg's oldest and most luxurious four-star hotels. The Zimnaya (Winter) Restaurant has good food, along with evening classical concerts.
Beliye Nochi, 'The White Nights Hotel', tel. 237–3193/2138, fax 237–3632, is on Primorskoye Shosse. Located in a pine forest on the Gulf of Finland, 38 kilometers from the city, it has all the amenities of a health resort and spa.
Commodore Hotel, moored on the Neva River near Nevsky Prospekt at 1 Morskoy Salvy Square, tel. 119–6666, fax 119–6667. A four-star ship-hotel has 334 rooms, restaurants, bars, shops, a night club, pool and a business center.

Cottage No. 1, 34 Kutuzova Embankment on Kammeny (Stone) Island, tel. 272-1500, fax 279-5024, is a magnificent old residence used often by visiting heads of State.

Hotelship Peterhof, a four-star Swiss venture, is located by Makarov pier near Tuchkov Bridge, and on the Neva by Lenin Stadium, tel. 213-6321, fax 213-3158. Reservations from abroad: tel. (41) 55-27-27-55, fax (41) 55-27-27-88. This four-star hotel has double and single cabins, restaurant, bars, night club,casino and fitness center.

Moskva Hotel, 2 Alexander Nevsky at the end of Nevsky Prospket, tel. 274-2115/2052; nearest Metro station Alexander Nevsky. This three-star hotel has restaurants, bars, shops, a sauna, and business center (fax 274-2130).

Neptun, 93a Nab. Obvodnovo Kanala, tel. 210-1707, fax 311-2270. A brand new hotel, but quite a long way from the center of town. South of Pushkinskaya Metro station.

Okhtinskaya Hotel, 4 Bolsheokhtinsky Prospekt, is a three-star hotel located on the Neva embankment across from the Smolny Cathedral, tel. 227-3767/4438, fax 227-2618. Two restaurants and bars, shops, a sauna and business center.

Olympia Hotel, on Sea Glory Square near Sea terminal Morskoy Vokzal on Vasilyevsky Island, tel. 217-8051 or 119-6800, fax 119-6805, is a three-star hotel aboard a Swedish ship. Nearest Metro station Primorskaya. Restaurant, bar, sauna, solarium and casino.

Pribaltiiskaya Hotel, 14 Korablestroiteley on end of Vasilyevsky Island on the Gulf of Finland, tel. 356-0263/0001, fax 356-0094/0372, is a de luxe four-star hotel (built by Swedes) with a bowling alley, business center, pharmacy, slot machines, restaurants, bars, beriozka and a sauna.

Pulkovskaya Hotel, 1 Pobedy Square, tel. 264-5022/5122, fax 264-5844, is a four-star hotel, with two restaurants and bars, a sauna and a business center. Nearest Metro station Moskovskaya.

St Petersberg Hotel, 5/2 Pirogovskaya Embankment across Neva River from Summer Gardens, tel. 542-9123, fax 542-9042, 248-8002; nearest Metro station Ploshchad Lenina. This de luxe four-star hotel has two restaurants, three night clubs, two pools and a sauna, a sports hall and business center .

MODERATE

Architect's House, 2 Pushchina Street in the town of Pushkin, tel. 466-6459, is a few hours ride outside of the city.

Chaika Hotel, 'The Seagull Apartment Hotel', is at 38 Serebristy Bulvar, tel. 301-7969/5663, fax 301-5622; nearest Metro station Pionerskaya. Restaurant.

Helen Hotel, 45/1 Lermontovsky Prospekt on the Fontanka Canal, tel. 251-6101, fax 113-0859, is a three-star hotel next to Hotel Sovyetskaya. Restaurant, bar, business center and International shop.

Hotel Rus, 1 Artilleryskaya Street, tel. 272-0321/279-5003. Nearest Metro station Mayakovskaya. Italian joint venture with café, bar, sauna.

Karelia, 27 Tukhachevsky Prospekt, tel. 226-3036/3515, fax 226-3511; nearest Metro station Ploshchad Lenina. Two restaurants, night bar, Eldorado Disco and sauna.

Kingswood, the old Druzhba Hotel, is at 4 Chapygina Street, tel. 234-1844. Nearest Metro station Petrogradskaya. Restaurant and bar.

Losevskaya Hotel is located in the Losevo National Park on the Karelia Peninsula, about a two-hour drive from city, tel. (279) 6-72-29. Restaurant, bar and sauna. Hiking in birch and pine forests. Boating, kayaking, swimming and fishing.

Mercury Hotel, 39 Tavricheskaya Street near the Smolny Cathedral, tel. and fax 278-1977, has a restaurant and bar.

Morskaya Hotel, 1 Morskoy Slavy at the head of the harbor on Vasilyevsky Island, tel. 355-1417/1387; nearest Metro station Primorskaya. Restaurant, night bar, shops and a sauna.

Octivian Hotel, the former Hotel Gaven, is situated at 88 Sredny Prospekt on Vasilyevsky Island, tel. 356-8504/8516, fax 355-6714. Restaurant, bar, shops.

Oktyabrskaya Hotel, 10 Ligovsky Prospekt off Nevsky Prospekt (centrally located), tel. 277-6330. Nearest Metro station is Ploshchad Vosstaniya on Znamenskaya Square Restaurants and bars. Many rooms are worn and shabby.

Olgino Motel, Primorskoye Shosse, tel. 238-3009/3489. For information in English, call 238-3553 or fax 238-3954. Located 18 kilometers from city center. It's situated in country, so transportation is difficult. Several restaurants, bars, shops, and a sauna.

Rechnaya and The Fural Hotels, 195 Obukhovskoy Oborony Prospekt, tel. 267-3196 or 262-8400, fax 279-6516, has a restaurant and bar. Nearest Metro station Proletarskaya.

Vyborgskaya Hotel, 3 Torzhkovskaya Street, tel. 246-2319/9141, has restaurants, bar and a sauna. Nearest Metro station Chyornaya Rechka.

Inexpensive

Elpis, 27 Kronverkskaya, 197101, tel. 232-9838, fax 332-2688. Besides B & B has one and two room apartments. Free business visa invitations. Try to book several weeks in advance.

Lingva, 7-ya Liniya 36. Vasilyevsky Island, tel. 218-7339. Inexpensive double rooms—can rent out monthly. A small charge for visa support and airport pick-up.

Natalino Motel, Krasnoye Selo, 20 kilometers southwest of the city, tel. 132-4589/8815. Restaurant and sauna.

Bed and Breakfasts / Hostels

Host Families Association (HOFA), 5 Tavricheskaya Street, no. 25, St Petersburg 193015, tel. 251-6101 or 552-6086, fax 113-0859, provides bed and breakfast facilities in 10 cities throughout Russia. Apartments arranged. Other cultural, educational and sightseeing services available. Visa invitations also ranged, try to book at least two months in advance.

Golden onion domes of Catherine the Great's Palace

State of Siege

What an incredible thing is this feeling of hunger. One can get used to it as to a chronic headache. For two successive days I have been waiting with blind resignation for one glutinous piece of bread, without experiencing acute hunger. That means the disease (ie hunger) has gone over from the acute stage to the chronic.

It's dark. I couldn't stop myself getting out that precious candle-end, hidden away in case of dire emergency. The darkness is terribly oppressive. Mila's dozing on the sofa. She is smiling in her sleep, she must be dreaming of a sandwich with smoked sausage or of thick barley soup. Every night she has appetizing dreams, which is why waking up is particularly tormenting for her.

The entire flat is appallingly cold, everywhere is frozen, stepping out into the corridor involves putting on one's coat, galoshes and hat. The bleakness of desolation everywhere. The water supply is non-existent, we have to fetch water from more than three kilometres away away. The sewage system is a thing of the distant past—the yard is full of muck. This is like some other city, not Leningrad, always so proud of its European, dandyish appearance. To see it now is like meeting a man you have become accustomed to seeing dressed in a magnificent, thick woollen overcoat, sporting clean gloves, a fresh collar, and good American boots. And here you suddenly meet that same man completely transformed—clothed in tatters, filthy, unshaven, with foul-smelling breath and a dirty neck, with rags on his feet instead of boots.

Yesterday's Leningradskaya Pravda published an article by the chairman of the Leningrad Soviet, comrade Popov, entitled 'On the Leningrad Food Situation'. After calling on all citizens to summon their courage and patience, comrade Popov goes on to speak of the very real problems of theft and abuse in Leningrad's food distribution network.

My candle-end has almost burnt down. Soon darkness will descend upon me—until morning...

17th January. Old age. Old age is the fatigue of the well-worn components that are involved in the working of a human body, an exhaustion of man's inner resources. *Your blood no longer keeps you warm, your legs refuse to obey you, your back grows stiff, your brain grows feeble, your memory fades. The pace of old age is as unhurried as the slow combustion of the almost burnt-out logs in a stove: the flames die away, lose their colour, one log disintergrates into burning embers, then another—and now the last flickering blue flames are fading—it will soon be time to shut off the flue.*

We are, all of us, old people now. Regardless of age. The pace of old age now governs our bodies and our feelings...Yesterday at the market I saw a little girl of about nine, wearing enormous felt boots which were full of holes. She was bartering a chunk of dubious-looking brawn—probably made from dog meat—for 100 grammes of bread. Her eyes, hardly visible beneath a pair of heavy lids, looked terribly tired, her back was bent, her gait slow and shuffling, her face puckered and the corners of her mouth turned down. It was the face of an old woman. Can this ever be forgotten or forgiven?

23rd January, 11a.m. Slowly, laboriously, like emaciated people toiling up a hill, the days drag by. Monotonous, unhealthy, withdrawn days in a now silent city. Leningrad's nerve centres, which have until recently kept the life of the city going, fed it vital impulses—the power-stations—have ceased to function. And all the nerve fibres extending over the city lie dormant, inactive. There is no light, no trams or trolley-buses are running, the factories, cinemas, theatres have all stopped working. It is pitch black in the empty shops, chemists', canteens—their windows having been boarded up since autumn (as protection from shell fragments). Only the feeble, consumptive flame of a wick-lamp flickers on every counter...Thickly coated in snow, the tram, trolley-bus and radio cables hang listlessly above the streets. They stretch overhead like an endless white net, and there is nothing to make them shed their thick snow cover.

The great city's nervous system has ceased its function. But we know that this is not death, but only a lethargic sleep. The time will come when the sleeping giant will stir, and then rouse himself...

Alexander Dymov, Winter of 1942, *translated by Hilda Perham*

The interior splendor of Catherine the Great's Palace

Hostel Altus, 15-ya Liniya 4–6, tel. 213-4738. An inexpensive small B & B with singles, doubles and triples, all with TV. It's on Vasilyevsky Island, about a 15-minute walk from Vasileovstrovskaya metro station.

IBV Bed and Breakfast Systems, 13113 Ideal Drive, Silver Spring, Maryland, 20906, USA., tel. (800) 428-2010 or (301) 942-3770.

Moscow International Hostel/Guest House, 50 Bolshaya Pereyaslavskaya Street, 10th Floor, tel:/fax. (7-095) 971-4059, fax 280-7686. (Mailing address: PO Box 27,51 Prospekt mira, 121110.) Ten minute walk from Prospekt Mira metro. This Western-style hostel has English-speaking staff, kitchen and laundry facilities, a lounge with TV, phone and fax service, train tickets and visas. Advance reservations recommended. You can also make reservations for the St Petersburg/Moscow/Helsinki Hostels (and Russian visas and travel) in the United States at **Russian Youth Hostels**, 409 Pacific Coast Highway, Bldg. 106, suite 390, Redondo Beach, California, 90277; tel (310) 379-4316, fax (310) 379-8420. In London at: **YHA Travel Store**, 124 Southampton Street, WC2 7HY, tel (44-71) 836-1036 or **Individual Travel**, Rm. 15, 47-51 Wharfedale Road, N1, tel (71) 278-2512.

RYH Youth Hostel, no. 28 3-ya Sovyetskaya (Rozhedstenskaya) Street, tel. (7-812) 277-0569, fax 277-5102. A five minute walk from the Moskva Train Station and Nevsky Prospekt (Ploshchad Vosstaniya metro). A newly renovated pre-revolutionary building that has rooms for three or four, breakfast included. Kitchen facilities and TV room. Also arranges visas, train travel (incl. Trans-Siberian), tours, theater and ballet tickets. Reservations should at least be made two or four weeks in advance.

Repinsky Hotel, 428 Primorskoye Shosse, is an hour from the city in the town of Repino on the Gulf, tel. 231-6509/6337, fax 231-6920. Restaurant, bar, beach, swimming and bicycle rentals. In winter, cross-country skiing and ice fishing.

Retur Motel, on Primorskoye Shosse along Finnish Gulf about 30 kilometers from city, tel. 237-7533, has cottages and camping facilities (need to make reservation far in advance). Restaurant, bar, sauna, heated swimming pool and tennis facilitites.

Rossiya Hotel, 11 Chernyshevskaya Square on Moskovsly Prospekt, tel. 296-7649/7349; nearest Metro station Park Pobedy. Restaurant.

Sovyetskaya Hotel, 43/1 Lermontovsky Prospekt, tel. 296-2656/2552, fax 251-8890; nearest Metro station Tekhnologichesky Institute/Baltiiskaya. Three restaurants, grill, bar, sauna and business center.

Sputnik Hotel, 34 Morisa Toreza Prospekt in the northwest part of the city, tel. 552-5632/8330, fax 552-8084. Restaurant, bar, sauna and business center.

Vyborgskaya Hotel, 3 Torzhkovskaya Street, tel. 246-2319/9141, has restaurant, bar and a sauna. Nearest Metro station Chyornaya Rechka.

Restaurants

Intourist and foreign hotels have restaurants, cafés and bars (accepting both hard currency and rubles). Swedish smogasbords (*Svedski Stol*) can be found at major hotels in St Petersburg and Moscow. Many new joint venture restaurants and clubs, offering the cuisines of France, Germany and India, have added new spices and variety to the Russian culinary scene. Discos, jazz clubs, casinos and other lively night bars now operate into the small hours. This is a tremendous change—not long ago all one could do was to have a hunk of meat and potato in a restaurant and then go home with friends to drink until midnight. For the first time since the Bolshevik Revolution, people have more choices than they know what to do with.

NEVSKY PROSPEKT

Café Bristol, 22 Nevsky, tel. 311–7490, serves pizza, caviar, khachapuri, pastries, ice creams, tea and coffee for rubles (open 10 am–8 pm).

Club Rendezvous, 9 Nevsky, is open daily from 1 pm–1 am. Restaurant, bar and dance hall at night, tel. 274–3502.

Druzhba ('The Friendship Café'), 15 Nevsky, tel. 315–9536, serves lunch and dinner (open 11 am–11 pm).

Kavkazy, 25 Nevsky, is a popular restaurant serving Caucasian dishes, tel. 311–3977. An orchestra plays in the evenings. Open noon–6 pm and 7 pm–midnight.

Literaturnoye Café (corner of the Moika Kanal, opposite Kazan Cathedral), 18 Nevsky, tel. 312–8543/6057, has good food and literary recitals (open noon–5 pm and 7–11 pm).

Ogonyok, 24 Nevsky, specializes in ice cream and drinks.

Stroganov, 17 Nevsky, tel. 312–1859, serves Russian and Italian food. Elegant decor, enhanced by traditional music. Open 11 am to midnight.

U Kazanskovo, 26 Nevsky, tel. 314–2745, offers Russian food. Open 11 am–10 pm.

The Grand Hotel Europe is on the corner of Nevsky and Mikhailovsky. The French-style **Brasserie**, tel. 119–6000, ext. 6340, offers a good variety of dishes and a wine list. Open daily 11 am–11 pm and Sunday 3–11 pm.

Café Mezzanine in the Atrium serves light food, wine, and coffee or tea. Open 11 am–10 pm and Sunday 3–10 pm.

Chop Sticks, tel. 119–6000, ext. 6391, has à la carte Chinese menu. Open noon–3 pm and 6–11 pm, reservations required.

The Italian La Trattoria, tel. 119–6000, ext. 6391, serves pasta and pizza for reasonable prices. Open daily 1–11 pm.

Restaurant Europe A three-course dinner for one will run to about $100. Open for breakfast 7–10 am and dinner 6–10 pm. It has Sunday brunch, closed for Sunday dinner. Tie and jacket required. Reservations, call 119–6000, ext. 6330. **Sadko** is Petersburg's hottest new hotspot. Open daily noon–midnight. For reservations call 119–6000, ext. 6390.

FARTHER ALONG NEVSKY PROSPEKT

Admiralteisky, 27 Bolshaya Morskaya, tel. 314–4514, Russian food. Open noon–11pm.

Afrodite, 86 Nevsky, tel. 275–7620, 17 different cuisines. Open noon–midnight.

The **Angleterre Restaurant** is in Block B. Open noon–11.30 pm.

The **Astoria Hotel**, at 39 Bolshaya Morskaya/St Issac's Square, tel. 210–5906, has: **The Astoria**, which offers European and Russian food, open 12–midnight; **The Astoria Grill** is in Block B, open noon–midnight; **Restaurant Christopher Columbus** in Block B has Italian cuisine, open noon–midnight; **Zimny Sad**, 'The Winter Garden' restaurant in Block A, offers Russian food in the beautiful winter garden. Food includes caviar, pelmeni, borshch and Chicken Kiev. Open noon–11 pm. Classical concerts in the evenings.

Avtomat Café, 45 Nevsky, tel. 311–1506, has snacks and coffee.

Baskin-Robbins, 31 flavours of ice cream. Open 10 am–10 pm.

The **Commodore Hotel** has a number of American-style restaurants and bars. The '**New York**' has à la carte cuisine, the '**Los Angeles**' has a buffet with jumbo burgers, the '**Las Vegas**' is a show and dance restaurant. The '**Sky Club**' is an intimate piano and cocktail bar with a view of the city.

Detsky is a 'Children's Café', at 42 Nevsky.

Dr. Oetker, Nevsky 40, tel. 312–2457. The restaurant serves hot dogs, pasta dishes, pizzas,desserts, and imported German beers. Open noon–midnight. Next door is **MARS**, a small café with candy, cakes, and coffee.

Dom Arkhitektora, 52 Bolshaya Morskaya, is located in a beautiful turn-of-the-century hall. Russian food. Reservations a must, tel. 311–4557; open noon–11pm.

The **Hotel Nevsky Palace**, 57 Nevsky.

The **Restaurant Admiralty** has Scandinavian food, the **Bier Stube** and **Café Vienna** are traditionally Austrian, The **Imperial Restaurant** has Russian style food, and the **Restaurant Landskrona** is the most luxurious. Open 7 am–1 am, tel. 113–1518.

Imperial, European food, open 7–11 am, noon–3 pm and 7–11 pm.

John Bull Pub, 79 Nevsky, tel. 164–9877, offers Russian and English food. Open lunch and dinner, closed 6–7 pm.

Le Café, 142 Nevsky, tel. 271–2811/3037, is a German restaurant, open from noon–midnight.

Palace of Paul I, Pavlovsk

Moskva Restaurant, Alexander Nevsky Square, in the Moskva Hotel, tel. 274–9503 has Russian food, orchestra and variety show. Breakfast 8–11 am, open noon–11 pm.

Neva, 46 Nevsky, tel. 110–5980, has Russian-European style food with a nightly floor show, dancing and orchestra. Open noon–4.30 pm and 7 pm–midnight.

Restaurant Nevsky, 71 Nevsky, tel. 311–3093, serves Russian food. A floor show and orchestra perform at night. Open noon–5 pm and 7–11 pm.

Rioni,136 Nevsky, tel. 277–5893, has Georgian and Caucasian food. Orchestra plays Georgian songs. Open 11 am–midnight.

Sever, 44 Nevsky, tel. 110–5503. An orchestra plays at night. Open noon–4.30 pm and 7–11 pm.

Veronika, 87 Nevsky, tel. 279–6733, is a grill bar. Open noon– midnight.

Vostochniye Sladosti ('Eastern Sweets'), 104 Nevsky, has Russian, imported, and Middle Eastern pastries.

Universal, 106 Nevsky, tel. 279–3350, serves Russian food, and an orchestra plays here at night. Open noon–11 pm. Nearby, at 35 Marata Street, is the **Iveriya Café** with Georgian food.

Warsteiner Forum, 120 Nevsky, has German food and beer, tel. 277–2914. Open noon–2 am.

Zastole, 74 Nevsky, tel. 272–9017, has Russian food. Open noon–midnight.

FONTANKA CANAL

Ambassador, no. 14, tel. 273–7440, offers Russian and European cuisine, with piano music, fireplace and candlelight. Open noon–midnight.

Korean House, no. 20, tel. 275–7203, is open 1–9 pm.

Na Fontanke, no. 77, one of the city's first cooperative restaurants; it offers good Russian food and nightly floor shows. Reservations, tel. 310–2547. Open 1–5 pm and 7.30–11.30 pm.

EKATERININSKY (GRIBOYEDOV) CANAL

Gino Ginelli ice cream, tel. 312–4631, is next to the Chaika and serves Italian pizza, pasta and, snacks. Open noon–10 pm.

Gridnitsa Grill, at no. 20, tel. 310–2883/3420, has hearty food, drinks and music. Open 11 am–10 pm.

Kolomna, at no. 162, tel. 144–3232, has grilled meats, pastries and tea. Open 11 am–10 pm.

Restaurant Sankt Petersburg, at no. 5, tel. 314–4947/2278, opposite the Cathedral of Spilled Blood. Decorated in 19th-century style, has a variety of Petersburg and German dishes (German joint venture). Wine list. During the day, a Russian folk band performs.

Tschaika, at no. 14 and on the corner of Nevsky, is a Russian-German joint venture with pub, serving hearty, medium-priced food and beer. Open 11 am–3 am, tel. 312–4631.

SADOVAYA (GARDEN) STREET

Diana Grill, at no. 56, tel. 310–3322, is open noon–11 pm.

The **Metropole**, at no. 22, tel. 310–1845 or 311–0233, is one of the oldest restaurants in the city, well-known for the meat and fish dishes, and desserts. An orchestra plays in the evenings. Open noon–midnight. **Lakoma** is near the Metropole and serves a delicious variety of pastries, pies and cakes.

Russkye Samovary, at no. 49, tel. 314–8238, serves Russian blini-pancakes. Open 8 am–8 pm. Closed 3.30–4.30 pm.

Shanghai, at no. 12/23, tel. 311–2751/5320, is one of the few Chinese restaurants. Open noon–midnight.

PETROGRADSKAYA SIDE

Austeria, tel. 238–4262, is at the Peter and Paul Fortress and offers dishes popular during the days of Peter the Great, if you're up for that! Open noon–midnight.

Aragvi, tel. 225–0082/0336, is located in the northeastern part of the city, at 41 Tukhachevskaya Street. Georgian cuisine. Open noon–11 pm.

Belaya Loshad, the 'White Horse' Café, is at 16 Chkalovsky Prospekt. It's a Russian beer bar, open noon–11 pm, tel. 235–1113.

Bukhara is located in the northeastern part of the city at 74 Nepolkorennikh Street, tel. 249–3481. Middle-Asian food. Open noon–11 pm.

The **Demyanova Ukha**, at 53 Kronversky Prospekt, tel. 232–8090, is a seafood restaurant with excellent soups. Open noon–10 pm.

Diamond Jack is at 32 Lenina (Shirokaya) Street, tel. 230–8830, Russian food and piano music. Open noon–midnight.

The **Fortetsiya Restaurant**, at 7 Kuibisheva Street, tel. 233–8488/9468, offers Russian food, orchestra and dancing. Open noon–midnight.

Galspe at Palanga is a Spanish Restaurant at 127 Leninsky Prospekt, for 254–5582; it also has bingo, casino, disco and bar, open 5 pm–2 am. The **Palanga** is a small Russian restaurant next door, tel. 255–6417; open 12.30–11.30 pm.

The **Goloboy Delfin**, a seafood restaurant, is at 44 Sredneokhtinsky Prospekt in the northeast, tel. 227–2135. Open noon–11 pm; closed 4–5 pm.

Grand Café Antwerpen, tel. 233–9746, serves European food at 13/2 Kronversky Prospekt. Open noon–midnight.

Hebei Chinese Restaurant is at 61 Bolshoy Prospekt, tel. 233–2046. Chinese cuisine. Open noon–11 pm. The **Zerkalny** restaurant, tel. 542–9155, also in the hotel, has Russian food and music. Open noon–11 pm.

Imereti, at 104 Bolshoy Sampsonievsky (formerly Karl Marx) Prospket, tel. 245–5003, has Georgian and Caucasian food. Open 11 am–10 pm.

Pushkin House Museum

The **Karelia** is at the Hotel Karelia at 7/2 Tukhachevsky Prospekt (near Piskorovsky Cemetery) in the northeast, tel. 226–3549. Russian food, disco and dancing. Open 8 am–11 pm.

Kingswood Trust Restaurant is in the Hotel Kingswood with Russian food and dancing at 4 Chapigina Street near TV Tower, tel. 234–4456. Open 11 am–10 pm; .**Nevskye Melodii** is at 62 Sverdlovsky Embankment, tel. 227–1596/2676, across river from Smolny in northeast. Russian food, disco (9 pm–1 am) and bar. Open noon–1 am. Casino and bar 10 pm–4 am.

Okean 'Ocean' Seafood Restaurant is at 31 Primorsky Prospekt, tel. 239–2877. Open noon–midnight.

Okolitsa, at 15 Primorsky Prospekt, tel. 239–6984, has Russian food. Open 11am–11 pm.

Petrovsky Zal is in the **Hotel Petersburg** at 5/2 Vyborgskaya Embankment, tel. 542–9155, near the TV Tower. Russian food and panoramic views of city.

The **Zerkalny** restaurant, tel. 542–9155, also in the hotel, has Russian food and music. Open noon–11 pm.

The **St Petersburg**, tel. 542–9121, has Russian food, orchestra and dancing. **Pizzunda Café**, at 12 Kamennoostrovsky (Kirov) Prospekt, tel. 232–2477, has Russian food. Open noon–11 pm.

Polese Restaurant is at 4 Sredneokhtinsky Prospekt, tel. 224–2917, in northeast, across river from Smolny. Belorussian and Slovenian food, grilled suckling pigs as speciality. Open 12.30–11 pm.

Primorsky, at 32 Bolshoy Prospekt, tel. 233–2783, has Russian and European food. Open noon–midnight.

Shchlotburg is in the east across the river from the Smolny at 41 Bolsheokhtinsky Prospekt. Old style-type 'Merchants Kitchen', reservations required at tel. 227–2924. Open noon–midnight.

Staraya Derevnya ('Old Village Café'), at 72 Savushkina Street (in northwest across from Yelagin Island), serves in the tradition of the 'Russian family salon' of the 1900s. Open noon–11 pm, tel. 239–0000.

Tbilisy, at 10 Sytninskaya Street (not far from Peter and Paul Fortress) has Georgian food and music. Make reservations at 232–9391. Open noon–11.30 pm.

Tête-A-Tête, 65 Bolshoy Prospekt, tel. 232–7548, serves stylish Russian dishes. Open 1 pm–midnight, closed 5–7 pm.

U Petrovichka, at 44 Sredneokhtinsky Prospekt in northeast, tel. 227-2135, is an intimate 19th-century 'Merchant-style' restaurant. Food sometimes includes venison, bear, fish, fowl, caviar. Open noon–5 pm and 6–midnight.

Victoria Restaurant is at 24 Kamennoostrovsky Prospekt, tel. 232-5130, with European-Russian cuisine. Open noon–11 pm, closed 4–6 pm.

Volshebny Krai is at 15/3 Bolshoi Prospekt, tel. 235-5984, with light food, pastries, tea and coffee. Open 10 am–8 pm.

VASILYEVSKY ISLAND

Fregat, at 39 Bolshoi Prospekt, tel. 213-4923, serves Russian food, including some dishes from the days of Peter the Great.

Hotelship Peterhof at Pier Makarov, tel. 213-6231, serves excellent European food and drink, coffee and Swiss pastries for hard currency only. Open noon–2 pm and 6–10 pm. Coffee shop 3–6 pm, piano bar 6–11.30 pm and night club 10 pm–2 am.

Oktivian, a restaurant in the Octivian (Gaven) Hotel, at 88 Sredny Prospekt, tel. 356-1206, is open from 7 am–10 pm.

In the **Olympia Hotel**, the **Piccolo Restaurant** has a view of the Gulf of Finland. Located at Sea Glory Square, tel. 119-6800.

The **Pribaltiiskaya Hotel**, at 14 Korablesroitleley Street, tel. 356-4409, has a variety of restaurants.

Venetsia, next to Pribaltiiskaya at no. 21, tel. 353-2054, 352-1432, serves Italian food; open noon–11 pm.

OTHER COOPERATIVES

A Thousand and One Nights, at 21/6 Millionnaya Street, tel. 312-2255, serves Uzbek and European food. Variety show and late night striptease. Open 9 am–5pm.

Alenushka, at 78 Moskovsky Prospekt, tel. 292-2996, has Russian food. Open noon–11 pm.

Baltika is at 4/1 Sennaya (Mir) Square, tel. 310-7121, with Russian food and a nightclub. Open noon–midnight.

Beliye Nochi, at 43 Voznesensky Prospekt, tel. 314-8432, has Russian food, orchestra, dancing. Open noon–11 pm, closed 6–7 pm.

Bella Liona, 9 Vladimirsky Prospekt, tel. 113-1670. Italian cuisine with piano music. Noon–midnight.

Brigantina is in the southwest at 3 Dvinskaya Street, tel. 259-0815, and has Russian-European food and 'Variety Show Manhattan'. Open noon–midnight.

Daddy's Steak Room is at 73 Moskovsky Prospekt, tel. 298-7744, has steaks, fish, salad bar. Open noon–10 pm.

Izmailoff, tel. 292-6838, at 22 Krasnoarmeiskaya Street, has Russian food, gypsy and folklore show. Open 1–4 pm and 8–11 pm.

Khachapuri, near the Baltiisky Train Station at 13/18 6-ya Krasnoarmeiskaya Street, tel. 292–7377, serves Georgian and Caucasian food. Open 1–11 pm.

The Meridian is in the Hotel Pulkovskaya at 1 Pobedy Square, tel. 264–5177, south of the city. Russian food, orchestra and cabaret. Open 8 am–midnight. **The Turku Restaurant**, tel. 264–5716, is here with Russian food. Open 7 am–4 pm and 5–11 pm.

Nevskye Zvyozdy, the Nevsky Stars is at 91 Babushkina Street in southeast, tel. 262–5490. Russian food.

Okhotnichny Klub, the Hunter's Club, at 45 Gorokhovaya Street, tel. 315–3694, Russian food and music. Open noon–midnight.

Pietari, across the street from Pulkovskaya Hotel at 222 Moskovsky Prospekt, tel. 293–2397/1809, steaks and pizza. Open noon–3 am, bar and disco midnight–2 am.

Pogrebok, at 7 Gogol Street, tel. 315–5371, Russian food. Open 11 am–10 pm.

Rossiya Restaurant is in the Rossiya Hotel by the Tauride Park at 11 Chernyshevskaya Street, tel. 296–7549, Russian food, orchestra and dance floor. Open noon–midnight.

Saigon-Neva, at 33 Kazanskaya (a side street off the back of Kazan Cathedral), tel. 315–8772, is a Vietnamese Restaurant. Open 12.30 pm–11 pm, closed Tuesdays.

Schwabski Domik, at 28/19 Krasnogvardisky Prospekt, near Baltiisky Station, tel. 528–2211/0669, German food, with a European wine selection and music. Open 11 am–2 am.

Sovyetsky Restaurant at Hotel Sovyetsky, 43/1 Lermontovsky Prospekt in southwest, tel. 259–2454, Russian food. Open noon–11 pm.

Troika is at 27 Zagorodny Prospekt, in between Fontanka and Vitebsk Station, tel. 113–5343. They have salmon, Chicken Kiev, caviar and champagne, vodka and European wines. Variety show known as the 'Moulin Rouge of Petersburg'. Open 7 pm–midnight.

Stores

To bring antiques out of the country you will need to get an exit-permit at the Ministry of Culture, 107 Ekaterininsky (Griboyedov) Embankment, tel. 314–8234.

BERIOZKA SHOPS
Most large hotels have their own Beriozka (foreign currency) shops. The largest of these is on the side of the **Pribaltiiskaya Hotel**. Also the **Astoria**, **Grand Europe**, **Moskva**, **St Petersburg**, **Kareliya**, and **Pulkovskaya Hotels** have them. Other stores are at 9 Nevsky, 26 and 38 Herzen Ulitsa, 9 and 15 Morskaya Embankment, and at the Pulkovo airport.

MAJOR DEPARTMENT STORES
Best, 15 Kupchinskaya St (open 9 am–8 pm);
Dom Peterburg Torgovli ('Trade House'), 21–23 Bolshaya Konyushennaya Street,

(open 10 am–8 pm. **Fruzensky Univermag**, 60
Moskovsky Prospekt. **Gostiny Dvor**, 35 Nevsky
Prospekt (open 10 am–9 pm,); **Kirovsky
Univermag**, 9 Narvskaya Square (open 10 am–9
pm, closed Sunday); **Moskovsky Univermag**, 205–220
Moskovsky Prospekt (open 10 am–9 pm, closed Sunday);
Narvsky Univermag, 120–138 Leninsky Prospekt;
Passazh, 48 Nevsky Prospekt (open 10 am–9 pm, Satur-
day 10 am–6 pm, closed Sunday); **Shopping Center**, 1
Novosmolenskaya, Embankment (open 10 am–7 pm,
Saturday 10 am–3 pm closed Sunday);

INTERNATIONAL SHOPS
Bosko, at 8 Nevsky, 8 Zhukovskaya and also at 8/10
Millionnaya, tel. 219-1856 or 273-7092 (open 11 am–
8 pm, closed 3–4 pm); **Castor Shop**, at 30 Makarova
Embankment, tel. 213-7161 (open 10 am–5 pm); **Joy
Boutique**, 9 Zagordny Prospekt, Women's fashions,
tel. 315-5315; **Lenwest**, at 119 Nevsky Prospekt, has
German shoes, tel. 277-0635 (open 10 am–7 pm,
closed 2–4 pm); **Levis**, at Hotel St Petersburg, tel.
542-8032 (open 10 am–9 pm, closed 2–4 pm);
Littlewoods, in the Gostiny Dvor on Nevsky
Prospekt, sells Western items; **Mon Paris Shop**, 13

Nevsky Prospekt, **Panasonic**,14/2 Narvskaya Square,
tel. 252-4403 (open 9 am–6 pm, closed Saturday and Sunday); **Rifle**, at 54
Kamennoostrovsky Prospekt, tel. 234-4377; **Sovinteravto Service**, 73 Moskovsky
Prospekt, with imports from Germany and Holland, tel. 296-5790 (open 10
am–7 pm and closed Sunday and Monday); **Troika Mini-Market**, at 28 Zagorodny
Prospekt (open 10 am–7 pm).

BOOKSTORES
Antikvarnaya Bukinisticheskaya Kniga,18 Nevsky, tel. 312-6676 (open 11–8 pm, closed 2–3
pm and Sunday; **Bukinist**, 59 Liteiny Prospekt, tel. 273-2504; **Children's Book World**,105
Ligovsky Prospekt, tel. 164-2394 (open 10 am–7 pm; **Dom Knigi**, 28 Nevsky Prospekt, tel.
219-9443 (open 10–8 pm and closed Sunday); **Iskusstvo**, 16 Nevskyel, tel. 312-8535 (open 10
am–7 pm, closed Sunday); **Knizhnaya Lavka Pisateley**, 66 Nevsky Prospekt, tel. 314-5458
(open 10–7 pm, closed 2–3 pm and on Sunday and Monday); **Leningrad**, 52 Nevsky Prospekt,
tel. 311-1651; **The Mask**, 13 Nevsky, tel. 311-0312 (open 10 am–7 pm); **Planeta**, 30 Liteiny
Prospket, tel. 273-8815.

Belozersky Palace, Fontanka River

Entertainment

THEATERS AND CONCERT HALLS

Theater performances usually begin at 7.30 pm, and concerts at 8 pm. The time of the performance and seat number are written on the ticket. It is usually required to check your coat in the cloakroom before entering the theater. Here you can also rent opera glasses for a small charge.

Academic Bolshoi Drama Theater, 65 Fontanka Embankment, tel. 311-4577 or 310-9242/ 0401. Metro Gostiny Dvor.

Alexandrinski Theater (or Pushkin Drama Theater), 2 Aleksandriskaya (Ostrovsky) Square, tel. 312-1545, 311-6139. The oldest drama theater in Russia. Metro Gostiny Dvor.

Bolshoi Puppet Theater, 10 Nekrasov Street, tel. 273-6672, 272-8215. Metro Gostiny Dvor.

Bryantsev Theater for Children, 1 Pionerskaya Square, tel. 112-4102, 164-0679. Metro Pushkinskaya.

Buff Theater, 1 Narodnaya Street, tel. 263-6767/6512. Metro Lomonosovskaya.

Central Concert Hall, 1 Lenina Square, tel. 542-0944. Metro Ploshchad Lenina.

Circus, 3 Fontanka Embankment, tel. 210-4390/4411 or 314-8478. Metro Gostiny Dvor.

Comedy Theater, 56 Nevsky Prospekt, tel. 312-4555, 314-2610. Metro Gostiny Dvor.

Concert Hall in Hotel St Petersburg, 542-8051/9056. Metro Ploshchad Lenina.

Experiment Drama Theater, 'Theater of Miniatures', 35/75 Kamennoostrovsky Prospekt, tel. 233-9428/9276. Metro Petrogradskaya.

Glinka Capella Choral Hall, 20 Moika Embankment, tel. 314-1058/1159, 233-0243. Metro Nevsky Prospekt.

Komissarzhevskaya Drama Theater, 19 Italyanskaya Street, tel. 311-3102/0849. Metro Nevsky Prospekt.

Maly Drama Theater, 18 Rubensteina Street, tel. 113-2078/2028. Metro Vladimirskaya.

Maly Theater for Opera and Ballet, 1 Iskusstv ('Arts') Square, tel. 314-3758. Metro Gostiny Dvor.

Maly Zal ('Small Hall' Philharmonic), 30 Nevsky Prospekt, tel. 311-8333, 312-4585. Metro Nevsky Prospekt.

Mariinsky (Kirov) Theater of Opera and Ballet, 1 Teatralnaya ('Theater') Square, tel. 114-4344/1211/4441, fax 114-4540.

Molodezhny Theater ('Youth' Theater), 114 Fontanka Embankment, tel. 292-6870. Metro Gostiny Dvor.

Musical Comedy Theater, 13 Italyanskaya Street, tel. 277-8731, 542-1460. Metro Gostiny Dvor.

Music Hall, 4 Park Lenina, tel. 232-9201, 233-0243. Metro Gorkovskaya.

Oktyabrsky Concert Hall ('October' Hall), 6 Ligovsky Prospekt, tel. 277-7487/6960/7400. Metro Pl. Vosstaniya.

People's Theater, 13 Rubinshteina Street, tel. 312-3484. Metro Vladimirskaya.

Philharmonic Concert Hall of St Petersburg ('Grand Hall'), 2 Mikhailovskaya Street, tel. 110-4085/4257, 311-7333. Metro Gostiny Dvor.

Puppet and Marionette Theater, 52 Nevsky Prospekt, tel. 311-1900. Metro Nevsky Prospekt.

Rimsky-Korsakov Conservatory, 3 Teatralnaya ('Theater') Square, tel. 312-2519/2507.

Russian-American Theater, 4 Alexandrovsky Park, tel. 232-8576. Metro Gorkovskaya.

St Petersburg Ballet on Ice Jubilee Palace of Sport, 18 Dobrolyubov Prospekt, tel. 238-4049.

St Petersburg State Theater (the former 'Open' Theater and Town Merchant's Club), 12 Vladimirsky Prospekt, tel. 113-2190/2191/2207. Metro Vladimirskaya and Dostoevskaya.

Theater on the Liteiny, 51 Liteiny Prospekt, tel. 273-5335/6363. Metro Vladimirskaya.

Theater of the Musical and Drama Institute, 35 Mokhovaya Street, tel. 273-1592. Metro Chernyshevskaya.

Theater of Puppets' Tales, 121 Moskovsky Prospekt, tel. 298-0031. Metro Moskovskye Vorota.

Variety Theater ('Estrady'), 27 Bolshaya Konyushennaya (Zhelyabova) Street, tel. 314-7060. Metro Gostiny Dvor.

Zazerkale Children's Theater ('Through the Looking Glass'), 11 Strelninskaya Street, tel. 235-3618. Metro Petrogradskaya.

JAZZ AND ROCK

Indie Klub 223 Obukhovsky Oborony in Lenin House of Culture. Heavy metal bands on weekends. Concerts advertised on posters through town

Jazz Philharmonic Hall (formerly Jazz Club), tel. 164-5683/8565 or 113-5331, 27 Zagorodny Prospekt. Jazz programs nightly at 8 pm; on weekends jam sessions past midnight. Metro Vladimirskaya.

Kvadrat Jazz Club, 10 Pravdy Street, tel. 164-5683. Metro Vladimiskaya.

Rok Club, 13 Rubinshteyna Street, tel. 314-9629, 312-3483. Basement club where old Leningrad Bands as Akvarium and Kino hung out. Opens around 7pm; bands play till 3 am in summer. Near metro Mayakovskaya.

Saturn Show, 27 Sadovaya Street, one block from Nevsky. Live rock'n'roll from 9 pm–6 am. Food for high prices in rubles.

Tam-Tam Club, on Maly Prospekt, corner of 16th Line on Vasilyevsky Island. It's run by a former member of the rock band Aquarium. Live music and local rock bands frequently play here. Offers the latest in avant-garde music. Concerts are usually on Tuesdays and Fridays. (Check first to see if it's open.)

GAY AND LESBIAN NIGHTLIFE

As yet, has no official or established venues in St Petersburg. (In Russian, the word for gay is *goluboy*, meaning 'sky blue', and the word for lesbian has been taken from the English.) At times, though, the old Lenin Komsomol Theater hosts all-night parties; one finds out through word of mouth.

CASINOS

JOY Nightclub and Casino, corner of Griboedova Canal and Lomonosovskaya Street, one block from Nevsky Prospekt.

The Bronze Horseman

Where lonely waters, struggling, sought
To reach the sea, he (Peter the Great) paused, in thought...
The haughty Swede here we'll curb and hold at bay
And here, to gall him, found a city.
As nature bids so must we do:
A window will we cut here through
On Europe, and a foothold gaining
Upon this coast, the ships we'll hail
Of every flag, and freely sail
These seas, no more ourselves restraining.
A century passed, and there it stood,
Of Northern lands the pride and beauty,
A young, resplendent, gracious city,
Sprung out the dark of mire and wood...
Now there rise great palaces and towers; a maze
Of sails and mastheads crown the harbor;
Ships of all ports moor here beside
These rich and peopled shores; the wide,
Majestic Neva slowly labors,
In granite clad, to push its way
'Neath graceful bridges; gardens cover
The once bare isles that dot the river,
Its glassy surface still and grey.
Old Moscow fades beside her rival.
A dowager, she is outshone,
Overshadowed by the new arrival
Who, robed in purple, mounts the throne...

Alexander Pushkin

777 **Kazino**, 22/24 Nevsky Prospekt, tel. 311-3141. Open 1 pm–midnight.
Nevskye Melodii (at restaurant), 62 Sverdlovskaya Embankment, tel. 227-2676. Hours 10 pm–3 am.
Nordvest, 4 Kima Prospekt, tel. 350-1291. Slot machines.
Spielbank Casino (Hotel Pribaltiiskaya), 14 Korablestroiteley Street, tel. 356-4153. Open 8 pm–3 am.
Zoo, 1 Park Lenina, Zoological Gardens. Open 10–7 pm.

GALLERIES AND EXHIBITIONS

Alivekt, 22/24 Nevsky Prospekt, tel. 315-5978. Open 10 am–7 pm.
Anna, 16 Nevsky Prospekt, (also at 39 Plekhanova Street), tel. 312-8535 (311-8755). Open 11 am–8 pm, closed Sunday.
Autograf, 5 Lomonosova Street, tel. 310-2602. Open 9–6 pm. Contains etchings, lithographs, book illustrations and graphics.
Ariadna, 11 Konnogvardeisky Bul., no. 17, tel. 311-6997. Modern art gallery.
Art Gallery '10/10', 10 Pushinskaya Street,
Atus (Russian-Austrian joint venture), 7 Ispolkomovskaya Street, tel. 277-0263.
Block Library Art Gallery, 20 Nevsky Prospekt, tel. 311-7777.
Exhibition Hall, 57 Liteiny Prospekt, tel. 279-7135. Open 11 am–7 pm, closed Monday. Across the street, at no. 58, is the **Borey Art Gallery**, tel. 273-3693.
Flowers Hall, 2 Potemkinskaya Street, tel. 272-5448. Open 11–8 pm; closed Monday and Thursday. Metro Chernyshevskaya.
Griffon, 33 Bolshaya Morskaya Street, Paintings and folkart.
Hall of the Artists Union, 64 Sverdlovskaya Embankment, tel. 224-0633. Open noon–7 pm; closed Monday. Metro Ploshchad Lenina. The **Lavka** (Gallery of Artists Union) is at 8 Nevsky Prospekt, tel. 312-6193.
Heritage, 116 Nevsky Prospekt, tel. 279-5067. Open 10 am–7 pm. Arts and crafts store, with paintings, boxes, jewelry and china.
House of Nature, 8 Bolshaya Konyushennaya (Zhelyabova) Street, tel. 314-8859. Open 11–7 pm.
Kolomna, 24 Rimsky-Korsakov Prospekt, tel. 114-3150.
Lenkommisiontorg Shop, 39 Plekhanova Street, tel. 312-7253.
Manege (the Central Exhibition Hall), 1 Isaakievskaya Ploshchad, Open 11–7 pm, closed Thursday. The outdoor market, **Klenovaya Alleya**, is also on Manege Square, tel. 219-2129.
Modern Art Gallery, 83 Moika Embankment, tel. 314-4734. Modern paintings and graphics. Open 1–6 pm, closed Sunday and Monday.
Milena Art Gallery, 11 Millionnaya Street, tel. 235-3901, 311-0513, fax 312-7884. Private collection of painters; call first.

Palitra Art Gallery, 166 Nevsky Prospekt, tel. 277–1216.

Petersburg Antique Store, 54 Nevsky Prospekt, open 11 am–8 pm, closed Sunday.

Rosdesign, 13 Solyanoy Prospekt, tel. 279–4196. Colored glass designs.

St Petersburg Branch of the Artists' Union, 38 Bolshaya Morskaya Street. Open 1–7 pm; closed Monday (exhibits and sells art works). The Blue Drawing Room (Golubaya Gostinaya) featuring well known artists is also at this address, tel. 315–7414.

The Russian Arts, 53 Saltykova Shchedrina Street. Decorative arts. Closed Monday.

Russian Collection, 19 Konnargvardeiskaya Street, tel. 311-1945.

Trojan Horse Art Gallery, 6 Krasnoarmeiskaya Street, tel. 355-9740.

Varyag Art Shop, at Hotel Octivian, 88 Sredny Prospekt, tel. 356-6139. Collection of Russian crafts. Open 7 am–2 am.

During the White Nights Festival, artists exhibit their works on Dvortsovy Bridge by the Hermitage. The paintings are hung late at night and exposed to view when the bridge is raised around 2 am. Other arts and crafts spots are around the Catherine the Great monument at Aleksandriskaya (Ostrovsky) Square off Nevsky and across the street from the Circus at 3 Fontanka.

Miscellaneous

SPORTS STADIUMS

Dynamo Stadium, Park Pobedy (Victory Square).

Kirov Stadium, 13 Morskoi Prospekt on Krestovsky Island, tel. 235-4877/5494.

Lenin Stadium, 2 Petrovsky Island, tel. 238-4003, 233-1752.

Palace of Culture, 42 Kamennoostrovsky Prospekt, on Vasilyevsky Island.

Sports and Concert Complex, 8 Gagarin Prospekt on Petrovsky Island, tel. 298-4196/ 4847. Metro Park Pobedy.

Yubileiny Sports Palace, 18 Dobrolyubov Prospekt, tel. 238-4122.

Winter Stadium, 2 Manege Square, tel. 315-5710, 210-4865.

HEALTH CLUBS

Bast Sports Centre, 16 Raevskovo Proezd, tel. 552-5512. Open 24 hours. Tennis courts, exercise rooms, sport halls, sauna and massage.

World Class Fitness Centers, with pool, gym, sauna, solarium and massage. A Swedish-Russian firm. At Astoria Hotel Square, tel. 210-5869/5010. Open 7.30–10 am and 3–10 pm; weekends 9.30 am–9 pm. At Grand Hotel Europe, tel. 312-0072, ext. 6500 or 113-8066. Open 7 am–11 pm; weekends 9 am–11 pm. At 26/28 Kamennoostrovsky Prospekt, tel. 232-7581. Open 9 am–11 pm; weekends 11 am–8 pm.

Olymp-Co-operative, 41 Plekhanova Street, tel. 311-5734.. Exercise room, sauna and mini pool.

Rossiya, at Hotel Rossiya, tel. 296-7221.

Solyaris, 203 Obvodnovo Embankment, tel. 251-3641. Sport and fitness complex. Also check at your hotel desk for indoor and outdoor pools, and *banya* (sauna-pool) locations. There are over 30 Russian *banya* baths in StPetersburg. One *banya* complex is at 5 Marat Street just off Nevsky Prospekt (no. 100), near Metro station Mayakovskaya. It is open 7 am–11 pm; closed Monday and Tuesday (tel. 312-1379). Each part has two saunas and a small swimming pool. In the summer, birch branches are usually sold out front for the baths. The baths are known by numbers, not names. Some others:

Banya no. 43, at 82 Moika Embankment, tel. 312-3151, is east of the Yusupov Palace, near the Forarny Bridge. Women on Wednesday, Friday and Sunday; men Tuesday, Thursday and Saturday. Open 8 am–10 pm, closed Monday.

Banya no. 17, at 1 Chaikovsky Street, tel. 272-0911, is near the Bolshoy Dom. For men and women, open Wed–Sun 8 am–10 pm.

Banya no. 13, at 29a Karbysheva Street, tel. 550-0985. For men and women, open 8 am–10 pm, closed Wed and Thurs. Southwest of Ploshchad Muzhestvo Metro.

Banya no. 46, at Olgi Forsh Street, tel. 592-7622. For men and women, open 8 am–10 pm Wed–Sun. About three blocks west of Grazhdansky ProspektMetro.

Banya no. 57, at 5 Gavanskaya, tel. 356-6300. Women Wed, Fri and Sun; men Thurs and Sat. Open 8 am–10 pm. On Vasilyevsky Island, off end of Bolshoi Prospekt. Another *banya* on the island is at 5-ya Line 41, tel. 213-4275 for schedules.

FARMER'S MARKETS

Most markets, or *rinoks*, are open daily 8 am-7 pm, Sunday 8 am-4 pm.

Prospekt Stachek, 54 Narvskaya Street. Metro Kirovsky Zavod.

Klenovaya Alleya, at Manezhnaya Square, tel. 219–2129, is the latest popular flea market. Lots of souvenirs and illegal money changing. Open daily 9 am to sunset.

Kondratyevsky Alleya, 45 Polyustrovsky Prospekt, is a food and pet market. Closed Sunday. Near Ploshad Lenina Metro.

Kuznechny, 3 Kuznechny Pereulok. Metro Vladimirskaya.

Morovsky, 12 Reshetnikova. Metro Elektrosila.

Nekrasovsky, Nekrasova Street. Metro Ploshchad Vosstaniya.

Nevsky, 75 Obukhovskoy Oborony Prospekt.

Oktyabrsky/Sennoy, Moskovsky Prospekt. Metro Sennaya Ploshchad.

Sytnyı, 3/5 Sytninskaya Ploshchad. Metro Gorkovskaya.

Torzhkovsky, 20 Torzhkovskaya. Metro Chyornaya Rechka.

Vasileostrovsky, 16 Bolshoi Prospekt. Metro Vasileostrovskaya.

Veschovy Rinok, on Sadovaya Street, behind the Apraksin Dvor, is a large flea market. Metro Gostiny Dvor .

Churches

Alexander Nevsky Church, 10 Shuppa Street, tel. 136-4616. Metro Prospekt Veteranov. Open 9 am–2 pm and 7–10 pm.

Cathedral of the Holy Trinity (Svytotroitsky Sobor), Alexander Nevsky Monastery, tel. 274-0409. Metro Ploshchad Alexandra Nevskovo. Open 8 am–2 pm and 5–7.30 pm, till 9 pm on holidays (Alexander Nevsky Day September 11- 12).

Cathedral of Prince Vladimir (Knyzia Vladimira Sobor), 16 Blokhina Street, tel. 232-7625. Metro Gorkovskaya. Open 10 am–noon and 5–8 pm.

Ilyinskaya Church, 75 Troitskaya (Revolutsy) Square, tel. 227-8815. Metro Ploshchad Lenina. Open 10 am–12.30 pm and 5–7 pm; closed Monday and Tuesday.

Our Lady of Vladimir Icon Church, 20 Vladimirskaya Street, tel. 113-1614. Metro Vladimirskaya. Open 9 am–8 pm.

St Isaac's Cathedral, Isaakeivskaya Square, tel. 312-0721, is closed Wednesdays.

St Nicholas Cathedral (Nikolsko-Bogoyavlensky Sobor), 16 Nikolskaya Pl., tel.114-0862. Metro Ploshchad Mira. Open 7 am–8 pm; services 10 am–noon and 6–8 pm.

St Peter and Paul Cathedral (Sobor Svyatovo Petra i Pavla), 32 St Petersburgskaya Street, tel. 427-9268.

Yeliseyev's, Nevsky Prospekt

CAR RENTALS
Astoria Rent-A-Car, 39 Gertsena St, tel. 210–5858, fax 542–8798; **Avis**, 34/4 Konnogvardeisky Blvd, tel. 312–6318, fax 312–7292, 13 Remeslennaya, tel. 235–6444; **Interavto** (Hertz Representative), 9/11 Ispolkomskaya St, tel. 277–4032, fax 274–2562; **Mobil–Service**, rm 2, 65/11–13 Borovaya St, tel. 164–6066, fax 108–5105.

FILM DEVELOPMENT
Agfa, 20 Nevsky Prspkt, tel. 311–9974; **Fuji**, 23 Nab. reki Fontanki, tel. 314–4936; **Kodak**, 7 Malaya Konyushennaya St, tel. 110–6497, 32 Gertsena St, tel. 110–6403

OTHER
Bicycle Rental at Bicyling Club 'Burevestnik' at 81 Engelsa Prospekt, tel. 554–1741. Admiralteyets Velosipedny Klub is at 6 Blagoveshchenskaya (Truda) Square, tel. 311–2590; Sport-School for Children, 34 Vyborgskoe shosse, tel. 553–3203. **Boating Rental**: Akva Excurs, 34 Vozrozhdenskky Prospekt, tel. 237–1436, 110–1192, many public boat tours of rivers and canals; Breakwater, 94 Martynova Embankment, tel. 235–2722; Yacht rentals at Malakhit, tel. 264–6510; The Baltic Shipping Co. Yacht Club on Krestovsky Island sails the Gulf of Finland. Contact: Kostya Klimov, captain of the *Argus*, tel. 166–0222. **Bowling** at Pribaltiiskaya Hotel, 14 Korablestroiteley St, tel. 356–1663. Open 12–9 pm. **Chess** at 25 and 45 Bolshaya Konyushennaya (Zhelyabova) St, tel. 314–7561. **Horse rentals**: Olgina Hotel on Primorskoe Shosse, tel. 238-3132; Kirov Stadium on Krestovsky Island, tel. 235–1851; 20 Krestovsky Island, the Prostor-Park Riding School and Stables, tel. 230–3988, 9 am–8 pm, Horseback instruction given. **Skating**: Central Park of Culture, Yelagin Island, tel. 239–0911; Tavrichesky Garden at 50 Saltykova-Shchedrina Street, tel. 272–6044; Katok Moskovskovo Parka Pobedy, 25 Kuznetsovskaya Street, tel. 298–3411; Le Sportclub, 112 Fontanka Emb, tel. 292–2081 (has a summer skating rink). **Tennis**: The Tennis Club, 23 Konstantinovsky proezd (on banks of Neva), tel. 235–0407, training, court and racquet rentals, open 8 am–10 pm; Bast Sports Center (open 24 hrs); Lawn Tennis at 116 Metallistov Prspkt, tel. 540–7521/6092; Kirov Stadium on Krestovsky Island from April–September tel. 235–4877; Primorsky Park Pobedy, tel. 235–2077. **The Women's Center**, 13 Stekhanovsteva Street, tel. 528–1830.

Street Name Changes

OLD SOVIET NAME OF THE STREET	NEW RUSSIAN NAME OF STREET
Anny Ulyanovoy ul.	Polozova ul.
Brodskovo ul.	Maly Sampsonievsky pr.
Dekabristov pl.	Mikhailovskaya pl.
Detsky park Oktyabrskovo rayona.	Yusupovsky sad.
Dzerzhinskogo ul.	Gorokhovaya ul.

OLD SOVIET NAME	NEW RUSSIAN NAME
Fofanovoy ul.	Enotaevskaya ul.
Fotievoy ul.	Eletskaya ul.
Gaza pr.	Staro-Petergofsky pr.
Griboedova kan.	Ekaterininsky kan.
Kalyaeva ul.	Zakharyevskaya ul.
Karla Marksa pr.	Bolshoy Sampsonievsky pr.
Khalturina ul.	Millionaya ul.
Kirovsky most	Troitsky most
Kirovsky pr.	Kamennoostrovsky pr.
Kommunarov pl.	Nikolskaya pl.
Komsomolsky most	Kharlamov most
Krasnaya ul.	Galernaya ul.
Krasnoy Konnitsy ul.	Kavalergardskaya ul.
Krushteyna kan.	Admiralteysky kan.
Maksima Gorkogo pr.	Kronversky pr.
Marii Ulyanovoy ul.	Grafsky per.
Mayorova pr.	Vosnesensky pr.
Mira pl.	Sennaya pl.
Ogorodnikova pr.	Rizhsky pr.
Olega Koshevogo ul.	Vedenskaya ul.
Ostrovskogo pl.	Aleksandriskaya pl.
Park Chelyuskinstev	Udolny park
Pestelya most	Panteleymonosky most
Pestelya ul.	Panteleymonoskaya ul.
Petra Lavrova ul.	Furshtatskaya ul.
Pionersky most	Silin most
Podbelskogo per.	Pochtamtsky per.
Profsoyuzov ul.	Konnogvardeysky ul.
Rakova ul.	Italyanskaya ul.
Revolyutsii pl.	Troitskaya pl.
Sad im. F.E. Dzerzhinskogo	Lopukhinsky sad
Shchorsa pr.	Malyy pr. P.S.
Skorokhodova ul.	Bolshaya Monetnaya ul.
Skver na Ostrovskogo pl.	Ekaterininsky skver
Smimova pr.	Lanskoye shosse
Sofi Perovskoy ul.	Malaya Konyushennaya ul.
Stachek pl.	Narvskaya pl.
Svobody most	Sampionievsky most
Tolmachyova ul.	Karavannaya ul.

From Cradle to Grave

Melissino and I were present at an extraordinary ceremony on the Day of the Epiphany, namely the blessing of the Neva, then covered with five feet of ice.

After the benediction of the waters children were baptized by being plunged into a large hole which had been made in the ice. On the day on which I was present, the priest happened to let one of the children slip through his hands.

'Drugoi!' he cried.

That is, 'Give me another.' But my surprise may be imagined when I saw that the father and mother of the child were in an ecstasy of joy; they were certain that the babe had been carried straight to heaven. Happy ignorance!

*Giovanni Jacopo Casanova de Seignalt, Memoirs,
translated from the Italian by Arthur Machen*

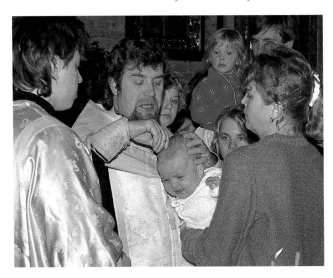

OLD SOVIET NAME	NEW RUSSIAN NAME
Truda ul. & pl.	Blagoveshchenskaya ul. & pl.
Voinova ul.	Shpalernaya ul.
Vosstaniya pl.	Znamenskaya pl.
Voytika ul.	Vitebskaya ul.
Zhelyabova ul.	Bolshaya Konyushenaya ul.

KEY

úlitsa (ul.) = street
prospekt (pr.) = avenue
most = bridge
plóshchad (pl.) = square
kanal (kan.) = canal
sad = garden
rayón = region
pereúlok (per) = lane

Russian Glossary

Although you will find that English is spoken in major hotels and on all tour routes, elsewhere it is not spoken so widely. Here are some Russian phrases and vocabulary to help you make yourself understood in a number of everyday situations.

General words and phrases

Yes	*da*
No	*nyet*
Hello	*zdrahst'voitye*
Good morning	*do'broye oo'tro*
Good afternoon	*do'bree dyen*
Good evening	*do'bree vye'cher*
Good night	*spakoi'ne no'chee*
Goodbye	*da sveedahn'ya*
Please	*po`zhal'sta*
Thank you	*spasee'bah*
Excuse me	*eezveenee'tye*
How are you?	*kahk dyelah'?*
My name is...	*menyah'zavoot'...*

Do you speak...?	*vii govoree'tye poo...?*
English	*Ahnglee'ski*
German	*Nemyet'ski*
French	*Frantsooz'ski*
I don't speak Russian	*Ya ne gavaryoo'po roos'ski*
I (don't) understand	*Ya (ne) poneemah'yoo*
I'm from America/England	*Ya eez Ahmer'eekee/Ahn'glee ee*
I am a tourist	*Ya tooree'st*
Please help me	*pamagaitye mnye pazhalusta*
May I?/Is this OK?	*moz'hna?*
Forbidden/impossible	*nyel'zya*
Who?	*ktoh'?*
What?	*shtoh'?*
When?	*kagdah'?*
Where?	*gedye'?*
Why?	*pachemoo'?*
How?	*kahk'?*
How much/many?	*skol'ka?*
How much does it cost?	*skol'ka stoi'eet?*
Big/small	*ballshoi/mal'enkee*
Good/bad	*kharoshaw/flo'kha*
Open/closed	*atkri'to/zakri'to*
Left/right	*le'vo/prah'vo*
Much (many)/few	*mino'ga/mah'lo*

Transport

Aeroplane	*samolyot'*
Airport	*aeraport'*
Aeroflot office	*agen'stva aeraflota*
Train	*poyezd*
Railway station	*vokzahl'*
Metro station	*metro'*
Taxi	*tahksee'*
Bus stop	*astanof'kaz afto'boosa*
Customs	*tamo'zhnya*
Left-luggage Office	*khranyeniya*
Ticket	*beelyet'*
Is there a plane/train/ bus to...?	*yest li samalyot'/poye'zhd avtobus do...?*

A ticket to...please	*adin beelyet do..., pozhal'sta*
Is there a bus to the	*khodit li avtobus do*
airport/the town?	*aeraporta/goroda?*
Road	*daro'ga*
Street	*uli'tsa*
Boulevard	*bul'var*
Avenue	*pras'pyekt*

Food and Drink

Food	*pishcha*
Restaurant	*rest'aran*
Café	*ka'fe*
Tea-house	*chai-khana*
Bar	*bar*
Food shop	*gastronom*
Menu	*myen'yu*
Starter	*vervye blyuda*
Main course	*vtarye blyuda*
Caviar	*ikra*
Meatballs	*bitochki*
Mushrooms	*griby*
Steak	*bifshteks*
Drink	*napit'ky*
Water	*vada*
Mineral water	*mineral'naya vada*
Tea	*chai*
Coffee	*kofye*
Fruit juice	*sok*
Wine	*vino*
Beer	*piva*
Milk	*milako*
Vodka	*vodka*
Cognac	*kanyak*

Recommended Reading

GENERAL HISTORY AND CURRENT AFFAIRS

Billington, James. *The Icon and the Axe: An interpretive History of Russian Culture,* Vintage, 1966.

Burlatsky, Fedor. *Khrushchev and the Russian Spring: The Era of Khrushchev Through the Eyes of His Advisor,* Charles Scribner's Sons, 1988.

Binyon, Michael. *Life in Russia,* Random House, 1983.

Brown, Edward. *Russian Literature Since the Revolution,* Macmillan 1969.

CNN Reports: 7 Days That Shook the World and the Collapse of Soviet Communism, Turner Publishing, 1991.

Cohen, Stephen. *Sovieticus: American Perceptions and Soviet Realities,* W.W. Norton, 1986

de Jonge, Alex. *The Life and Times of Grigorii Rasputin,* Dorset Press, 1987.

Goldman, Marshall. *Gorbachev's Challenge: Economic Reform in the Age of High Technology,* W.W. Norton, 1987.

Gorbachev, Mikhail. *December, 1991,* 1993.

Gorbachev, Mikhail. *Perestroika: New Thinking for Our Country and the World,* Harper and Row, 1987.

Hammer, Armand and Neil Lyndon. *Hammer,* Putnam, 1987.

Hayward, Max. *Writers in Russia: 1917-1978,* Harvest, 1984.

Kaiser. *The People and the Power,* Pocket, 1976.

Kagarlitsky, Boris. *The Thinking Reed: Intellectuals and the Soviet State, 1917 to Present Day,* Verso, 1988.

Lenin. *What Is To Be Done?* Written 1902, published by Pengiun, 1988.

Lincoln, W. Bruce. *The Romanovs,* Dial Press, 1981.

Massie, Robert. *Nicholas and Alexandra,* Atheneum, 1967.

Massie, Robert. *Peter the Great,* Ballantine, 1980.

Massie, Suzanne. *Land of the Firebird: The Beauty of Old Russia,* Simon and Schuster, 1980.

Massie, Suzanne. *The Living Mirror: Five Young Poets from Leningrad,* Doubleday, 1972

Medvedev, Roy. *Let People Judge,* Alfred Knopf, 1971.

Medvedev, Z & R. *A Question of Madness,* W.W. Norton, 1979.

Medvedev, Zhores. *Gorbachev,* Blackwell, 1987.

Mirsky, D.S. *A History of Russian Literature,* Alfred Knopf, 1958.

Morrison, John. *Boris Yeltsin: From Bolshevik to Democrat,* EP Dutton, 1991.

Moynahan, Brian. *Comrades: 1917 Russia in Revolution,* Little, Brown & Co., 1992.

Pozner, Vladimir. *Parting With Illusions,* Avon Books, 1991.

Reed, John. *The Ten Days That Shook the World.* (1919), International, 1967.

Remnick, David. *Lenin's Tomb: The Last Days of the Soviet Empire*, Random House, 1993.

Riasanovsky, N. *A History of Russia*, Oxford University Press, 1984.

Richard & Vaillant. *From Russia to the USSR*, Independent School Press, 1987.

Riehn, Richard. *1812: Napoleon's Russian Campaign*. McGraw Hill, 1990.

Salisbury, Harrison. *Nine Hundred Days: The Siege of Leningrad*, Avon, 1970.

Service, Robert. *The Russian Revolution: 1900–1927*, Macmillan, 1986.

Smith, Hedrick. *The New Russians*, Random House, 1991.

Sobchak, Anatoly. *For a New Russia: The Mayor of St. Petersburg's Own Story for the Struggle for Justice and Democracy*, Macmillan, 1992.

Thomas, Bill. *Red Tape: Adventure Capitalism in the New Russia*, Dutton, 1992.

Trotsky, Leon. *The Russian Revolution*, Doubleday, 1959.

Ulam, Adam. *The Bolsheviks*, Macmillan, 1965; *The Communists: The Story of Power and Lost Illusions 1948–1991*, Charles Scribners Sons, 1992. *Stalin: The Man and His Era*, Beacon Press, 1989.

Walker, Martin. *The Waking Giant*, Sphere, 1987.

Yeltsin, Boris. *Against the Grain*, Summit Books, 1990.

PICTURE BOOKS; ART AND CULTURE

A Day in the Life of the Soviet Union, Collins, 1987.

Before the Revolution: St. Petersburg in Photographs 1890–1914, Harry Abrahms, 1991.

Saved for Humanity: The Hermitage During the Siege of Leningrad 1941-1944, Aurora, Leningrad, 1985.

A Portrait of Tsarist Russia, Pantheon, 1989.

Stanislavsky on the Art of the Stage, translated by D. Margarshack, Hill &Wang, 1961.

Harlow Robinson's *Sergei Prokofiev: A Biography*, Paragon, 1988.

Russian Masters: Glinka, Borodin, Balakirev, Mussorgsky, Tchaikovsky, W.W. Norton, 1986.

Russian Fairy Tales, Pantheon, 1973.

Citizen Diplomats: Pathfinders in Soviet American Relations - And How You Can Join Them, Continuum, 1987.

Bird, Alan. *A History of Russian Painting*, Oxford, London, 1987.

Feigan, Leo. *Russian Jazz and the New Identity*, Quartet, 1985.

Chamberlain, Leslie. *The Food and Cooking of Russia*, Penguin, London, 1983.

Gray, Camilla. *The Russian Experiment in Art 1863-1922*, Thames and Hudson, 1986.

Konchalovsky, Andrei. *The Inner Circle: An Inside View to Soviet Life Under Stalin* (based on his film), with Alexander Lipkov, New Market Press, 1991.

Pokhlebkin, William. *A History of Vodka*, Verso, 1993.

Popova, Olga. *Russian Illuminated Manuscripts*, Thames and Hudson, 1984.

Prince Michael of Greece. *Nicholas and Alexandra: The Family Albums*, Tauris Parke, 1992.

Rudnitsky, Konstantin. *Russian and Soviet Theater 1905–1932*, Harry Abrams, 1988.

Shead, Richard. *Ballets Russes*, Wellfleet Press, 1989.

Skvorecky, Josef. *Talking Moscow Blues*, Ecco Press, 1988.

Snowman, A. Kenneth. *Carl Fabergé: Goldsmith to the Imperial Court of Russia*, Crown, 1983.

Strizhenova, Tatiana. *Soviet Costume and Textiles 1917–1945*, Flammarion, 1991.

Tamarov, Vladislav. *Afghanistan: Soviet Vietnam*, Mercury House, 1992.

Troitsky, Artemus. *Back in the USSR: The True Story of Rock in Russia*, Faber & Faber, 1987.

Troitsky, Artemus. *Children of Glasnost*, 1992.

NOVELS AND TRAVEL WRITING

Absyonov, Vassily. *In Search of a Melancholy Baby*, 1985.

Akhmatova, Anna. *The Complete Poems of Anna Akhmatova, Vol. I & II*, translated by Judith Hemschemeyer and edited by Roberta Reeder, Zephyr Press, 1990; Akhmatova, Anna. *My Half Century, Selected Prose*, edited by Ronald Meyer, Ardis, 1992; *Anna Akhmatova: Poems*, translated by Lyn Coffin, Introduction by Joseph Brodsky, W.W. Norton, 1983.

Chekov, Anton. *The Portable Chekhov*, Viking Penguin, 1968.

Dostoevsky, Fyodor. *Crime and Punishment*, Translated by C. Garnett, Bantam, 1982.

Filippov, Boris. *Leningrad in Literature. The Complete Prose Tales of Alexandr Sergeyevitch Pushkin*, translated by G. Aitken, W.W. Norton, 1966.

Finder, Joseph. *The Moscow Club*, Signet, 1992.

Gogol, Nikolai. *Dead Souls*, translated by D. Magarshack, Penguin, 1961.

Hansson and Liden. *Moscow Women*, Random House, 1983.

Kelly, Laurence. *Moscow: A Traveller's Companion*, Constable & Co, London, 1983, and *St Petersburg: A Traveller's Companion*, Atheneum, N.Y., 1983.

Mochulsky, K. *Dostoevsky: His Life and Work*, Princeton University Press, 1967.

Morris, Mary. *Wall to Wall* (a trip from Beijing to Berlin across Russia on the Trans-Siberian), Penguin, 1989.

Oakley, Jane. *Rasputin: Rascal Master*, St. Martin's Press, 1989.

Pasternak, Boris. *Dr Zhivago*, translated by M. Hayward, Ballantine, 1988.

Radzhinsky, Edvard. *The Last Tsar: The Life and Death of Nicholas II*, Doubleday, 1992.

Rutherfurd, Edward. *Russka: The Novel of Russia*, Crown, 1991.

Rybakov, Anatoly. *Children of the Arbat*, Dell, 1988.

Salisbury, Harrison. *Moscow Journal*, University of Chicago Press, 1961.

Solzhenitsyn, Alexander. *One Day in the Life of Ivan Denisovich*, Bantam, 1963, *The First Circle*, Harper & Row, 1968, and *The Gulag Archipelago*, Harper and Row, 1973.

Taubman, W & J. *Moscow Spring*, Summit, 1989

Theroux, Paul. *The Great Railway Bazaar.* A trip across Russia on the Trans-Siberian Railway.

Thubron, Colin. *Where Nights are Longest,* Atlantic Monthly Press, 1983.

Tolstaya, Tatyana. *On the Golden Porch,* l988.*Sleepwalker in a Fog,* l992.

Tolstoy, Leo. *The Portable Tolstoy,* and *War and Peace,* Penguin, 1978.

Turgenev, Ivan. *Fathers and Sons,* translated by D. Magarshack, Penguin, 1961.

Ustinov, Peter. *My Russia,* Little Brown & Co, 1983.

Van Der Post, Laurens. *Journey in Russia,* Penguin, 1965.

Voinovich, Vladimir. *Moscow 2042,* Harcourt Brace Jovanovich, 1987.

Wechsberg, Joseph. *In Leningrad,* Doubleday, 1977.

Wilson, A.N. *Tolstoy Biography,* Ballantine, 1988.

FILMS AND VIDEOS AVAILABLE FOR RENTAL OR PURCHASE

National Geographic's *Inside the Soviet Circus,* 1988, and *Voices of Leningrad,* 1990

Durrell in Russia

Moscow: The Other Russians

Reds 1981

Moscow on the Hudson, 1984.

Basic Russian by Video.

Eisenstein's *Potemkin,* USSR, 1925.

October: Ten Days that Shook the World, USSR, 1927.

Alexander Nevsky, USSR, 1938.

Ivan the Terrible, USSR, 1946.

Eisenstein, USSR, 1958.

Pudovkin's *Mother,* USSR, 1926.

The End of St Petersburg, USSR, 1927.

Vertov's *The Man with the Movie Camera,* USSR, 1928.

Petrov's *Peter the First: Parts I, II,* USSR, 1937.

Tarkovsky's *Andrei Rublev,* USSR, 1965.

Maya Plisetskaya Dances, USSR.

Backstage at the Kirov, USSR, 1984.

Menshov's *Moscow Doesn't Believe in Tears,* 1980.

Abuladze's *Repentance,* USSR, 1987.

Pichul's *Little Vera,* USSR, 1988.

20th Century Fox, *Back in the USSR,* 1991, shot in Moscow.

ANNA AKHMATOVA

In 1889, the Gorenko family of Odessa added a new daughter, Anna. She was destined to become one of Russia's greatest 20th-century lyric poets.

When Anna was one year old, the family moved north to Tsarskoye Selo (now Pushkin) near St Petersburg, where she lived until she was 16. 'My first memories are those of Tsarskoye Selo', she later wrote, 'the green grandeur of the parks, the groves where nanny took me, the hippodrome where small, mottled ponies jumped, and the old train station . . . .'

She wrote her first poem at the age of 10. But poetry was a licentious pastime, according to her father, and he admonished her not to 'befoul his good and respected name'. So, Anna, while still in her teens, changed her surname to Akhmatova, honoring her maternal great-grandmother's Tatar heritage which, supposedly, was traced back to the last khan of the Golden Horde in Russia, 'Achmatkhan', a descendant of Ghenghis.

Her first book of poetry, *Evening,* appeared in 1912, and was an immediate success. 'Those pathetic verses of an empty-headed girl', the astonished author wrote, 'have, no one knows why, been reprinted 13 times'. And yet every young person of the time could recite her 'Gray-Eyed King.' Prokofiev later set the lyrics to music.

> *Hail to thee, everlasting pain!*
> The gray-eyed King died yesterday...
> I will wake up my daughter now.
> And look into her eyes of gray.
> And outside the window the poplars whisper.
> 'Your King is no more on this earth.'

Her second collection, *The Rosary,* was published in 1914.

With the publication of Akhmatova's *White Flock* collection, Russian poetry hit the 'real' 20th century. Her recurrent themes of romance and love and the wounded heroine of these poems speaks with intimacy and immediacy.

> *There is a sacred boundary between those*
> who are close,
> And it cannot be transcended by passion or love
> Though lips on lips fuse in dreadful silence
> And the heart shatters to pieces with love...
> Those who strive to reach it are mad,
> and those
> Who reach it are stricken with grief...
> Now you understand why my heart
> Does not beat faster beneath your hand.

In 1910, Anna married the talented poet Nikolai Gumilev, who had begun to court her when she was 14. Together they traveled to Italy, and then to France where Modigliani made a series of drawings using Anna as his model. Along with her talent, she had tremendous physical beauty. Anna was five-foot-eleven-inches tall, dark-haired, lithe and feline; someone once compared her light green eyes to those of a snow leopard. Positively stunning, she caught the eye of many an artist and sculptor. In addition, a whole volume could be filled with poetry and prose written just about her.

Recollections of the years with Gumilyev echoed many times throughout her poetry.

> He loved three things in the world,
> Singing at night, white peacocks
> and Old maps of America.
> He hated when children cried,
> He hated tea with raspberry jam
> And women's hysterics.
> ...and I was his wife.

Anna was 28 and at the center of Petersburg's artistic world of cabarets and intellectuals when the Romanov Dynasty was ousted during the 1917 Revolution. She was 32 when, under Stalin, her husband Gumilev was arrested on a charge of plotting against the Soviet government. He was executed soon afterwards. Her only son, Lev, was later twice arrested and sentenced to many years in a labor camp.

Anna Akhmatova's name began to disappear from the literary scene and from 1925 until 1940 there was an unofficial ban on the publication of all her poetry. In 1935, her second husband Nikolai Punin, an art critic and historian of Western art, was arrested; he soon died in prison. The disappearance and death of friends, harassment by officials, no place to live, hours of waiting in lines for news of her arrested son, all took their voice in her prose-poem *Requiem*, dedicated to those times. Not daring to write anything down on paper, her friends memorized the verses. She wrote it between 1935 and 1940, but it wasn't allowed to be published in Russia until 1987.

In the terrible years of the Yezhov horrors, I spent 17 months standing in prison lines in Leningrad. One day somebody recognized me. There standing behind me was a woman with blue lips. She had, of course, never heard of me, but she suddenly came out of her stupor so common to us all and whispered in my ear (everybody there spoke only in whispers) 'Can you describe this'? and I said 'Yes, I can.' And then a fleeting smile passed over what had once been her face . . .

Even though Akhmatova had opportunties to leave the country during Stalin's Terror, she refused to emigrate. To her, being Russian meant living in Russia, no matter what the government did to her or her loved ones.

Pictures of Akhmatova show a beautiful woman with an aristocratic profile and a proudly raised head—a lioness with sad eyes. In the Summer of 1936, a friend of hers wrote, 'She is extraordinary and quite beautiful. Those who have not seen her cannot consider their lives full'.

In November 1941, during the Siege of Leningrad, Akhmatova was evacuated to Tashkent. There she began writing her *Poem Without a Hero* set in the Fontanka House (off of the Fontanka canal) in St Petersburg. The work consumed her for 22 years; she finished it in 1962. In 1946, after the war, Akhmatova returned to Petersburg, where her popularity was again immense. Because of her growing celebrity, and also possibly because of a meeting with Isaiah Berlin, she was expelled from the Writer's Union and denounced by Zhdanov, Stalin's cultural watchdog, who accused her of poisoning the minds of Soviets; he called her a 'half-nun, half-harlot'.

After this denunciation, Akhmatova was no longer published. She earned her money through translations and writing about accepted poets such as Pushkin. With no official residence, she lived off the help and kindness of friends. The West suspected that she was no longer writing poetry; many in Russia thought that she was no longer alive. But, somehow, she always knew that it was her fate to live through an epoch of interminable grief and upheaval.

In 1956, Akhmatova's son was released from the camps, and the last decade of her life became somewhat easier. She continued to live in the House on the Fontanka and was given the use of a tiny summer house in Komarovo, a writer's colony outside Petersburg. She was allowed to travel twice abroad. In 1964, Anna Akhmatova received the Etna Taormina Literary Prize in Catania, Italy; and in 1965, in England, she received an honorary doctorate from Oxford.

After her death on March 5, 1966, a memorial service was held at the Cathedral of St Nicholas the Seafarer, a 20-minute walk from her house on the Fontanka. It was said that the crowd attending her memorial looked like a human sea. The poet Joseph Brodsky, a close friend, wrote:

At certain periods of history only poetry is capable of dealing with reality by condensing it into something graspable, something that otherwise couldn't be retained by the mind. In that sense, the whole nation took up the pen name of Akhmatova, which explains her popularity and which, more importantly, enabled her to speak for the nation as well as to tell it something it didn't know . . . her verses are to survive because they are charged with time . . . .

And timelessness. She captured the sense of the eternal in her last dated poem of February 1965, at the age of 75.

> *So we lowered our eyes,*
> Tossing the flowers on the bed,
> We didn't know until the end,
> What to call one another.
> We didn't dare until the end
> To utter first names,
> As if, nearing the goal, we slowed our steps
> On the enchanted way.

A literary critic who visited the house on the Fontanka described her room: 'A bed, or rather a stretcher, covered with a thin, dark blanket stands by the wall: on another wall is a mirror in an ancient gilt frame. Next to it, on a shelf, is a porcelain object, not really valuable but antique. In the corner is a folding icon. By the wall next to the door stands a small rectangular table, with a simple ink stand and a blotter—the desk. There are also one or two old chairs and a worn armchair, but neither wardrobe nor bookshelves. Books are everywhere, on the desk, the chair and on the windowsill.'

Today at 34 Fontanka is the Anna Akhmatova House Museum, which displays these rooms, where she lived and wrote, along with photos, letters and her poetry. Akhmatova never stopped writing about life's tumultuous truths.

> *These poems have such hidden meanings*
> It's like staring into an abyss.
> And the abyss is enticing and beckoning,
> But never will you discover the bottom it,
> And never will its hollow silence
> Grow tired of speaking

(Opposite page, top) Budding young gymnasts,
(bottom) St Petersburg school children with Mickey Mouse ears.

THE FIREBIRD

Once upon a time, a very long time ago, there was a beautiful girl named Marushka, who was orphaned at an early age. This maiden was capable of embroidering the most beautiful and exquisite patterns on cloths and silks; no one, on all the earth, could match her talents.

Word of her marvelous works spread far and wide, and merchants from all over the world sought Marushka, trying to lure her off to their kingdoms. 'Come away with us', they pleaded, 'riches and fame will surely be yours'. Marushka always replied, 'I shall never leave the village where I was born. But if you indeed find my work beautiful, then I will sell it to you. If you don't have the money, you can repay me whenever you can. I get my pleasure from the work itself; the money I distribute throughout my village'.

Even though the merchants would leave the village without Marushka, they spread their stories of her incredible talent across the world. The tales finally reached the ears of Kaschei the Immortal, the most wicked of the sorcerers. Kaschei was immediately curious and enraged to think that such beauty existed somewhere that he had never seen. He learned too that Marushka was quite beautiful herself, so he turned himself into the handsomest of princes and flew out over the mountains, oceans, and almost impassable birch forests until he found Marushka's village.

'Where is the maiden who embroiders the most exquisite of patterns?' He was led to her very door, as the villagers were used to the many visitors. When Marushka answered the door herself, the disguised sorcerer asked to see all the needlework and tapestry that she had ready to show. Marushka fetched all her shirts and sashes, towels and trousers, handkerchiefs and hats. Kaschei could hardly contain his delight.

Marushka said, 'My lord, I hope my work pleases you. Anything that meets your fancy is yours to keep. If you don't have the money, you needn't pay me. My happiness comes from your delight'.

Although the great Kaschei could not believe that this girl could fashion things even better than he, he was also taken by her beauty and kindness. He decided that if he could not make such things himself, then he most possess her and take her home to his kingdom.

'Come away with me, and I will make you my queen. You shall live in my palace, all the fruits of my kingdom shall be yours, your clothes shall be covered with jewels, and birds of paradise will sing you to sleep every night. You shall even have your own chamber, containing the most exotic of threads and materials, where you will embroider for me and my kingdom'.

Marushka listened quietly to all this, then she softly replied, 'I couldn't ever leave this village where my parents are buried, where I was born. Here my heart shall always be. There is nothing sweeter than the fields and woods and neighbors of my own village. I must give my embroidery to anyone who receives joy from my work. I could never embroider for you alone'.

The Great Kaschei had never been refused, nor had he ever failed to bewitch a mere girl. Furious, his face suddenly changed from that of the handsome prince to his very own, dark and raging. At this sight, Marushka gasped and tried to flee the room. But it was too late.

'Because you will not leave your village and come to be my queen, because you dared to refuse the Great Kaschei, from this moment on I cast a spell on you. You shall be a bird! I shall make sure that you fly far, far away and never see your village again!'

As he spoke these terrible words, the beautiful Marushka turned into a magnificent, flaming red firebird. In the same moment, the Great Kaschei turned himself into a great black falcon, who swooped down on the firebird, grasping her in his enormous claws. He carried her high into the clouds so she would never return to her birthplace.

Marushka knew that she had to leave something behind. As the great falcon carried her through the sky, the firebird began to shed her flaming plumage. Soon, feather after feather floated down, dusting her beloved homeland. A rainbow of colors dotted the meadows and forests; and by the time the falcon had reached its own kingdom, all her feathers had fallen, leaving a shimmering trail right back to her cottage.

Even though the firebird died, all her magical feathers continued to live forever. The firebird's feathers carried their own spell: All those who loved and honored beauty in themselves and others, as Marushka, and who sought to create beauty for others, without expecting anything in return, would always be able to see the firebird's feathers.

12th-century icon, the Hermitage

The Black Madonna, 12th-century icon

Index